Advanced Praise for *A New Kind of Union*

"The emergence of Unifor has been a key catalyst in the revitalization of the Canadian labour movement after decades of stepped-up aggression from the corporate world. In this inspiring and well-told account, long-time progressive activist Fred Wilson tells the inside story of the hopes and dreams and battles that led to Unifor's creation."

— Linda McQuaig, *Toronto Star* columnist

"Unifor is a powerful new force in the Canada's labour, social and political movements, and this is a riveting insider's account of the unique process that created the union and motivated its actions. *A New Kind of Union* explains the challenges facing the labour movement and Unifor's crucial role in opposing the Conservative assaults on democracy and worker rights. It is important also for its timely and urgent call for a wider social solidarity to counter the demagogic appeal of right wing populists seeking to exploit the frustrations of working people and to impose their intolerant and regressive agenda on us all."

— Maude Barlow, Honorary Chairperson, Council of Canadians

"In this fascinating account of the creation of Unifor, Fred Wilson skillfully weaves three perspectives into this tale of union renewal: that of a lifelong activist drawing on a wealth of experience and practical insight; that of an insider who was a key figure in the creation of this new kind of union; that of a visionary who understood the role that Unifor could play in meeting the larger challenge of labour renewal at a critical time for working women and men in Canada."

— Gregor Murray, Canada Research Chair on Globalization and Work, School of Industrial Relations

"A very readable, enjoyable and instructive history of how two unions came together, put aside their egos, and built a new larger organization dedicated to 'class unionism' for Canadian workers in the twenty-first century. It was no small feat — in five short years Unifor has shaken up the twentieth Century labour establishment and breathed new life into worker organization and the fight for equality. This story of union renewal in Canada should be read and debated not only in Canada, but south of the border as well. The workers' movement will be better off for it."

— Peter Knowlton, National President, United Electrical, Radio and Machine Workers of America (UE)

A NEW KIND OF UNION

Unifor and the birth
of the modern
Canadian Union

Fred Wilson

Forewords by Jerry Dias and Peter Kennedy
Afterword by Jim Stanford

James Lorimer & Company Ltd., Publishers
Toronto

To the next generation of organizers and activists who will define working class solidarity in this century.

James Lorimer & Company Ltd., Publishers acknowledges funding support from the Ontario Arts Council (OAC), an agency of the Government of Ontario. We acknowledge the support of the Canada Council for the Arts, which last year invested $153 million to bring the arts to Canadians throughout the country. This project has been made possible in part by the Government of Canada and with the support of Ontario Creates.

Cover design: Tyler Cleroux
Cover image: Alamy

Photo Credits: All photos by John Maclennan except the following: p. 84 (right) and 148, CAW photo archive; p. 163, Fred Wilson; p. 171 Kim Elliott; p. 182, Lis Pimentel.

Library and Archives Canada Cataloguing in Publication

Title: A new kind of union : Unifor and the birth of the modern Canadian union / Fred Wilson ; forewords by Jerry Dias and Peter Kennedy ; afterword by Jim Stanford.
Names: Wilson, Fred, 1951- author.
Description: Includes bibliographical references and index.
Identifiers: Canadiana (print) 2019004991X | Canadiana (ebook) 20190050128 | ISBN 9781459414235 (softcover) | ISBN 9781459414242 (EPUB)
Subjects: LCSH: Unifor (Organization)—History | LCSH: CAW-Canada—History. | LCSH: Communications, Energy and Paperworkers Union of Canada—History. | LCSH: Labor unions—Mergers—Canada—History. | LCSH: Labor unions—Canada—History.
Classification: LCC HD8102.U55 W55 2019 | DDC 331.880971—dc23

James Lorimer & Company Ltd., Publishers
117 Peter Street, Suite 304
Toronto, ON, Canada
M5V 0M3
www.lorimer.ca

Printed and bound in Canada.

Contents

Foreword
Jerry Dias

This is a book about the extraordinary accomplishment that changed the labour movement, changed Canada and changed the lives of thousands of people, including me.

Unifor was a brilliant idea, and it came just in time. Right-to-work (for less) laws had marched north from the United States to our border, and our presumed future was staring at us from Michigan and Wisconsin. Emboldened corporations such as Caterpillar were ripping up social contracts that had governed relationships for a half-century. The labour movement seemed to be paralyzed and incapable of confronting the challenge in front of it. We were written off as yesterday's news by journalists, politicians, businesses and a growing number of working class people trapped in the low-wage world of precarious work, where unions are largely irrelevant.

Five years after Unifor's founding, we continue to face huge economic and social challenges. But we have also stepped back from the edge and re-established credibility and influence. Trade union freedoms have been restored in our federal jurisdiction, and our Supreme Court has affirmed the right to strike and organize as protected by the Canadian *Constitution* and the *Charter of Rights and Freedoms*. Conservative politicians have been forced to have second thoughts about political campaigns to single out and attack workers and their unions. We continue to watch our back against another assault on our rights, but as of 2019 we are looking forward and have our sights set on economic and social progress.

Unifor does not claim all the credit for our fight back to where we are in 2019. We were among millions and many social movements in the defeat of Tim Hudak, Stephen Harper, Jim Prentice and Christy Clark. But from the crucial turnaround campaign against Hudak in Ontario in our first year as a union, Unifor unquestionably has been a new and powerful force that has changed politics and the labour movement.

If Unifor has changed how unions are seen in Canada, I am most proud of our union's commitment to ending violence against women and the achievement of legislation to provide paid leave for victims of domestic violence. I think of the platform that Unifor's Canadian and regional councils provided for truth and reconciliation, the demand to establish the inquiry into murdered and missing Aboriginal women and support for the heroic work of Cindy Blackstock to win justice for First Nations children. I am immensely satisfied that Unifor took these issues to the bargaining table with major employers and negotiated the Canadian Community Fund to fund social justice.

Unifor is the first trade union in Canada to wield the bargaining power of hundreds of thousands of workers in twenty separate industries and sectors. Employers are well aware of the strength we bring to every negotiating table, large and small. Our longest labour disputes have been in defence of the smallest groups of workers, who have, in almost every case, lasted one day longer to win fairness. Our bargaining power when tens of thousands linked arms across industries was intended to be a force for progress, and it has been. Negotiating $1.5 billion of investments in our auto sector and raising the floor for retail workers by improving minimum wages and standards of work are only two examples. Collective bargaining can and must be more than protection and fairness: unions must use their power to be a force for social and economic advancements.

There is no question that Unifor was created to act differently. And we have. When you decide to break with past failures and make change, you can expect that not everyone will like it. Unifor has been labelled as opportunists, empire builders, thugs, Liberals and even Nazis. This book describes what Unifor is and what it was created to do. Unifor's structure and its rank-and-file democracy, its decision to be a union for everyone and its fiercely independent politics were debated in detail and then affirmed by thousands of union activists. Our principles and our strategic goals are not mysterious — they were set out in detail in the New Union Project. To know the history of the project and its vision is to understand Unifor and the decisions we have made. This is essential reading for anyone who seeks to know what Unifor represents.

Of course, Unifor's principles did not send us on an explicit mission to create controversy or become embroiled in disputes within the labour movement or social democracy. We certainly did not set out with the intention of changing the leadership of the labour movement and then withdrawing from the Canadian Labour Congress. We did not expect that twice within one year US-based unions would put Canadian local unions under trusteeships and that these workers would turn to us for support. But as this book explains well, rank-and-file democracy and an independent Canadian trade union movement are part of our DNA. The creation of Unifor as the only large Canadian union in the private sector also brought with it the responsibility to be "Canada's union." Unifor's separation from the Canadian Labour Congress is certainly temporary and in no way signals a direction away from our labour movement. Inside Unifor, we see these conflicts as an expression of our solidarity and commitment to democracy in our movement.

Herein is also the story of the great founders and leaders who, through the New Union Project, created Unifor. Ken Lewenza and Dave Coles were two selfless leaders whose spark of genius made everything possible. Peter Kennedy and Gaétan Ménard shepherded the project and overcame what many thought were irreconcilable differences between the Canadian Auto Workers and Communications,

Energy and Paperworkers unions. Fred Wilson and Jim Stanford, and the project team of staffers, were always a step ahead. And the outstanding union leaders and activists on the Proposal Committee and the working groups became entirely consumed in the two-year-long New Union Project. The project handed over to the Unifor National Executive Board, regional directors and staff a blueprint to build a new union, create its structures and councils and then take on critical struggles to change the country. Within a year, they had done all that and more. I could not be happier that this book recognizes their contributions for future generations of Unifor members and leaders.

Had Ken Lewenza decided to stay on and become Unifor's first president, my life would have been very different. But, with his big heart, he decided to return to Windsor. When Ken made his decision and the Canadian Auto Workers leadership proposed that I be nominated to lead the new union, I called my family together and put to them that this was both the opportunity that all my training and development in the union had led to and a life-altering event.

And so it has been for me — a roller-coaster ride and romp through the halls of power from coast to coast. The making of Unifor opened doors that had been closed to workers for decades. I have been immensely proud and honoured to walk through those corporate and government doors on behalf of our members. As I write this foreword, I have the job of speaking for labour on the inside of the renegotiation of the North American Free Trade Agreement — the first labour leader to have such an assignment. From the New Union Project and the mentors who guided me, I will never forget that I am speaking for Canadian workers at large, whether they have a union or not. Nor does it ever escape me that our power and influence come from the most important halls of power: the union halls and the councils of Unifor, where hundreds and thousands of union activists make decisions to change the labour movement, the country and our world.

Foreword
Peter Kennedy

On August 31, 2013, Canada's newest national union, Unifor, was born. So begins the narrative you are about to read. Turn the clock back forty-one years, almost to the day: August 28, 1972, the day I became a union member. Although I knew when I started work at 3M Canada that I would join the union, I would never have dreamed it would begin the start of a personal journey that would culminate in becoming an officer of Canada's largest and most influential private sector union. Nor could I have imagined that I would have a ringside seat and be part of the process to create Unifor — the most transformative event in the Canadian labour movement, certainly in my lifetime as a union member.

Although unions were born as a result of challenging the status quo, the evidence will show that we have been hesitant to challenge our own status quo. After three-plus decades of declining relevance, influence and membership density, an institutional malaise has taken hold of the labour movement in Canada and abroad. Apart from the necessary but not enduring business-as-usual daily activities and the occasional demonstration to protest this or to support that, labour's responses to the defining issues of our time have become predominantly rhetorical.

At conventions and conferences of various unions, at the local labour councils and Federations of Labour and the Canadian Labour Congress, I heard many gifted speakers rail against the neo-liberal agenda, wage stagnation and the decline in union membership. The problems and the responsibilities of others were always clear. But much less clear was what we were required to do. It seemed we were saying that all would be well if we only had this government, or a new piece of labour legislation or that leader — or if we could only turn back the clock to when I joined the movement. As they say, hope is not a strategy.

This is the story of how two labour leaders intuitively understood that for real change to happen, the labour movement itself had to change. We needed, and still need, a strategy. Their vision provided the impetus for many others to engage in a historic moment not only to create Unifor but also to begin the process of continuous change and innovation that is necessary to renew the labour movement.

There had been a number of preliminary meetings in 2011 among the leaders and key staff of the founding unions who grappled with the idea of a new union. However, the real work of shaping Unifor began about twenty months before its founding in a process we called the New Union Project. It was full of intense, emotional, time-consuming and even harrowing experiences. There were takeoffs and landings that took us to every part of Canada and deep dives into the essence of what trade unions are and must do in the twenty-first century. Like that time when we were en route to New Brunswick and our aircraft blew a tire on the runway, there were occasions when our fast-moving project seemed about to crash.

The Proposal Committee that I had the privilege to co-chair with Gaétan Ménard and our six dedicated staffers on the project team spent countless hours together and in caucus to put our thoughts together about what this yet unnamed union would look like. We determined early that the new union would not be named after the sectors in which our members worked or be an amalgamation of the current names of the predecessor unions — the National Automobile, Aerospace, Agricultural, Communications, Energy, Paper, Transportation and General

Workers Union of Canada — and not simply because it would be way too much to embroider on a T-shirt or ball cap.

We wanted to build a new union with a new identity, but we could not start with a clean slate. We had all been influenced by our histories and cultures, experiences in and loyalties to our former unions. But we were able to agree that if the only or best argument that could be made in favour of a feature of the new union was "that is how we have always done it," that argument would not carry the day.

Our respective pasts inevitably led to many intense, sometimes fractious, deliberations. This was not only true of our joint meetings but also within our caucuses. In either case, everything that was said came from the heart.

On several occasions, I felt as if we were not going to make it; it seemed the discussion was going off the rails. All of us knew we did not have to do this for the sake of our respective unions. We could have walked away and continued as we were before the New Union Project; to walk away would have been the easier path. But we also knew that this was something more than that and worth the hard work and the risks — something bigger than numbers and more than the sum of our parts.

This was about a new way of practising trade unionism. The more we met, the more we discussed, the more we debated and sometimes even laughed, the more this idea guided those thoughts. The more we became of one mind. This was too important to fail. The pressures of time and restrictions of schedules forced us to be focused and to find resolutions to issues that sometimes seemed insurmountable.

And so we did. Everyone you will read about in the pages of this book played an invaluable role in the final outcome. But neither was any one person irreplaceable. The group dynamic made Unifor come together.

The genesis of Unifor is the shared vision of a renewed trade union movement, but this vision remains a work in progress. The new union we created continues to grow and evolve, adapt and change, as we believed it must.

Unifor represents a combined history of change and evolution punctuated by mergers and breakaways from international unions —

all bold initiatives in their day. But change is constant, and the labour movement today must embrace change in a new and meaningful way, not just with rhetorical flourishes and "resolutionary politics," where much more is said than done.

Unifor is an example of how to make change. We did not see ourselves as creating a model of change management, but the project forced us to design a process that would take us past the insecurities and institutional roadblocks that all too often prevent or divert change. Unifor is to me a beacon of hope. Although I said earlier that hope is not a strategy, without hope we are lost.

I often said about my former union that I would like to have a magic wand to put the organization in suspended animation so that we would have the time to reinvent, restructure and rebuild without the daily pressures of crisis management that all unions face. In many ways, the twenty months of the New Union Project was just that time.

Although we had the skills of and advice from highly educated and deeply experienced trade union activists and leaders, none of us who made Unifor went to school to learn or be prepared to make a new union. Our project was that school, and our experience was unique for trade unionists in our country and globally. The New Union Project has already been a case study for trade unionists in other countries who also see the necessity of change and renewal. If nothing else, I know that we have changed the discussion around union renewal and what it means.

I want to thank the leadership and membership, past and present, of all our former unions whose DNA has been embedded into Unifor. The opportunity provided to all of us who were part of this process was something very special and rewarding. I am eternally grateful to have been able to play a role in the creation of Unifor and to help lead it through its first three years. I am likewise privileged that Unifor, as a "union for everyone," provides me and many thousands of others with the ability to continue my activism in our movement. In the words of the acclaimed singer-songwriter Steve Earle, "the revolution starts now."

Introduction

On August 31, 2013, Canada's newest national union, Unifor, was born. This is the story of the process that led to its formation: the New Union Project. It is a Canadian labour story that is especially important because Unifor was created to be a new kind of union. Unifor was conceived and delivered as a change agent in the labour movement. It was intended to disrupt conventions and act differently for the purpose of reversing a forty-year decline in economic and political influence.[1]

The creation of Unifor was also a response to profound structural changes in the economy and the working class and the need for unions to adapt and modernize outdated operating principles, structures and models of representation — a need talked about for years and sometimes called "union renewal."

There were 776 Canadian trade unions in 2015, broadly defined. But less than a third of those unions represented 95 per cent of union members. New unions and mergers of old unions are common events, but it is rare indeed that a new union with a different purpose and strategy makes any real difference for the labour movement or its role in Canadian society.[2]

The formation of Unifor stands apart. It is important because of its size and economic significance, with members in all the main regions of Canada. It is easily the most diverse of Canada's unions by sector, spanning the spectrum of production from resource extraction to manufacturing, transportation, communications and retail. It is the largest industrial or private sector union in Canada but also includes tens of thousands of public sector members.

By global standards, Canadian unions have maintained levels of union density higher than in many other Western industrial countries. However, that achievement is highly relative and cannot obscure Canadian labour's own struggle for survival. Canadian trade unions are holding on to their relative positions within a paradox of rapid economic and cultural change and their own deep-seated traditions and internal conservatism. Sometimes the disparity between trade union organizations and revolutionary changes in technology, communications and workplace organization can be baffling and bemusing. If you have ever wondered who would belong to a "guild," "lodge" or "chapel" or who would be meeting behind closed doors guarded by sentries called "sergeants-at-arms," welcome to the world of trade unions. Among the oldest continuously operating civil society institutions, unions are junior only to churches and a few societies and political parties. That tradition and baggage are accompanied by a worrisomely aging membership surrounded by growing numbers of precarious and non-traditional workers who have little sense of how a union could help them. At the same time, modern trade unions are remarkably complex and constantly evolving. Viewed as mass democratic organizations of ordinary citizens, the largest and best-organized trade unions surpass the size and sophistication of political parties, charities and service or community groups. The degree to which large modern unions hold a central place in the economic and democratic affairs of masses and the extent to which they impact the daily lives of working people have no comparator. On any given day, many thousands of the almost five million union members in Canada look to their union to be their negotiator and provider of a legal and binding collective agreement that determines compensation and writes the rules of their workplace. On any other day or the same day, the union is a political lobbyist, human rights advocate, lawyer, adult educator, personal coach, safety officer, epidemiologist, ergonomist, investment analyst, crisis and addictions counsellor, pension actuary and retirement planner, researcher, office assistant, webmaster and communications professional. These and other roles and services have evolved over time and continue to adapt and expand, responding to emerging needs, technologies and changing workplace environments.

Unions are widely seen as the most important human infrastructure of the so-called middle class. It is indeed hard to imagine the working class achievements of the twentieth century without trade unions. Yet it is also a troubling reality that political and economic changes over the past fifty years have led to a serious decline in the proportion of workers represented by a union in Canada — a proportion we describe interchangeably as the rate of unionization or "union density." Among Canadian men, the unionization rate fell from just over 42 per cent in 1981 to 27 per cent in 2014, a decline of almost 15 percentage points. The largest decrease — 8 percentage points — took place in the 1990s. Young men were lost to unions in the greatest proportion, whereas the only demographic that has grown since the 1980s has been older women. Women and the public sector jobs they dominate have saved Canadian labour from cataclysmic decline.[3]

In 2011, the dominant narrative about unions in Canada was that the gig was just about up. Private sector industrial unions were portrayed as facing an unstoppable decline and relegation to the margins of Canadian economic and social life. The idea of Unifor came from this existential challenge.

From its radical origins in the nineteenth and early twentieth centuries, long before workers' rights secured legal recognition, the labour movement has been shaped by leaders and organizers who challenged the accepted prescriptions and proscriptions of what unions could and could not do. Those conventions and limits on the role of unions were established by employers, governments, courts, scholars, the media and sometimes the labour movement itself. But at each stage of this history, the truly important events were carried out by leaders and activists who refused to accept the boundaries imposed on the role of unions or what they could achieve. They were prepared to break moulds and create movements for change that would expand workers' rights.

In the spring of 2011, Dave Coles, president of the Communications, Energy and Paperworkers Union (CEP), and Ken Lewenza, president of the Canadian Auto Workers Union (CAW), had an informal discussion during a meeting of the Canadian Labour Congress (CLC) and agreed to explore the possibility of a new Canadian union. Their encounter was not altogether coincidental. There had been preliminary discussions in Quebec about a potential CAW-CEP initiative. But when the two national leaders opened a discussion on "something new," they were still operating on instinct, unsure of what could be done. They were stepping into a dimension without any known parameters or precedents. It was a leap of faith that would begin an astonishing change process that would come to be known as the New Union Project.

This is the story of the New Union Project and the decisions it made and carried out to create Unifor. It is an exposition of the ideas and choices that drove the process. It is equally a story of change itself and how unions that are steeped in their own histories can be transformed when there are no guidebooks and more reasons to fail than to succeed.

The main characters who made up the New Union Project did not come together directly from their close association or background, nor was the process dominated by the agenda or vision of the chief officers of the two founding unions. This uncharted journey of discovery was driven instead by an unlikely combination of secondary leadership, staff, rank-and-file activists and retirees. None of them had expected to be thrown into a project to reinvent the labour movement, nor did they anticipate the exhausting demands of a project to create a new union in less than two years. Fuelled by idealism and adrenalin, the New Union

Project was a unique collaboration and the product of their creative energy.

Lewenza and Coles were both outspoken and larger than life in their public personas. Each had well-honed populist instincts, and they shared an openness to radical solutions. Their sheer audacity in proposing the start of a discussion towards a new union was later matched by their willingness to step back and allow a new union to define itself.

The helm of the New Union Project was directed instead by the second-in-command from each union, Peter Kennedy and Gaétan Ménard, and their personalities and temperaments kept the fledgling process from running aground on multiple shoals. Assembled around the workshop table was a diverse collection from each union, largely unknown to each other. The participants reflected the secondary leadership in each union: for the CEP, its regional vice-presidents, and for the CAW, current and retired assistants to the president and senior staff. Rank-and-file executive board members from each union rounded out the group that came to be known as the "Proposal Committee." Its mandate was daunting: to develop a vision of a new union with a new identity and structure.

Another key person in the CAW leadership, Assistant to the President Jerry Dias, was an early supporter of the proposal to begin discussions on a new union. However, Dias was focused on the day-to-day bargaining of the union and was not assigned to the Proposal Committee. He would emerge strongly a year later in leadership discussions leading to the founding convention. When Ken Lewenza announced that he would not stand for leadership in the new union, Dias's personality would quickly become central to the emergence of Unifor as a political and social force in Canada.

The organizational centre of the New Union Project was led by six key staffers who did the heavy lifting of research, policy development and facilitation: from the CEP, Duncan Brown, Patty Barrera and me; from CAW, Jim Stanford, Jo-Ann Hannah and David Robertson. Jim Stanford and I were asked to hold initial meetings to map out the possibilities for what would become the New Union Project. From our first meeting at the Sheraton Centre in Toronto to discuss what could be new about a new union, we formed a bond over the historic opportunity that the idea of the new union presented.

The second stage of the New Union Project brought a wider group of players into the working groups who developed the founding documents and shaped the operational practices of the new union. Several are noted in this account, but many others played key roles and made significant contributions. They are listed in the appendix and also referenced in several of the endnotes. By the time Unifor held its second convention, almost all of the New Union Project players who served on the Proposal Committee or the working groups had retired or moved on. The transition of leadership and staff that drove the New Union Project was nearly complete when both Peter Kennedy and I retired at the end of 2016.[4]

The intense engagement of the New Union Project activists over its two-year process and in the early years of Unifor was immensely productive. They left behind a history-making legacy in the making of Unifor and a transformation of political fortunes for the trade union movement. By the time of Unifor's second convention in 2016, the perfect storm that seemed to be engulfing organized labour at Unifor's founding had been resisted by inspired labour campaigns, unpredictable political events and Supreme Court of Canada decisions affirming the constitutional rights of workers and unions. The organizers and innovators who immersed themselves in the New Union Project could not have imagined that the winds of change would turn in their direction so soon. Of course, the turn of events for Canadian labour cannot simply be ascribed to Unifor, but neither can the renewed strength and influence of Canadian labour be imagined without Unifor's role.

Unifor, and the labour politics it unleashed, was a material factor in defeating labour's worst political adversaries in critical provincial and federal elections, and it established a political influence for Canadian labour unseen in recent history. It almost immediately launched high-profile dynamic organizing drives, although with mixed results. And it upended labour movement politics by defeating an incumbent president of the Canadian Labour Congress for the first time in modern Canadian labour history.

The degree to which Unifor has brought and will bring the transformational change set out in its founding documents remains to be assessed by its actions and accomplishments over a longer period. But supporters and critics will agree that, at the very least, it has been bold and disruptive in its early history.

The prospects for Canadian unions and workers' rights remain precarious. Like their American counterparts, Canadian unions face a depressing mathematical reality, where the normal rate of organizing new members is regularly surpassed by the growth in the labour force such that economic growth itself leads to a decline in overall union density, especially in the private sector. Unless and until unions dramatically increase their rate of organizing and secure a significantly larger base in the growing service, technology and financial economic sectors, these trends will lead to an ongoing marginalization of unions, the most powerful voice of working people.

Stating this reality is not a cry of despair. The trade union movement retains powerful public sector and industrial bases in the Canadian economy and has demonstrated its ability to rebound politically and organizationally. In his afterword to this book, my colleague Jim Stanford describes a recent stabilizing of the unionization rate in Canada and with it a small but important turn to what unions are supposed to accomplish in distributing a greater share of wealth to working people. As Stanford points out, this organizational success must be seen in the context of political achievements since 2011 that are unique in the industrialized world and turned back a planned legislative assault that would have brought a very different outcome for Canadian unions.

Reversing a long retreat begins with holding your ground, and Canada's labour movement is tentatively at that point. But this critical juncture demonstrates that the union renewal Unifor represents is central to truly countering the trends underlying the diminishment of union power over the past many decades. Especially in the United States and Canada and the few other countries that follow the "*Wagner Act*" model of exclusive majority representation (*Wagner Act* is the informal name of the *National Labor Relations Act*; see Chapter 3), there is a growing gap between the "union-advantaged" islands of relatively high-wage, standard jobs and the steadily growing oceans of the "precariat": low-income, part-time and non-standard workers mostly but not exclusively in the service sector. The great challenge for unions is to bridge this gap and to redefine the relationship between the organized working class and the unorganized. Hanging in the balance is not just union density or the percentage of unionized workers generally and in particular industries, but also relevance. Put simply, unions will either be a social movement for economic and social justice, speaking and acting for the vast majority of workers, or they will increasingly be the special interest groups that labour's adversaries decry, representing an ever-smaller share of the workforce.

There is little prospect for increasing or even maintaining economic and political influence if private sector trade union density continues to decline. The relatively strong position of our public sector unions, with an effective union density of more than 70 per cent, is not sustainable if private sector density declines much further. As concessions are wrung from private sector workers and precarious work becomes the new normal, these same conditions will inevitably be extended to the public sector. With each additional drop in density, employers and anti-union politicians will be emboldened to launch new assaults on trade union rights. The danger of the country relapsing into a resurgent right-wing populism with anti-labour and racist attacks on democracy will persist.

That was the case at the end of 2018. Labour movements in Europe, Latin America, the United States and Canada faced political hostility not only from conservative political forces seeking to undermine their rights and role in society but also a potent ideological challenge from a new right-wing populism aimed at the hearts and minds of their working class base. I argue in the conclusion of this history that five years after Unifor's founding, there is a renewed urgency for union renewal and that this demands a redefining of solidarity. To become the social movement they must be, unions must move beyond "transactional solidarity" based on jurisdictional lines and cost-benefit analyses. Unions must renew their organizing, representation and political models on the basis of values and genuine social unionism. The seeds of that renewal were planted in the New Union Project, but the making of Unifor was never intended to be a set of definitive answers and prescriptions for the labour movement. "Change is constant" was embedded in Unifor's founding principles — a call for continuous innovation, experimentation and adaptation.

These are all good reasons why the story of how a new and different Canadian union was created, and an elaboration of the foundational principles that define Unifor should be written down and shared with trade union activists in Canada and around the world.

This is a history primarily of the New Union Project, but the defining characteristics of Unifor continued to develop after its founding. The final chapter on Unifor's political policy and impact and its turbulent relationship with the Canadian labour movement remains an unfolding story. These events are included in this history because they were shaped by the principles and goals of the New Union Project, and, in turn, these events represent an evolution of Unifor's character and purpose.

I am mindful of the valid critiques of Unifor in its first years. Some of the principles and objectives that are set out here will be measured against Unifor's actions, decisions and compromises. Without doubt, the union's power and influence have been wielded inconsistently — at times standing alone on principle, with hardly a chance of success, and at times overtly pragmatic to move on to the next predicament or battle.

There are also ideas and roles in this account that those close to Unifor will immediately identify as unfulfilled or altered in basic ways. Sometimes what was intended as new and different but not entirely understood became a casualty to what was known and preferred by the gatekeepers of change at different levels of the union.

In particular, Unifor's decision to be a "union for everyone" was a deliberate, self-conscious starting point for union renewal, but it was only a point of embarkation. The full commitment of resources and focus that are needed has yet to be delivered. This central but unfulfilled objective remains a work in progress with unresolved conceptual and organizational issues. But the idea and design of Unifor are nonetheless a beacon for a new kind of trade unionism. The foundational goals and principles that are built into Unifor's DNA will always be a reference point for the union's leadership and activists and a spark for new initiatives and experimentalism.

The significance that this history assigns to Unifor is not intended to in any way diminish the innovations and achievements of other Canadian unions, councils or federations. The portrayal of Unifor reflects my pride and self-identification with Unifor and my belief that the creation and building of Unifor was the most important development in the Canadian labour movement since the neo-liberal assault against labour began in the 1980s. In the following chapters, the story of the New Union Project is set out based on the agendas, documents, notes and recollections of the great leaders and organizers, researchers and communicators who made the creation of Unifor their daily priority.

CHAPTER 1
A Moment of Truth

In May 2011, there were two defining events for Canadian unions that focused contrasting outlooks on the future of the Canadian labour movement.

On May 2, Stephen Harper won a majority government, bringing to power what many saw as the most extreme right-wing government in Canadian history. But for most trade union leaders, the shock of the election result was offset by the "orange wave" that elected a historic number of New Democratic Party (NDP) members of Parliament and made Jack Layton leader of the Official Opposition. For many NDP stalwarts the terrible results for the Liberals were satisfying and they were quite prepared to weather four years of a Harper majority for the chance of converting the first NDP Official Opposition into government. For them, May 2 was all about the NDP and a taste of victories to come.

I was among hundreds of NDP supporters in Ottawa watching the returns that fateful night, desperately hoping for a minority government with a strong NDP presence. As a very different result became clear, the doors of the Sala San Marco banquet hall burst open for the triumphant entry of Member of Parliament Paul Dewar and Ed Broadbent. In the victory speeches that followed, we heard soaring rhetoric of the historic breakthrough that had occurred, but there was no mention of the Conservative majority and what it represented for working people and the labour movement. "Sipping Orange Crush from cases of the beverage placed on tables in lieu of flowers, they regularly cheered and applauded as television reported NDP successes across Canada," as the *Ottawa Citizen* described the evening.[1] The NDP celebration was understandable, but among the smaller group of labour activists who retreated to the sidelines to share their premonitions, there was a palpable disconnection from the festive atmosphere. In our smaller circle we were reflecting on Stephen Harper's reputed quote, "You won't recognize Canada when I'm through with it."[2]

Our equivocal emotions that night reflected a larger analysis that was shared by many others in the labour and social movements, including the leadership of both the CAW and CEP. The Canadian Auto Workers Union had appealed to Jack Layton in 2006 not to bring down the Martin government and in 2011 it seemed to the CAW that the no-confidence vote in Parliament that precipitated the election was manipulated by Conservatives eager to go the polls and secure a "stable majority." The CAW had developed a strategic voting strategy to block a Conservative majority with recommendations for their members in fifty swing ridings.

In the CEP, we had enthusiastically supported the 2008 proposal for an NDP-Liberal coalition government supported by the Bloc Québécois, as the CAW did also. Our smaller election effort in 2011 was aimed at electing New Democrats where CEP members were numerous enough to make a difference. But we were also fearful of a Harper majority and held no illusions that an NDP government was possible, instead calling on our members at large to vote for another minority Parliament.

On May 10, the Canadian Labour Congress met in convention in Vancouver. In addition to the euphoric welcome to Jack Layton, the congress had two large items on its agenda. The first was a multimillion-dollar television advertising campaign called "Fairness Works" to improve the image of unions. Telling the story of the "union advantage" and the positive role of unions in society was the orthodox answer to the danger represented by the Harper government. As Canadian Labour Congress President Ken Georgetti said to the convention: "Too often unions are portrayed negatively, inaccurately and unfairly. Put simply, we've been framed. Framed by our opponents, by big business, in the media they own and by right-wing governments . . . We must examine our public image as unions and be willing to reconsider our strategies to address it . . . We are going to step completely out of their distorted frame, starting at this convention."[3]

The other major business at the Canadian Labour Congress convention was a set of constitutional changes arising from a review and purported "renewal" of the trade union movement. Expectations for anything approaching renewal were low, especially after the Canadian Labour Congress Executive Committee appointed itself the Structural Review Committee. Although a few trial balloons were floated on issues such as revitalizing local labour councils through full participation by all congress affiliates, it was no surprise that the review did not result in any important change in or renewal to labour's public role or structures. The main upshot of the two-year structural review was a revised internal code of conduct aimed at stopping the "raiding" of members in an affiliated union by another union. The solution to this long standing divisive issue between unions was a Canadian Labour Congress process for members who wanted to change their affiliation.

In short, the conventional trade union movement's answer to the storm clouds gathering over it in 2011 was to up its public relations game and circle the wagons.

The Canadian Labour Congress's wagon train was directed by its fifteen-year president, Ken Georgetti. Emblematic of the movement's public image challenge, Georgetti was unknown to most Canadians and not much better known by union activists. He was an aloof figure who would arrive at occasional speaking events at union conventions and leave without meeting anyone except the leaders who invited him. Georgetti was known to say that he reported and was accountable to a membership of ten: the presidents of the five largest private sector and five largest public sector Canadian unions represented on the congress's Executive Committee. Congress leadership could revolve around an even smaller group of leaders — usually all men — who would from time to time broker decisions over private dinners at a Preston Street Italian restaurant in Ottawa.

Georgetti had succeeded the most high-profile and popular Canadian labour leader of his generation, Bob White of the CAW. But whereas White had led the breakaway union and was a favourite of social activists across the country for his strong vision of social unionism, Georgetti was closely associated with the private sector international unions, and his Canadian Labour Congress had fewer and more tense relations with social movements. Although White had been a leader of the labour movement and civil society coalition that campaigned against the Canada-United States Free Trade Agreement and the North American Free Trade Agreement (NAFTA), the congress under Georgetti had no real campaign on trade issues. Nor was the congress at the centre of broad-based social justice alliances as it was during and in the aftermath of the free trade struggles.

The Canadian Labour Congress under Georgetti's leadership was caught flat-footed by the election result and had not prepared an action plan to unite the convention. Rank-and-file activists were meeting in caucus and were demanding emergency resolutions committing the congress to a militant response to the anticipated strike-breaking and anti-labour legislation from the new majority government. An ad hoc committee made up of the assistants to the presidents of major affiliates was thrown together to draft a fight-back plan that would answer the call. After several iterations, an action program was drafted reminiscent of many labour movement convention resolutions to forge solidarity around mutual commitments to take "necessary actions" to defend workers and to build political community coalitions. Typically, this kind of resolution would be introduced near the end of a convention, when labour leaders and activists would come together in a show of unity. Georgetti knew well how that worked in trade union culture, but in this case, he refused to let the resolution come to the floor of the convention for adoption. He had long before lost any appreciation or patience for the calls to militancy and action from rank-and-file voices, and he was determined instead to deny the left-wing action caucus delegates their turn at the microphone. It was not simply the result of an increasingly imperious style that had grown over his tenure but also a deliberate departure from that kind of unionism. The action plan was distributed as a statement without debate, publicity or any intention of implementing it.

One of the peculiar terms that emanated from the Georgetti leadership was "intelligent militancy" — a euphemism for wielding influence without protest and social activism that was seen as counterproductive. Needless to say, militants in the labour movement hardly appreciated the suggestion that they lacked intelligence, nor were they inclined to agree that it was a smarter approach to shift emphasis and resources away from activism and co-ordinated struggles towards public relations and professional lobbying. In 2011, Georgetti intended to apply intelligent militancy to establish a relationship with the Conservative government in Ottawa and to prepare for expected anti-labour legislation with television ads and a public relations program.

There was little debate over the plan, which was taken by the vast majority as a prudent approach that, although not particularly exciting, would at least counter a perceived threat. For Ken Lewenza, CAW president, and Dave Coles, CEP president, there was a hollowness to the response that did not match the urgency of the situation or hold out much promise of stopping the Harper government. But the two leaders did not have an alternative plan ready to propose at that meeting. The larger problem was the state of the labour movement, which left them with little comfort. The frustration they shared was the limited reach and power of the labour movement and the ability of their respective unions to win key fights and change outcomes for their members.

*Top: CEP President Dave Coles leading CEP members to
a Toronto rally in defence of telecommunications workers,
August 23, 2012.*
*Right: Ken Lewenza, CAW National President, holding
Adele Siddall, a daughter of a CEP member, at the rally.*

Lewenza had on his mind the CAW's epic confrontation in London, Ontario, with Electro-Motive, the locomotive manufacturer. Bargaining had broken down after the former General Motors subsidiary was purchased by the notoriously anti-union US giant, Caterpillar Corporation. Caterpillar's venture into Ontario followed more than a decade of union busting in the United States highlighted by two long strikes between the United Auto Workers (UAW) and the company at Peoria, Illinois, that resulted in the union returning to work on the company's terms. Caterpillar led the way in the United States, demanding two-tier wages and benefits implemented through take-it-or-leave-it bargaining that barely recognized the existence of the union. At Electro-Motive, Caterpillar demanded that wages be cut in half and the pension plan gutted. The CAW saw it for what it was: a provocation to start a labour dispute and an excuse to close operations and take production to low-wage, "right-to-work" states in the United States. All of this would play out in the coming months. Within a year, the $35/hour jobs at Caterpillar in London would be moved to Muncie, Indiana, where the new starting rate was $12 to $18 per hour. A *Washington Post* article on the company's labour strategy that had been brought to Ontario in 2011 summed up what Lewenza was up against: "Caterpillar to Unions: Drop Dead."[4]

The CAW's firebrand leader broke the mould of career trade union leaders in the CAW and in many of the other large affiliates. Like his predecessors in the CAW, Bob White and Buzz Hargrove, Lewenza had a larger-than-life presence. However, he was the first CAW president to bypass the staff promotion ladder and go directly from local union leader to national president. Lewenza was known for his passionate oratory and occasional malapropisms, gregarious manner and grassroots style. Deeply committed to his home community of Windsor, he was a regular visitor to workplaces, community events and hospitals where members or retirees would be found.

Dave Coles was an organizer who had climbed through the ranks of the Canadian Paperworkers Union and CEP with a colourful brand of left-wing activism. He gained national attention soon after his election as CEP president by exposing police agent provocateurs during the protests against the 2007 "Three Amigos Summit" with Stephen Harper, George W. Bush and Felipe Calderón in Montebello, Quebec. One of a few union leaders at the protest, Coles marched at the head of a parade through a phalanx of riot police in a symbolic effort to deliver a petition opposing the corporate-inspired "Security and Prosperity Partnership." As the march was ending, three apparent protesters wearing masks appeared, and one was carrying a rock. Coles confronted him, demanded that he put down the rock and then called him out as a cop. When Coles demanded that he remove his mask, Quebec police arrived on the scene and quickly escorted the three through the police lines, but not before a video and photographs revealed that the provocateurs were wearing boots identical to those worn by the Sûreté du Québec, the Quebec provincial police. The video of the whole affair went viral on social media, and the CEP later filed complaints with the Sûreté that led to an admission that the three masked men were indeed undercover officers. Dave Coles enjoyed and nurtured his image as a labour radical.

Coles and the CEP had come through several years of restructuring in the forest industry, which at one point saw almost the entire forest industry and several media companies under *Companies' Creditors Arrangement Act* bankruptcy protection. The *Act's* processes invariably led to cuts to worker pensions, which are largely unprotected by Canadian bankruptcy laws. The experience of being unable to stop the painful cuts and concessions imposed by the industry was profound for the CEP, which declared "Change the Rules" as the theme of its 2010 convention.[5]

These and other brutal experiences had a deep impact on both private sector labour leaders. Although many labour leaders pointed to a 30.8 per cent union density in Canada — one of the highest in the industrialized world — Coles and Lewenza were focused instead on private sector union density, which had declined from 20 per cent in 2000 to 17 per cent in 2011.

Hostile politicians were eager to pile on, assuming they were jumping on a populist bandwagon against unions. Stephen Harper's extreme anti-labour politics had been largely kept in check during two minority governments between 2006 and 2011, but any reasonably informed and engaged trade unionist knew that they could expect hostile attacks on their rights once Harper could brandish power unchecked. The Conservative anti-labour agenda was already well known: restricting bargaining rights, rolling back union security provisions and requiring public financial reporting by unions intended to curtail labour's political campaigns and support for social movements.

In 2012, Harper intervened in airline and railroad bargaining to end or prevent labour disputes. Harper was making it clear that his government would not allow free collective bargaining and legal labour disputes to determine economic outcomes in major sectors of the economy. Nor did it take long for the Conservative majority to launch a broadside against trade union political activities and workers' rights. By October of 2011, the Conservatives had moved against union financing of campaigns and social causes with legislation requiring the publication of all significant union expenses. The controversial legislation that singled out unions among all other Canadian organizations was strategically introduced as a private member's bill and co-ordinated with anti-union employers. A few months later, the Conservatives followed up with legislation restricting the right to strike in the federal public service and eliminating long-standing workers' rights in the *Canada Labour Code* to refuse unsafe work. Yet another assault on trade union rights reversed a key provision that had been the law for seventy years known as "card check." Card check certification allows workers to form a union and be certified by organizing a majority to sign membership cards, without the requirement of holding labour board votes that are often influenced by employers.[6]

At the provincial level, between 2004 and 2010, a series of anti-labour laws were enacted in British Columbia, Alberta and Saskatchewan. In Saskatchewan and Alberta, these laws restricted public sector bargaining rights and imposed sweeping essential services rules that invoked public safety or "welfare" to prevent large numbers of public sector workers from participating in a labour dispute. Increasingly, these restrictions far surpassed any need for public safety and effectively undermined the right to strike in the public sector. In British Columbia, legislation had been used to rip up negotiated health care agreements and to make illegal the right of teachers to negotiate class size. These laws were challenged in Canadian courts and would eventually lead to Supreme Court decisions to overturn them. The contempt for free collective bargaining or any measure of good faith in their dealings with the unions in these cases led the court to affirm the constitutional protection of trade union rights in Canada under the freedom of association provisions of the *Charter of Rights and Freedoms*.

The largest threat to the labour movement was in Ontario. The leader of the Ontario Progressive Conservatives was Tim Hudak, who had made anti-labour rhetoric the centrepiece of his stab at right-wing populism. Hudak was campaigning to end the "Rand formula," which has been a cornerstone of union security in Canada since the 1940s. The provision is named for Supreme Court justice Ivan Rand, who ruled in 1946 that when a trade union secures a majority in a workplace, the union would be required to fairly represent all workers, and, in turn, all workers covered by the certification would be required to pay union dues. The Ontario Conservative party was leading in polls and widely expected to form a government in the next election, making his promise to outlaw the Rand formula ominous.

Union security and the Rand formula were inextricably bound up with the history of the CAW. Local 200 of the CAW's predecessor international union, the UAW, organized a historic strike for union rights by 11,000 workers at Ford's manufacturing operations in Windsor in 1945. After ninety-nine days and an epic blockade of the factory by hundreds of workers' cars, the dispute was referred to arbitration and the resulting history-making decision by Ivan Rand. However, the Rand formula did not become universal practice in Ontario until the 1980s, in the wake of another renowned UAW strike at Fleck Manufacturing near London, Ontario. The first-contract strike of about eighty low-paid, mostly female workers was punctuated by scabbing and picket line confrontations over the demand by the union for the Rand formula to be put into the collective agreement. Later, Conservative Premier Bill Davis legislated that no employer could refuse such a demand by a duly certified union, and the Rand formula became standard practice in the province.

Militant struggles such as the Ford and Fleck strikes were much less common after the turn of the century and decades of shrinking union density and numbers of strikes. The reasons for the union security provisions that earlier strikes had fought for were receding in public memory. This gap in consciousness was fertile ground for Hudak's rhetoric of ending "forced unionism." Demagogues were jumping on pedestals to champion the rights of individual workers to stand outside the majoritarian principle of union certification.

An additional and powerful context in Ontario was the dramatic push in the United States to strip trade union rights and enact so-called "right-to-work" laws. Right to work was not a new threat to US unions, but it had suddenly pushed north and was being implemented in

Ontario's neighbouring states of Michigan and Wisconsin. It was no coincidence that the battles for union recognition that led to the Rand formula had taken place in Windsor, connected by a bridge across the Detroit River to the historic centre of the auto industry. It seemed now that a counter revolution against everything labour had achieved since the 1930s could come to Canada across the same bridge.

These virulent anti-labour provisions have nothing to do with any right to secure employment. They are instead laws preventing a union from negotiating any provision that would require employees to join the union ("closed shop" or "union shop") or to pay dues in a unionized workplace even if they decide not to join the union (Rand formula in Canada).

The spin of casting these laws as rights for workers is outrageous and perverse, particularly given their roots. The first coining of the term dates to the 1940s and the campaign of the anti-Semitic Christian American Association, which railed against Roosevelt's "New Deal" pro-labour social legislation and jobs programs in the 1930s, casting these policies as a Marxist-Jewish conspiracy. So-called right-to-work laws were passed in Arkansas and Florida, where the Christian American Association alleged that unions would break the colour barrier and force black and white workers to work side by side as members of the same union. From these unseemly origins, contemporary right-to-work ideologues have modified their arguments and today use libertarian arguments about "forced unionism." They also use job blackmail to frighten workers that their employers will flee if union security provisions are allowed in a workplace.

In 2011 and 2012, there was a co-ordinated offensive by employers and their Republican political allies to vastly expand right-to-work legislation in the United States. Right-to-work initiatives were debated in sixteen US state legislatures in 2011 and in nineteen state legislatures in 2012. Indiana and Michigan passed right-to-work legislation in 2012, to be followed by Wisconsin in 2015.

With Hudak, Harper and Canadian Conservatives increasingly echoing US Republicans and using anti-labour laws as red meat for their extremist base, it was no wonder that the dominant narrative in Canadian media was about labour's fall from power and its precarious clinging to the past at the margins of economic and political relevance. The storyline was somewhat exaggerated but based in a core truth that the labour movement had yet to come to terms with. It was facing an all-sided attack on labour rights that was evolving much faster than the movement's organizational and political response.

At the Canadian Labour Congress Executive Council meeting prior to the Vancouver convention, Coles and Lewenza were seated next to each other listening to the discussion among Canada's labour leadership. The orange wave was still being applauded, but beyond that there was little to cheer about so far in 2011. Employment levels had only barely climbed back to 2008 levels, and more than half of the jobs created over the previous year were part time. Union wages were lagging well behind inflation and since the start of the year had declined a bit. A report released in March revealed that black workers in Canada on average faced a wage gap of about 10 to 15 per cent compared with non-visible minorities, with education and location taken into account. None of this was helping union fortunes. The McGuinty Liberal government of Ontario had passed legislation banning the right to strike for Toronto transit workers, Toronto's populist right-wing mayor Rob Ford wanted to contract out unionized garbage collection and union members were now hearing rabid anti-union rhetoric on CBC television. Conservative bombaster Kevin O'Leary had begun a year of union bashing on CBC by telling *CBC News Morning* in January, "just get rid of unions every-where. They add no value whatsoever. I love to get out there and union bash, and you know, frankly, I think it's a good thing."[7] Now the labour movement would have to contend with a hostile federal government that could act against them with impunity. Coles and Lewenza were taken aback by the passivity and apparent hopelessness they heard, and the lack of a credible plan to defend the movement. Coles said to Lewenza, "We have to be able to do better than this." Lewenza replied, "We should have a conversation about how we can get stronger." Later that day, they agreed that they would explore "doing something new."

Both leaders were aware of discussions that had started in Quebec about the possibility of a CEP-CAW project. Some months before, Lewenza had contacted Coles to ask his permission for a discussion with the CEP to be initiated in Quebec. However, the two had not yet followed up and taken it to a "'what if' stage," as Coles put it to me. "We had only planted a seed, but in my heart I knew that if anything emerged, it would entail a bigger discussion and process."

In Vancouver, Lewenza and Coles bonded over the need for a stronger force with the potential to succeed where the movement to that point was failing, and it was an opening to connect the earlier Quebec contacts with the opportunity of a Canadian discussion. But there was no clarity on what form that new force might take. Coles was thinking that a new union or alliance was the answer; Lewenza was thinking that a combined union could wield the strength that was needed and that, as in the many mergers in the past, this would mean the smaller union becoming part of the larger. It was not the time or place to go further. Instead, they agreed to assign me, Coles's assistant, and CAW economist Jim Stanford to explore what might be possible. Coles knew that Stanford and I had known each other for some years and could speak frankly and off the record about both the opportunities and the challenges of building something new.

When Coles broached the subject with me, we agreed to keep the matter confidential until after the summer. The problem we saw was that in the smaller CEP, there was no likelihood of agreement on a merger into the larger CAW. There had been no discussion in the CEP about merging into another organization, and it was already deeply divided over proposed organizational reforms to reduce its top-heavy structure of fourteen elected full-time officers. Although in most parts of Canada, CEP's sectoral officers had evolved general administrative responsibilities, in Quebec, the paper, energy and telecommunications officers retained a clear division of responsibilities, with each taking the lead on internal matters within their sector. In the months prior to the New Union Project, CEP's attempt at a structural reform to eliminate the sector-based officers had hit a wall of opposition in Quebec. The CEP officers in Quebec maintained that competition with the nationalist localism of the rival Confederation of National Trade Unions made their regional sectoral leadership necessary. The sharp disagreements had stalled the process, and there were few ideas circulating to break the impasse.

Jim Stanford and I arranged to meet in Toronto on August 10, 2011. Jim had carved out a distinctive role in the Canadian labour movement as CAW's economist and public intellectual, author of several books, a *Globe and Mail* columnist and a TV commentator. He was director of the union's public policies, an authority on auto industry economics and a sought-after consultant by government and the Bank of Canada. In the CAW, he was a membership favourite who had honed his communication skills to popularize labour economics through offbeat methods that broke down the barrier between economist and workers. Leaders and members called him "Jimbo."

I had a much smaller public profile but had spent a lifetime in labour and left-wing politics. My background was in Vancouver, where I learned my politics from socialist fishermen and loggers and managing campaigns for the left-wing Committee of Progressive Electors. I was the first national representative hired by the CEP after its founding in 1992 and represented the union in forestry and environmental affairs during the "War in the Woods" on the West Coast.[8] After arriving in Ottawa in 2001 to become the CEP's assistant to the president, I became involved in union administration, industry bargaining in paper and energy and directing CEP's policy work, notably the union's forestry and energy policies. When I moved to Ottawa, I became a close associate of Maude Barlow and, with the union's support, joined the board of directors of the Council of Canadians.

Our meeting on the forty-second-floor lounge of the Sheraton Centre began with nothing clarified over our marching orders from Lewenza and Coles. As Stanford would later recall, "I was still labouring under the misapprehension that the CEP would simply merge into the CAW . . ." In our discussion, it quickly became clear that "something new" had to mean something different than the CEP joining the larger CAW, and Jim left the meeting to check in with Ken Lewenza. There was no obvious interpretation other than a new union, but the suggestion was so startling that it had to be confirmed. When we met again for lunch at the Spadina Gardens on Dundas Street, we had the green light we needed to begin discussing what a new union could be and how it might come about. "You and I knew full well it was about something much bigger than any union name or logo," Jim later reflected. "It was about building a stronger, more modern and effective vehicle for Canada's working class to collectively advance its interests, in all areas of life: in the workplace, in their communities, in politics, in the world. The fact that you and I both knew that — and that you and I both knew the other person knew it, too — was crucial in laying a groundwork of trust and shared vision."

But where to start? There was no crisis or pressing need in either union for a "merger." Neither union was desperate. In fact, both unions were very capable of carrying on business-as-usual operations. Although each had lost tens of thousands of members over the previous decade, including through the global economic crisis of 2008–2009, by 2011, those job losses had been reduced to a slow attrition. The CAW had roughly 200,000 members, and the CEP had about 100,000 members. Both unions had stable

Jim Stanford, left, and me, right, August 31, 2013.

annual budgets that were in balance and strike and defence funds that were ample for their needs. The CAW's strike fund was in the range of $90 million, and the CEP's defence fund was about $43 million. However, major strikes were exceptional events, and the two unions had relatively successful bargaining outcomes with a premier list of Canada's major corporations. A diverse multisectoral membership was a shared advantage. The majority of CEP's members were spread across four large industries: energy, forestry, telecommunications and media. The CAW members were even more diverse, based in automobile manufacturing and parts, aerospace, airlines and railroads, mining, retail, health care, public transit and more.

It was immediately clear that the traditional approach to union mergers, where unions agree to pool resources and bargain leadership positions, would not lead to the new force that Lewenza and Coles suggested. To launch the idea of a new union required starting from a different place. There would have to be an agreement that a new union was needed, as well as some common vision of how it could be different and more successful.

There were other considerations about how to begin. Jim had a copy of a document produced by the Quebec leaders of the two unions suggesting a joining of forces, but neither of us knew any of the background to it or its implications for a national process. Moreover, the English Canadian relationship between the two unions was quite different. Although the two unions had amicable relations, they had not been very close. That was the case especially in Ontario, where the CEP regional leadership and the CAW had been on opposite sides of labour rivalries in that province. Those differences dated back to the NDP government of Bob Rae and the "social contract" legislation that he imposed on public sector unions.[9] Although the CAW had supported the public sector unions and opposed Rae's legislation, the CEP in Ontario had joined the "pink caucus" of private sector unions that supported Rae. The pink caucus went so far as to propose dividing the labour movement into separate public and private federations. Although fifteen years had passed, those divisions continued to cut deeply across Ontario labour politics. A dialogue about a new union would have to start with introductions and building trust between leaders who barely knew each other.

The first meeting was organized for November 1 and 2 in Toronto to explore whether there could be an opening consensus towards a vision and process. This tentative meeting included only Lewenza, Coles and their respective secretary-treasurers, each the second ranking officer in their union, along with Jim and me.

Peter Kennedy, the secretary-treasurer of the CAW, was a counterpoint to Lewenza. His rise in CAW leadership was classic. A worker in the London, Ontario, 3M manufacturing plant, he was elected a local leader at a young age and then appointed staff representative, national education director and assistant to the secretary-treasurer before his election as national secretary-treasurer on the retirement of his predecessor, Jim O'Neil, in 2009. Kennedy eschewed tub-thumping oratory and was known for his measured tone and deliberative style. He had an easygoing manner shaped as a young man in the heyday of the 1970s counterculture and a lifelong passion for blues music. As a union officer, he presented a more refined image than many of his contemporaries, although he was as tough as any at the bargaining table. Behind the style, Kennedy was always an organizational man, completely committed to the union and a product of its culture.

CAW Secretary-Treasurer Peter Kennedy accepting his acclamation as Unifor's first secretary-treasurer.

Kennedy's CEP counterpart, Gaétan Ménard, was the youngest in the room and possibly the most complex character. A Quebecer from the Outaouais, he trained as a social worker but went to work in the Masson paper mill near his hometown of Buckingham. He became a staff representative for the CEP and was elected national secretary-treasurer to cement the regional alliance between Western Canada and Quebec that had elected Coles. Immensely

CEP Secretary-Treasurer Gaétan Ménard addressing the CAW convention in Toronto, August 22, 2012.

talented, Ménard identified strongly with the progressive left of the CEP but had clashed with Coles on administrative matters. His larger challenge, however, was his relationship with the Quebec region of the union. The Quebec leadership that had promoted him to national leadership had been succeeded by a different Quebec leadership with a more uneasy relationship with Ménard. Ménard, a passionate sovereigntist, found himself playing a national Canadian role, with his heart still in Quebec.

At 1 p.m. in the forty-third-floor boardroom of the Sheraton Hotel, the meeting opened with introductions; for some in the room, this was the first time they had met. Jim and I outlined a tight agenda, drafted to avoid the many issues that could easily sidetrack the discussion or undermine the chance of success. The agenda on the table began with two short "ground rules":

> We are here to see if a new Canadian union can fill a void in the labour movement and help us all do our work better than we are doing it today.
>
> This is a genuine exploration of that possibility; we don't know the answer yet. We have to answer the question affirmatively for the process to continue.

In a meeting spanning the afternoon and the morning of the next day, the four officers tackled three main questions. The first question was to evaluate the current condition of their respective unions, setting out the strengths and weaknesses they saw. The second question was an evaluation of the strengths and weaknesses of the broader labour movement and "what the movement is missing today."

The last and decisive question for the process to continue was a brainstorming session on "what a new union can do that existing unions cannot do." The guideline for the discussion called on the leaders to go beyond rhetoric. "We must be very specific and concrete in this discussion. Simply being bigger won't be enough, as we have seen with other mergers." We challenged each other to be specific and to speak to how a new union would impact "branding and image in the eyes of individual workers, organizational/leadership capacity to try new things, financial capacity, organizing new members (would it concretely change?), political impact and impact on the behaviour of labour centrals." We had expected it to be nearly impossible to keep the group focused, but there were only a few departures from the outline on the table. The discussion was cautious and low key, with each side carefully sketching out the daunting challenges they faced in bargaining and the threats posed by Harper. In response to the question of how each union was coping with those challenges, both unions affirmed that they were holding their ground and not facing a crisis. As the discussion moved towards what was needed, there was an early and strong agreement that the threats to the labour movement loomed larger than its capacity to respond. Before long, the question was posed directly: could a new union be larger in impact than the existing force and influence of the two unions? Each in turn answered that a new and stronger strategy and dynamic were needed and that a new union could be that force. By the time the discussion carried over into a working dinner at a nearby steakhouse, the officers were focusing more on getting to know each other on a personal basis. They had already agreed that the bold idea of a new Canadian union should be shared with a broader leadership group in each union.

The momentous decision was still a baby step. The first meeting had revealed a host of potentially deal-breaking issues, from different

histories and cultures to political strategies and organizational structures. Only a very small circle knew of the first meeting, and there
could be no certainty that the idea of a new union would pass through
a larger leadership filter. For the smaller CEP, the proposal would be
seen by some as just another route to a merger into the larger CAW.
In the CAW, there was a strong attachment and loyalty to the well-
known brand of the CAW, arguably the strongest of any Canadian
trade union.

With these concerns in mind, the officers made a strategic call not
to simply repeat their process with a larger group. Instead, they asked
Jim and me to summarize their consensus and flesh out the case for a
new union and how it would be different in a discussion document that
could be brought to the leadership of each union.

The opening argument for the new union that emerged just ten
days later was a provocative call for change in the labour movement.
The outline of the draft was prepared by Stanford, with added content
from me, and together we made revisions. Our seven-page document,
called *A Moment of Truth for Canadian Labour*, laid out a hard-hitting
assessment of the state of unions in Canada and a stark choice between
renewal and decline.[10]

"After two decades of fighting mostly defensive battles against the pressures of globalization, employer aggression, hostile government policy, and
public cynicism, the trade union movement in Canada faces an enormous
and historic moment of truth," said the discussion paper. The "truths" that
labour had to face up to were extensive, profound and threatening:

- Continuing erosion of union density, especially in the private
  sector
- Failure of union organizing to offset plant closures and keep
  up with labour force growth
- A decline in labour's share of national wealth and stagnant
  and falling purchasing power for working people
- New levels of political hostility, citing Stephen Harper's three

interventions in collective bargaining in the previous six months and anti-labour laws enacted in twenty US states

- Aggressive attacks by global employers on contract provisions and the foundations of unions, such as the Vale and US Steel attacks on Canadian steelworkers
- Dramatic generational change with the retirement of union veterans and the problem of appealing to and organizing young workers
- Growing negative public opinion of unions and the view that unions are self-interested and outdated
- Paralysis and dysfunction of some labour centrals
- Failure of the labour movement to significantly restructure and to initiate and lead powerful campaigns
- Lack of co-ordination and duplication of labour movement services and resources

The answer to this challenge, the paper argued, had to be "a new kind of unionism." The paper also asserted that the new union must have a new identity, neither the CAW nor the CEP:

> We believe there is a need for a new force in the Canadian labour movement with the ability to succeed and grow in a way that our present unions cannot. Such a new union could open important opportunities to build on our traditions and past successes, and also to create a new identity, a new presence, a new brand, and new power for worker rights and social change . . . Such a new union would have to speak to Canadians in a new way. It must reflect a dynamic, sectoral and community based workers' movement that is more attractive and more relevant to workers' needs than our present day organizations.

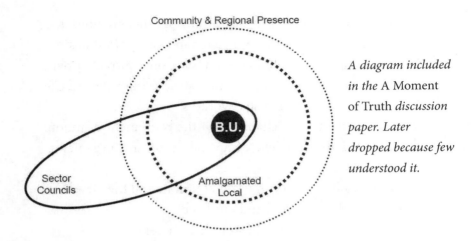

A diagram included in the A Moment of Truth *discussion paper. Later dropped because few understood it.*

A Moment of Truth acknowledged that the qualities and strategies of what was being proposed "must be the product of extensive dialogue, debate and visioning." But it nonetheless set out a series of starting propositions for that process that would take most of the next two years. Many of these ideas spoke to increased resources and innovation, but with the caveat that bigger was not necessarily better and that more than the combining of resources would be needed for success. Several of these propositions confronted much of what CAW and CEP leaders knew about their union and what the purpose of the labour movement was.

On the starting point of brand and identity, the paper proposed that a new union would be defined "not by who we are (e.g. autoworkers, paper workers etc.) but by what we think and what we do."

On mandate, the paper asserted that a new union must "define itself as a force fighting for all workers — not just its own members" and "offer services and support to non-union workers engaged in struggles and conflicts."

On outlook, vision and politics, the new union would articulate a critique of neo-liberal capitalism and "position itself as fighting for long run social and political change, not just incremental economic progress for its members." This radical vision was part of a "culture shift" that would "go beyond servicing" and view the work of union activists as "movement building."

On its role in the labour movement, the paper called for inspiring, pushing and embarrassing labour centrals into becoming more forceful bodies and, failing that, for the new union "to undertake those broader movement functions itself." The suggestion captured our collective disappointment in the larger movement, which seemed to be sleepwalking.

If the goal of A Moment of Truth was to start a debate on the need for change and a break with the past, it delivered. Too short to answer the myriad of questions it opened and too long and theoretical for some to see it as a practical proposal, it had everything needed to provoke strong responses from inside the two unions and across the labour movement.

The debate was sharpest within the CEP, and it led to a decisive leadership meeting on December 5 in Ottawa. The CEP's full-time elected officers met in a face-to-face showdown over the proposal of joining with the CAW. The meeting was tense and sharp, with strong misgivings from the Ontario leadership, who had been allied with the United Steelworkers against the CAW in Ontario labour politics. The three Ontario officers argued that CEP's major industries did not overlap with CAW's and they pointed to their disagreements with the CAW in the past.

However, when the smoke cleared, the new union idea survived the test. One key reason was the strong support from Quebec, where the CEP-CAW connection had its genesis. Those beginnings dated to 2007 when CEP Quebec leader Michel Ouimet developed a close working relationship with Luc Desnoyer, CAW director in Quebec. "We were looking for partners back then, but CAW was not the highest on our list, because there were other Canadian unions with closer sectoral relationships," Ouimet recalled. "But Luc and I began discussions at the FTQ executive board about working together. It didn't go anywhere at the time because he left the CAW to go into politics." Desnoyer left the CAW in 2008 when he was elected as an member of Parliament with the Bloc Québécois.

In the winter of 2010, Desnoyer contacted Ouimet to restart the discussions. "Luc called me to have lunch with him and we talked about our earlier discussions. The two of us then met with Jean-Pierre Fortin,

CEP Executive Vice-President Michel Ouimet, first Quebec director of Unifor, at the Unifor founding convention, September 2013.

who had become the CAW director." Ouimet added, "We agreed to start some discussions, and I confidentially spoke with Dave Coles and Jean-Pierre spoke with Ken Lewenza."

Ouimet and Fortin met multiple times over the winter of 2010–2011 and sketched out a diagram and bullet points on a possible integration of the CAW and the CEP in Quebec. Ouimet subsequently showed it to Coles in a meeting in the CEP Montreal offices in March 2011. The memo from Ouimet and Fortin discussed leadership, finances, staffing and services. "I briefed Dave in my office in Montreal, and he was surprised at what we had done," Ouimet said. "He said it would be controversial but to go ahead, that it was a good idea."

Coles and Lewenza were both surprised by the extent of the Quebec memo but had no substantive discussion about it before the Canadian Labour Congress convention in May. The Québécois beginnings of the New Union Project were crucial but would soon be eclipsed by the idea of an entirely new kind of union.

The possibility of a CEP-CAW relationship also had some roots in English Canada. In 2006, Brian Payne, CEP president prior to Coles, met discreetly with CAW President Buzz Hargrove, the predecessor of Ken Lewenza. Hargrove was eager to add to the forty-four mergers that the CAW had negotiated since 1985, and the CEP would almost equal in size all of the previous mergers. Payne did not believe that the CEP was ready or willing to join with the CAW or any other union in 2006. However, he was convinced that when that time came, the CEP could not become an international union, and he wanted to open a door to the only large Canadian industrial union that could be a partner.

Although few knew of any of these tentative beginnings as the CEP officers in Ottawa confronted each other on their options in 2011, it became clear that the fiercely Canadian CEP would not return to its past by joining an international union. If the CEP was interested in the idea of a new union, the CAW was the only Canadian industrial union that could be a viable partner.

Eventually, the debate moved towards process. Although some remained skeptical, Coles and Ménard argued forcefully that a merger into the CAW was not on the table; rather, what would occur was a process leading towards something entirely different. In the end, the CEP leadership was reassured that the ideas in A Moment of Truth and every other aspect of what the new union might be would be subject to a comprehensive, inclusive and transparent examination that would proceed one step at a time.

On the CAW side, there was less controversy when the paper was circulated to its national executive board. But there were serious and direct questions from the leaders of the large CAW locals and the assistants to Lewenza and Kennedy about where this process was leading. The CAW leaders were granted a vote of confidence, even if they had few definitive answers to those questions.

The critical question in the CAW debate was its identity; for many, the evolution from the UAW to the CAW was definitional. Its name and history from its breakaway from the UAW in 1985 were core to the union's self-image and internal solidarity. But by 2011, the roots of the union in the traditional automobile sector accounted for only about one-quarter of the total membership. There had been discussions for some years about how to expand the union's identity to include the many other large sectors that had joined the union since 1985 (including transportation, health care, retail and more). The national leaders, including those from the auto industry, were willing to consider a remaking of the union's identity and brand. The CAW leadership agreed to proceed with the same assurances that had been necessary in the CEP leadership, namely that a long and detailed process lay ahead before any ultimate decisions to change the CAW would be considered.

By mid-December, the debates in the CAW and CEP leadership had started to filter into the membership and to the media. On December 15, Lewenza sent a message to Coles:

> *Dave, Toronto Star has obviously received our document and have asked me questions. I simply said that there are multiple unions discussing, in a real way, how the labour movement can be strengthened in the interest of our members moving forward. The discussions are preliminary and nothing will get resolved without the approval of the respective executive boards of the unions. This is a long term discussion and things will not happen overnight. The star reporter Tony VanAlphen may be giving you a call.*

Two days later, stories had run in both the *Star* and the *Huffington Post*, and both leaders were trying to provide the context for the as yet unauthorized project. The *Star* story said that merger talks had opened between the two unions, but the *Huffington Post* story a day later stated that "Coles took issue with the characterization. 'What we're trying to do here is create a new union. It's not one joining the other, or merging together, it's actually starting from the ground up, and building a new union,' he says. 'It starts from the bottom up and it will require a significant amount of grassroots involvement.'" Lewenza also tried to modify the storyline. "It wouldn't be a takeover of CAW or vice versa," he told *Huffington Post*, "it would really be re-defining the labour movement based on best practices of our members, and trying to form a culture of providing the best of both organizations."[11]

With the media getting out in front of us, it was obvious that we had to act quickly and decisively to secure a mandate and establish a protocol with the backing of our national executive boards. The membership of both unions needed a full explanation of what was coming. We decided to bring together a broader and representative leadership from both unions as soon as possible after the New Year.

Jim and I were already thinking about the complications of the process ahead. On January 3, I wrote to Jim,

> *Key issue for process is how to construct a small*
> *representative group to get the work done and also*
> *reach out and include mainstream of each membership.*
> *Another concern is how to keep process focused*
> *on goals of a new union rather than just recreating*
> *ourselves . . . new qualities must be emphasized at the*
> *outset, because as process unfolds tendency will be to*
> *find comfort zones and increasingly focus on practical*
> *matters. Third concern is the intensity and time needed*
> *to do it right. Both unions will have to make this process*
> *a priority over a million other important things. A report*
> *by August means that the spring will have to be largely*
> *given over to the project.*

On January 16, 2012, in Toronto, seventeen people sat across from each other at the Sheraton in another first for the fledgling venture. The CAW group was led by Ken Lewenza, Peter Kennedy, the Quebec director Jean-Pierre Fortin and Sylvain Martin, his assistant and likely successor after his imminent retirement. With them were two assistants to the president, Jerry Dias and Deb Tveit, and Tim Carrie, the president of Local 27 in London and rank-and-file chair of the CAW Canadian Council. The CAW group was rounded out by Bob Chernecki, a recently retired assistant, and David Robertson, the recently retired director of workplace organization and training. The CEP side included Coles and Ménard, Executive Vice-President Michel Ouimet, National Media Vice-President Peter Murdoch, Ontario Regional Director Kim Ginter, Atlantic Regional Director Chuck Shewfelt and Western Regional Director Jim Britton. Stanford and I took one end of the table as facilitators.

For most of those in the room, it was the first time they had met. But there was little time for getting to know each other; they had given each other one day to reach a consensus on a protocol that would satisfy the constitutional and political requirements of both unions. This meant a process that would safeguard the interests of the larger CAW and the smaller CEP and be able to deliver a practical proposal before their respective conventions convened in August and October of that year.

By the end of the day, a protocol was agreed with a monthly time-table and an agreement to establish a "Proposal Committee" with equal members from each union to "develop the main principles of a new Canadian union with a new identity and structure." These proposals would be reported later that year to the CAW and CEP conventions for membership approval. The protocol demanded as well that "this process must be transparent with frequent reports to our members and democratic debate in each union. Where possible, joint meetings of CEP and CAW members should also be convened to discuss the work of the Proposal Committee and the principles of a new union."

With these decisions and the approval of the protocol by each union's executive board in the following days, the New Union Project was launched. A media statement was its first public declaration:

> *"Events like the lockout at Caterpillar have made it increasingly obvious that Canadian workers need a stronger more active and more innovative labour movement to defend them," said Ken Lewenza, CAW*

President. "Our movement cannot afford a business as usual approach in light of the attacks we face from business and government . . . Our goal is to create a new Canadian union," said Dave Coles, President of CEP. "We are examining every aspect of our work as trade unions, from organizing to bargaining to political activism. We are working to create a stronger union movement and a better future for workers."

Only a few months later, a feature article in the *Globe and Mail* newspaper asked, "Do unions have a future?" The tentative answer it offered up cited *A Moment of Truth*: "If unions do not change, and quickly, we will steadily follow U.S. unions into continuing decline."[12]

CHAPTER 2

Towards a New Union: The Proposal Committee Debates

There was a sense that the ambitious mandate set out in the "process protocol" would require immense intensity and effort to deliver. But no one in these first days of the project knew how large it would be.

The mandate to envision a new trade union with a new identity and structure was by itself unprecedented in Canadian labour, without comparable examples to draw on. When trade unionists talk about identity and principles, they almost always reference the sacrifices and struggles of previous generations of organizers, who, with few resources, fought for recognition and gains against hostile employers and governments. The storybook of recent role models and visionaries is much thinner. Even the left-wing tradition that many of the key players in the New Union Project identified with had much more to say about long-standing trade union principles than about how to successfully organize a process to break with decades of tradition and create a distinctly modern organization.

The sheer size and scope of the project were the first fault lines detected. It was clear that any misstep or delay would render the August deadline for the CAW convention unachievable. Nor could either union simply set aside bargaining or the day-to-day leadership of their large, complex organizations to focus on imagining the goals and principles of a union that did not exist.

The answer to that dilemma was as unconventional as the project itself. The two sides agreed that the Proposal Committee would consist of eight members and three staff members from each organization and that neither organization would appoint their president. This would free the presidents to continue to attend bargaining and take care of other priorities without the Proposal Committee being required to organize meetings to accommodate their schedules. Another benefit to having the presidents at arms' length was that it enabled them to stay above the fray of the inevitable debates and crisis points to come.

It was determined instead that the Proposal Committee would be co-chaired by the two secretary-treasurers, Peter Kennedy and Gaétan Ménard. The other members of the Proposal Committee from each side were a mix of national and regional leadership, senior staff and rank-and-file local union leadership.

New Union Project co-chairs, Gaétan Ménard, left, and Peter Kennedy, centre, with retired CAW Assistant to the President Bob Chernecki, right, at the May 30, 2013, launch of Unifor's name and logo.

For the smaller CEP, the Proposal Committee members were at the outset skeptical and cautious towards the new union idea and the larger CAW's centralism. They were made up of Ménard, the union's five principal regional and sectoral leaders, and two rank-and-file executive board members who came with a defensive mission to protect the CEP's decentralized democracy.[1] The CAW's appointees joining Peter Kennedy were characterized less by current leadership roles. Instead, they tended to be selected for their connection to CAW practices, culture and history. They included an assistant to the president, the director of the legal department, the chair of the CAW's Canada Council, the head of the union's General Motors Bargaining Council and two recently retired staffers. The CAW side of the Proposal Committee table had had its own doubts about the CEP, which seemed to operate in an alternative political and organizational reality.[2]

There was a very different set of relationships in the staff project team assigned to facilitate the process and to prepare the research that would be needed. Duncan Brown was the former Canadian director of the Graphic Communications International Union and had led a majority of its Canadian members into the CEP. Brown also had extensive experience in global labour structures and had a strong overview of recent approaches to organizing strategy. Patty Barrera was the youngest of the group and had left the Canadian Labour Congress two years earlier to direct the CEP's political work. A former national chairperson of the Canadian Federation of Students, she was known for her extensive political and movement connections. The CAW side of the project team included Jo-Ann Hannah, the CAW director of the pensions and benefits department, and David Robertson, the former director of the CAW's department on workplace organization. Both were expert policy analysts at the top of their game. Robertson was brought out of retirement because of his strong ideological grasp of CAW culture and trade union renewal issues. A talented facilitator and uncompromising debater, he and I would often spar over issues of union structures, democracy and renewal. By the end of the New Union Project, we had established a solid friendship. These four, Jim and I quickly formed a tight group and rarely disagreed on our proposals.

For the next seven months, this unique group of leaders, staffers, activists and retirees would engage each other in an open-ended process of discussing values, dispelling stereotypes and envisioning the principles and general structure of a new union. The project team's first task was to produce the material needed to kick-start the work of the Proposal Committee. Each union had to be mapped by industry and geography, finances, bargaining relationships and policies. Structures and constitutional provisions were compared. But as the binder grew, the information was tailored as context and background rather than as agenda items. There would be no new union by simply combining or rationalizing the old unions. A starting point for our work was that if the New Union Project was to succeed, it needed to be launched with idealistic goals and imagination that would carry it through the expected collisions of cultures, engrained practices and insecurities of leaders and staff.

A first meeting date for the Proposal Committee was set for February 26, 2013, but on the day before, the national executive boards of each union and a representative group of staff came together to workshop the promise and opportunity that had been set in motion. Three outside voices were asked to keynote the new union idea and generate debate among the eighty activists in the room. John Cartwright, president of the Toronto and York Region Labour Council, made a passionate case for an organizing culture that would close the gap between rhetoric and results. Pradeep Kumar, the dean of Canadian labour academics at Queen's University, warned against waning labour influence and argued for consolidation and building political power.

But it was the presentation by Gregor Murray from the University of Montreal that most sharply framed the challenge. Murray had recently completed a study of "union mergers" in Canada, and although the new union was not a standard merger, his analysis was sobering.[3] Murray deconstructed the themes that typically run through trade union mergers and reorganizations. He concluded that in most cases, the outcomes were far less than the promises. Mergers universally touted increased bargaining power, but most mergers actually left bargaining more fragmented and less focused on common demands. Neither was it a given that increased political influence resulted from making larger unions; political power was more dependent on the values, visions and styles of campaigning, which did not necessarily change with a change in affiliation. Instead, the fragmentation of amalgamated unions could result in less political cohesion. On organizing, Murray said there was no evidence that combining unions improved organizing results. Combined unions tended to maintain the organizing practices and results of the predecessor unions. In some cases, the temporary relief of increased resources reduced the motivation and focus for organizing.

Membership participation and engagement are another common casualty of mergers. Largely uninformed and left out of merger processes, members have been left bewildered by complex structures arising from a patchwork of former union structures or their forced integration into the structures of the larger organization. Murray found that members who lost a personal connection to governance and decision making that they had in their previous union were not at all likely to feel the same connection in their new union.

Not even the bottom line of economies of scale and efficiencies could be counted on to deliver better results in Canadian union mergers. Efficiencies were elusive in the face of more complex structures and political deals to maintain levels of servicing and employment. There were even common examples of merged unions that were incapable of integrating databases and systems in a timely manner, with a resulting diminishment in communications and general organization.

Murray told the workshop that success would depend on having clear political and organizational goals and building these into the project itself rather than expecting these outcomes to evolve naturally. The major benefits would come from the next generation of union activists, leaders and staff, who would develop an identity and culture in the new union.

Optimism survived Murray's cautionary notes, and the workshop ended with everyone writing down their personal goals for what the new union would mean. But a weight descended onto the shoulders of the Proposal Committee members, who were beginning to see the scope and the risks of the still-undefined process ahead.

Many of the concerns troubling the twenty-two-person Proposal Committee were not that different from those expressed at the very first meeting of CAW and CEP leaders. But they were now magnified by the numbers of participants and the strong, uninhibited personalities they brought to the table. Some were lightning rods for the misgivings and apprehensions in the room. For the CAW, the no-nonsense Bob Chernecki knew his role well from countless assignments to protect the interests of his union. Chernecki had a gruff exterior and was not inclined to trade the CAW practices that he had enforced for the still vague proposals about how a new union would act differently. The rough edge on the CEP side was its Ontario vice-president, Kim Ginter, a sawmill worker from Northern Ontario and a former union organizer who had scrapped his way to leadership of the Ontario region. Knowing that the issue of centralism and decentralism was a possible deal breaker, Ginter colourfully stated to the Proposal Committee at one of its early meetings, "The President doesn't come into my region unless I say so." It was not a true statement, and Ginter explained to me that he was referring principally to the politics of the Ontario Federation of Labour, where he was the ranking CEP officer, not the national president. But he wanted to get the CAW's attention, and he got the reaction he wanted from the stone-faced CAW side.

Organizational culture in both unions was the subject of considerable myth. It was beer talk in the CEP that the CAW's centralism smothered dissent and carried out decisions made by presidents who were bestowed with personality cult status. The CAW's view of the CEP was that the national union was a weak federation of regions that went in different directions according to the ambitions of regional politicians. They told stories of how CEP leaders were regularly pilloried by union members who lacked respect for their leadership or their union. In fact, both organizations were vastly more complex than the stereotypes, and to a considerable degree their different cultures reflected alternative aspects of Canadian reality. The CAW's centralist culture in part grew out of its regional context: 75 per cent of its members were in one province. They did not consider labour movement politics or any large matter in that province to be a local or regional issue. The CEP's members were more or less evenly distributed across the country, and the national leaders could as easily come from Western Canada as from Ontario and were not expected to be experts on provincial affairs.

However, these myths served to exaggerate the tensions between the sides. It fell to the co-chairs to demonstrate an openness and collaboration that would be needed and to keep the focus on the big picture issues on the agenda. As the Proposal Committee members probed and tested, Kennedy and Ménard deferred to the other and avoided disagreements.

The detailed comparisons of the two unions that had been compiled were stacked on the table, each page highlighting a category of differences. But the first item of business for the Proposal Committee set aside those differences and instead took the group into a visioning process around "hopes and fears" for the New Union Project and to reflect on "lessons of past mergers." It was a risky start and took all the extensive facilitation skills of David Robertson, but it delivered tone and perspective that cut across the divide in the room.

Two unifying themes stood out on the flip charts hanging on the walls. The common hope was for an open process that would take advantage of a unique opportunity to "think outside the box" and to "write our future" in a manner that would generate membership enthusiasm. Moreover, the overarching lessons from past experience for both sides was the need to create a new union without silos or the continuation of the old unions reproducing and reinforcing their cultures.

It still did not take long to identify the key differences between the CEP and the CAW and reveal the fault lines for the New Union Project. The two unions had substantially different leadership structures and local union organizations. The centralized CAW structure was dominated by large local unions, whereas the decentralized CEP was an amalgam of mostly small locals. Moreover, there were significantly different political strategies, particularly regarding participation with and within the NDP.

Before the first meeting of the Proposal Committee wound up, the members had made three critical decisions to step around the crevices. First, they agreed that local unions would remain intact, with no forced mergers, and that the broader issues of local union structures would be referred to as a "local union task force" to be carried out by the new union. Second, the issues of electoral strategies and the NDP would be taken off the table with an agreement that the political policy would be debated and adopted by the first convention of the new union.

Parking these hot-button issues made it more likely that the other pressing issues of union structures, leadership and innovation could be worked through in the tight time frame. At the same time, political principles in a broad sense could not be ignored if any true solidarity would be built. A third decision was proposed to clarify what the new union would stand for without prejudging specific political strategies. Although the New Union Project mandate at this point did not include drafting a constitution or particular policies, for this purpose, it was decided to draft the purposes and principles section of a new constitution to be included in the final report. This section would set out in detail what the founding principles of the union would be, including its community, social and political roles. It was yet another formidable undertaking, but the project team was assigned to have a draft before the summer, with David Robertson taking the lead. To underscore the momentum that was demanded, a New Union Project website was commissioned to be set up within two weeks, with background information on the process to date and updates on decisions after each meeting.

Over the next four months, the Proposal Committee would meet five times in exhausting sessions over structure and operating principles. The Proposal Committee meetings punctuated a continuous cycle of research, policy development, meeting preparation and communications. The seemingly unachievable demands of the process were met every time. The excitement of a once-in-a-lifetime opportunity to build a union from design to foundation and frame was both intoxicating and energizing for the project team. The New Union Project had become a workshop that built a defining principle of the larger project. Decisions could no longer be the "aspirational" goals that labour organizations subscribed to but never expected to fulfill. There would always be reasons why organizational plans and political objectives would fall short or never go beyond rhetoric. But when highly skilled activists are motivated and disciplined, goals can and will be met.

The central issue before the Proposal Committee was over structure. Every point of difference and most of what was held crucial in the existing characteristics of each union ultimately reduced to structure. Those issues would play out over two decisive meetings of the Proposal Committee in March and May.

The Proposal Committee's first full meeting on structural issues was scheduled for March 2012 in the CEP's national boardroom in Ottawa. Anticipating a possible deal-breaking rupture over the debate on the structure of the new union, both sides held caucus meetings while the project team worked to find overarching points of agreement to offset the differences.

Lewenza, Kennedy, Stanford and Robertson met in advance to develop a CAW plan. Their consensus view was that CEP politics were significantly driven by the jobs and job descriptions of the eleven CEP regional officers. In the days before the March meeting, those views hardened. "We will not go to a CEP regional structure," Lewenza and Kennedy firmly asserted, arguing that CEP and other large regionalized unions, such as the Canadian Union of Public Employees (CUPE), had weak national leadership as a result.

The CEP Proposal Committee members were indeed digging in to defend their system of elected regional vice-president and sectoral administrative vice-presidents, arguing to each other that this system empowered members. Moreover, the often contentious Ontario and Quebec regions had allied on the issue, and Michel Ouimet, who was a pivotal supporter of the New Union Project, was a particularly strong defender of regional sectoral officers.

On a parallel track, the project team met and searched for avenues through the road blocks. "We have to show movement at this meeting," Robertson impressed on his colleagues. Jim and I agreed, proposing that the structure debate should be preceded with a discussion on what would be "new" in the new union.

The March 15 Proposal Committee meeting was a watershed moment for the New Union Project. Each side prepared for the debate by producing a draft outline and a diagram of a governance structure. The two diagrams had considerable ideas in common, including a national executive board with industry representation and regional councils across the country. But although the CAW proposal suggested that the rank-and-file chairpersons of the councils would represent the regions on the national executive board, the CEP proposal countered that each regional council and the Quebec council would be led by elected national vice-presidents, similar to the existing CEP structure.

On the eve of the meeting, Jim and I met with Kennedy and Ménard to plan the agenda. We knew there would be no pathway through irreconcilable differences over either side's bottom line: for the CAW, a strong central union without regional or other bodies empowered to chart a separate political or ideological course at variance with the national union; for the CEP, with the majority of its members outside Ontario, the structure had to include meaningful regional structures and leadership beyond Quebec to reflect the diversity of the country.

The plan was to avoid an early confrontation by first asking each side to report on the "strengths and weaknesses" of its existing structure before turning to a set of principles that both sides could agree should guide the structural design of the new union. Instead of facing off on regional leadership roles, the emphasis would be put on rank-and-file democracy and structures that would allow members to be heard and included in every part of the country. Rather than trying to determine who would be spokespersons for the union and direct staff in the regions, we would look for agreement on the need for a "unified and effective union" with the ability to act rapidly as one union.

The Proposal Committee meeting eased its way into the main event, taking up the first day by returning to the information binders on the less contentious issues of organizing, political action, sectors and bargaining. The second day opened the structure issues, with each side caucusing and then reporting to the other on the strengths and weaknesses of its existing structures. Kennedy took the lead, maintaining that the CAW's Canadian Council and unified national leadership were the source of its strength and strong public profile. But he lowered CEP stress levels by also offering that the lack of significant regional structures was a weakness that the CAW was prepared to address.

Ménard responded in kind, citing the CEP's regional structure as a strength of its membership, which was divided somewhat equally across the country. But he, too, signalled flexibility by stating that the CEP had "too many elected people" and an oversized executive board. More importantly, he acknowledged that an "incapacity to downsize" had paralyzed the CEP's structural reforms. Ménard went further and critiqued the CEP system of assigning all members to one of three recognized sectors: forestry, energy and telecommunications-media. That system resulted in members outside of the mainstream of those industries being attached to structures that were not designed for their needs.

The centrepiece of the meeting that steered the group away from the rocks was a set of twelve principles introduced by Peter Kennedy as a foundational guide to determining the structure of the new union. Ninety minutes later, there was consensus in principle around the twelve points. Although some of the principles appeared to be self-evident and common-sense goals for labour activists, taken together, they spoke strongly to the essential elements of an "effective, democratic, militant union."

Our Structural Goals and Principles

- The new union must be democratic, progressive and active, and committed to the principles and practices of social unionism.

- The new union must structure and organize itself to provide excellent service to its members, to organize new members, to fight on behalf of all workers (our members and others) and to campaign for progressive change in all areas of society.
- The new union's democracy would be governed by the "rank and file principle" fostering maximum involvement by rank and file members at all levels of the union's democracy.
- The new union's power will be rooted in strong local unions and capable, accountable local leadership.
- The national character of Quebec will be reflected in the structure of the new union.
- The new union must be able to make decisions effectively, quickly and flexibly, responding rapidly and powerfully to issues and situations.
- The new union must be able to act in a unified, united integrated manner — as "one union."
- Leadership in the new union must be collective and accountable, implemented by a leadership team.
- The new union must be financially strong, including a strong defence fund with rigorous audit and financial control.
- The new union will be fully committed to equity and inclusion with strong representation and forums for women, racialized and aboriginal workers, LGBT members, workers with disabilities, young workers and other equity seeking segments of our membership at all levels of the union.
- The new union will be supported by the efforts and skills of engaged and committed staff.
- The structure of the new union must be open to new members through many channels: new organizing, mergers with other unions and possibly new forms of membership (such as individual or associate membership).

The second Proposal Committee meeting concluded without an overall agreement on a new union structure. But a breakup had been averted, and a statement emerged with agreement on three broad points: The new union would have an extensive system of equity committees and positions on its executive recognizing equity groups. A second agreement was an autonomous structure to reflect the national character of Quebec with the authority to "make decisions on matters pertaining to Quebec." On regions, it was agreed to have formal recognition for regions across Canada and positions on the national executive board that would be "elected in the regions by regional delegates."

Another important gesture to the regions was a cap on the number of persons on the national executive board from Ontario. The new union had significant membership across the country, but fully half of the members would be in Ontario. The power of that concentration of members could be used to dominate the national union, but the Proposal Committee agreed that the number of persons elected to the national executive board from any region could not exceed thirteen of twenty-five positions.

It was a bare bones consensus after three days of hard-hitting debate, but enough to carry the process to its next stage. Still on the table were a series of decisions that could break apart the emerging consensus. Those potential dividing points included equity and affirmative action issues, representation for retired workers and the CAW's unique recognition of "skilled trades" groups within bargaining units. There was no agreement yet on what regions would be established, who would be elected in regions and what authority they would wield.

There was just enough concurrence for the Proposal Committee to launch a series of membership meetings in April and May in Vancouver, Winnipeg, St. John's, Halifax, Edmonton, Regina, Toronto and Quebec City. The meetings were open to local union executives and members at large and drew more than one thousand union activists into the debates. The membership meetings were the first opportunity for rank-and-file members from the two unions to meet each other on common ground and were a crucial test for the project. Although tentative and probing, the rank-and-file engagement generated excitement from activist members about the possibilities for a stronger force in the labour movement. After hearing reports on the work of the Proposal Committee, most endorsed what they heard.

However, by the time the Proposal Committee returned to complete the structural issues in mid-May 2012, only the first two joint meetings in Vancouver and Winnipeg had taken place. Those meetings filled hotel ballrooms in these western locations, where the CEP membership was close to the CAW size. These first two meetings were positive but also revealed warning signs, with CEP members expressing misgivings that their regional identity and accountability of their leadership may be lost in a new, more centralized union. The trepidations were enhanced by the still incomplete presentation on how regional accountability would be maintained and what else would be gained in a new structure.

A nervous CEP group arrived in Toronto to complete the structure negotiation, and it would be the closest that the New Union Project came to failure. The careful step-by-step working through of issues had led the CEP regional officers into an uncomfortable corner. It was already determined that the new union would have a regional structure, but the developing concept of regions was focused on the roles of rank-and-file members rather than regional officers. The early-evening caucus meeting at the Sheraton began with a review of the Vancouver and Winnipeg meetings. Within minutes, it was asserted that CEP members would accept nothing less than the current system of regionally elected officers who directed staff and local politics. Unless they could assure members that this essential feature of the old union would be continued, they faced a rebellion in the CEP ranks. The CAW proposals for membership bodies in the regions without full-time elected leadership would transfer all power to Toronto, and the members would not stand for it. An hour later, the CEP group was doubling down on the CEP structure as a bottom line, and if it meant walking out on the process, so be it. "If we have to walk out, better now than later," it was asserted.

It was the only time I remember being silent in a new union debate, shocked by the aggressive rhetoric and the apparent unanimity of the group. When the caucus ended without making any constructive preparations for the Proposal Committee meeting the next morning, it seemed to me that they had come with the purpose of ending the New Union Project and that the meeting was a crude ritual to prepare for that outcome. Visibly upset and with only glares at Ménard and Ouimet, I walked out of the room, leaving the rest behind. Later that evening, I was nursing my wounds in a nearby bar when Gaétan Ménard called to reassure me that we were not at the end. I had misread the groupthink as consensus. As Ginter told me later, he wasn't surprised or impressed by the steam letting. He had already accepted that there could not be a continuing or similar role for him in Ontario, where the CEP was vastly outnumbered. But "the others were feeling jammed" and had not come to terms with the necessity for the new union to have a fundamentally new structure without any predetermined roles for them. Michel Ouimet had likewise offered support to his colleagues but also had no intention of letting the project fail.

The Proposal Committee meeting began with a debrief of the joint membership meetings and other membership responses to that point. Ginter led off with his report of the CEP energy and telecommunications council meetings. "People are nervous," he said, but quickly moderated his tone with the assurance that the CEP members had open minds and were waiting for "more meat on the bones." Others from both unions followed suit, echoing the need to provide members with answers to their questions around structure.

As expected, Kennedy opened the discussion on national and regional leadership with a critique of the CEP proposal to maintain its system of regional vice-presidents as formalizing a drift into silos and the risk of regional and sector-based unions with the union. "I am unable to reconcile that with the goals and principles that we have agreed on," he asserted. "It's not surprising we are having difficulty with this. We are trying to find commonality between two very different structures," he continued. "But if we really want to create a new union, we have to look at changing structures . . . We recognize the fundamental need to provide acceptable opportunities for regional and sectoral leadership. We have modified our proposal this morning to propose a governance structure that accommodates both."

Kennedy's proposal was to add to the leadership structure three elected regional directors, for Atlantic Canada, Ontario and Western Canada. These directors would, together with three national officers, be members of a national leadership team.

Ménard responded with an acknowledgement of the "big step" in the CAW proposal. The transition to this structure must maintain accountability to the regional members, he argued. Regional officers should have specific regional responsibilities and both specific and shared national responsibilities to maintain a leadership team without developing kingdoms, he said.

The logjam was broken, but a second impasse had to be resolved on whether the regional directors would be elected by regional members alone or nationally. That, too, was soon resolved with the compromise agreement that the regional directors would be nominated by a caucus of regional delegates at the national convention but elected by all delegates. Accountability to the regional membership would be established, but the structure would not allow any of the six to separate themselves from national decisions or to divide the union by playing to a regional or sectoral base. The Proposal Committee seized on the opportunity to flesh out a regional structure that was indeed new, bearing little resemblance to either of the existing structures. Unlike the CAW, there would be regions, but not the kind of regions that existed in the CEP. Those regions had elected full-time vice-presidents with extensive administrative and political authority and only voluntary councils of local unions for information sharing and education. The regions in the new union would be constitutional bodies bringing every local union into large rank-and-file councils with the mandate and authority to set policy and elect regional executives and standing committees.

The third report of the Proposal Committee to the memberships heralded a "milestone in creating a new Canadian union . . . a structure for a strong national union with a robust regional base." Two weeks later, the fourth meeting of the committee completed the structural proposals by detailing the regional council, sector, retiree and equity representation on the proposed national executive board of the new union.

The union that was taking form would be led by a president, secretary-treasurer and Quebec director, which closely resembled the existing CAW and CEP leadership. It would hold constitutional conventions every three years and on the off-years convene a Canadian Council for all local unions in the country. The Canadian Council carried forward a long-standing practice of the CAW, in effect a convention each year. The CEP also was fond of conventions and had held them every two years, on several occasions rejecting leadership proposals for three-year convention cycles.

The addition of the Quebec and four English Canadian regional chairpersons to the national executive board fulfilled the agreement to have direct representation on the board elected within regions and added muscle to the regional structures within the new union.

The largest group in the union leadership would be eleven sectoral representatives nominated by a structure of formalized industry councils. Like the regional councils, the industry councils would have autonomy but would choose leaders to be endorsed by the whole union. In this case, the eleven industry council representatives would be nominated by their industry peers but elected at meetings of the Canadian Council. The remaining three positions on the twenty-five-person executive board would represent Aboriginal workers and workers of colour, a council of skilled trades and retirees.

There was no doubt that equity issues would be one of the defining tests for the new union, and this posed a set of challenges that no Canadian union could yet claim success on. A commitment on equity was needed, particularly on gender balance. The down payment on that intention was a decision to entrench affirmative action for women in the constitution with the requirement that the number of women on the executive board could not be less than the proportionate share of women in the overall union membership — a unique provision in the statutes of any major Canadian union to that point.

Although the consensus on structure was partly a compromise on regions, in the end it was a substantially larger vision of a rank-and-file union that gave shape to the May agreement. The agreement embraced a balance between a democratic centralism and autonomous regional, sectoral and equity structures to ensure diversity and encourage local initiative and innovation.

Of twenty-five national leaders, only six would be full-time officers or directors; the balance of nineteen would be rank-and-file local union or industry leaders. The larger structure beyond the national executive board envisaged a network of regional, sectoral and equity councils that would engage thousands of members in constant decision making beyond their local unions and bargaining committees. Where would the members come from, and when would they have time to bring all of these councils and their meetings to life? The answer was another leap of faith: "They will."

The fourth meeting also brought to a conclusion the sleeper issues of budgets and financial accountability. For most members, the union was first and last a practical instrument to improve their standard of living. Members in both unions could be counted on to pay attention to money matters, and they would not allow membership dues to rise to the point where dues were perceived as diminishing their incomes. The New Union Project could not expect endorsement of a plan that did not guarantee equal or improved day-to-day services, from bargaining and strike support to education and technical assistance on health and safety, pensions and extended health benefits.

The new union would have dues income of about $110 million annually — by any measure a large operating budget. However, the impressive revenue also focused the need for financial accountability. One of the many consequences of the Enron accounting scandal in 2001 and the financial crisis of 2008 was heightened expectations of accountability for anyone managing large organizational budgets, and by 2011, these expectations hung over organized labour as well. In part, they resulted from the concerns of aware members with enhanced appreciation of financial competence, governance models and conflicts of interest. In the larger picture, financial scrutiny of unions was being fuelled by Bill C-377 and the attempt to make union expenditures the centrepiece of the ongoing anti-labour agenda.

Union dues were another difference between the CAW and CEP. The CAW had a system of collecting dues of two hours and twenty minutes pay from each full-time worker. It was a progressive dues system that required higher-waged workers to pay somewhat more than low-waged workers. The CEP had a progressive system as well but based on a percentage formula of 0.078 per cent of pay from regularly scheduled hours. The CAW dues structure was set centrally and set dues for both the national union and the local unions; the CEP's formula applied only to money for the national union, and local unions were free to set an additional dues structure for their needs.

Kennedy and Ménard ran the finances in their respective organizations, and although the debate over structure had played out, a financial analysis had been completed in the background. The numbers turned out to be a powerful argument for the New Union Project. Both unions had healthy balance sheets, and together they had an impressive financial base. The CAW brought $196.7 million with a projected $66.3 million in dues revenue in 2011; the smaller CEP's assets were $55 million with a projected $46.6 million in 2011 dues revenues. Each organization would be in the black for 2011 with surpluses of $4.9 million for the CAW and $4.99 million for the CEP.

For members looking at the financial bottom line and still expecting more, the new union was in a position to deliver. The Proposal Committee was able to promise increased strike pay and funding for organizing and services without significant dues increases. Strike pay would immediately jump to $250 per week, pro-rated to the first day of a strike or lockout — an improvement for both unions. Although most union members rarely collect strike pay, there isn't any other benefit more symbolic of the union's militancy and capacity.

The dues structure would go to the CEP model of a percentage-based system, but with a formula that would ensure that dues for CAW members were stable. The CAW side favoured the CEP-style percentage system over their status quo, in part because it provided greater fairness to their part-time workers, mostly in the retail sector. The recommendation on the dues structure was another highly visible demonstration that the new union was being shaped by consensus decisions on best practices rather than either the will or the experience of the larger organization. All of the dues income would be distributed into five designated funds: a general fund for day-to-day operations, a strike and defence fund, an organizing fund, an education fund and a convention fund.

In the first weeks of June 2012, the project team retreated to the Port Elgin, Ontario, Family Education Centre to write a draft report setting out the case for a new union and bringing together the decisions of the Proposal Committee. At the fifth meeting in Montreal at the end of June, the Proposal Committee announced that it had achieved its goal: "a comprehensive report describing the purposes, objectives, structure, finances and other main operating principles of a new union."

The final report of the Proposal Committee, *Towards a New Union*, was published in August, just in time for the CAW convention in Toronto. The decisions of the committee, made under pressure one by one, had been crafted into an integrated, visionary and polished presentation. *Towards a New Union* brought together for the first time a picture of the new union and its structures as a whole, visually clear in language and organizational charts. The structure and leadership proposals were combined with the persuasive case of the new union's potential breadth and influence.[4]

Starting out with 305,000 members, the new union would be the largest union in Canada's private sector, with thousands of members in every province and region working in more than twenty economic industries and sectors.

The largest sector, with 94,000 members, would be in manufacturing industries such as auto manufacturing and parts, trucks and buses, aerospace, electrical products, shipbuilding and food and beverage. The resource sector included over 50,000 workers in forestry, energy, mines, metals and fishing. The transportation sector would bring another 40,000 airline, railroad, trucking and marine workers, whereas an additional 41,000 were in telecommunications and media. But the second largest general area was services, including retail, hotels, gaming, health and social services. With health care workers across Ontario and the Atlantic, public transit workers in British Columbia and Crown corporations in Saskatchewan, private sector strength would be complemented by a significant public sector presence.

The scope and economic reach of the new union were clearly powerful and positioned it to be a force on economic strategy and job issues across the breadth of the economy that would make it a union of choice for diverse groups of unorganized workers. Increasingly, the term "a union for everyone" was heard in discussions about what would be new about the new union. Of course, most Canadian unions had long since abandoned the old "jurisdictions" that governed trade union organizing through the designation of predominant roles for major unions in each industry and sector, but there was no doubt that the scope of this amalgam was unprecedented for the Canadian labour movement.

"Our new union will represent another stage in the development of unions," *Towards a New Union* boldly asserted. The union development that it was getting at began with "craft unions" that in the nineteenth century brought together workers with common trades. Some CEP locals, such as printers, were remnants of this early form of union organization. In the 1930s, the Congress of Industrial Organizations (CIO) led a new stage of union organizing in mass production industries by uniting in one union all workers in an enterprise regardless of their trade or jobs and then combining these workplaces across an industry.

This form of union solidarity was known as "industrial unionism." The CAW's auto worker locals came from that era, as did the paper workers and energy workers in the CEP. In the late twentieth century, multi-sectoral industrial unions evolved, with unions such as the CAW and CEP representing industrial unionism in multiple sectors within the same union. The CAW became a Canadian industrial union for auto workers, aerospace workers, railroad workers, health care workers and others. The CEP had four industrial sectors: forestry, energy, telecommunications and media. The new union now declared its intention to go further again by bringing into one organization large numbers of workers representing the production cycle from natural resources to transportation, manufacturing and retail trade, as well as media, communications and social services such as health care and education. With this qualitatively wider scope across twenty distinct economic sectors, the new union could describe itself as a union for everyone. Herein also was the basis for the assertion of the evolution of trade unionism beyond both craft and industrial unionism to a "class unionism" for Canadian workers.

This class solidarity was to be cemented in an interlocking network of industrial, equity and regional councils that formed the architecture of the proposed new union. A key idea was its openness to additional groups of members that could be given representation and profile by expanding membership councils within the model.

All this left an obvious gap for a "union for everyone" — the vast sections of the working class with little practical opportunity to organize. This was an issue put on the table by *A Moment of Truth*, with its call for "a force fighting for all workers" that would "offer services and support to non-union workers engaged in struggles and conflicts." *Towards a New Union* took that commitment to a new level with the proposal to provide union membership for workers excluded by existing traditional unions. The report was cautionary and promised careful development of the details, but it was a bold announcement of a new kind of union that would open its membership to workers in non-union workplaces, including those who joined the union during organizing drives that failed to secure a traditional certification. Temporary or contract, freelance and self-employed workers would also be welcome as members. Membership would also be open to students and the unemployed.

The most definitive part of the Proposal Committee's final report was its delivery on the assignment made months before to craft the preamble, principles and objectives section that would set out the *raison d'être* and foundational statements to be inserted into the constitution of the new union. The language of the preamble and constitution is usually not a hot item for most members. But, of course, both would nevertheless be read by thousands and put to a test over whether the organization being described accorded with the values of members.

The statement of principles spoke to a union in which "change is constant." Its goals were "transformative": to "change our workplaces and our world." It would be a union about much more than collective bargaining: "to fundamentally change the economy, win equality and social justice, restore and strengthen democracy and achieve an environmentally sustainable future."

For those in the crucible of the New Union Project, a mountain had been climbed. After the Proposal Committee's June meeting and unanimous final report, there was a party late into the night. On the blurry morning after, the recognition of the heights yet to scale was sobering. Chief among them was the necessity for the final report and its recommendations to pass two conventions with the adoption at each of a common resolution.

The Proposal Committee had long known that the bar would be high when the recommendations went to convention. Seasoned convention delegates would not easily agree to move to a not yet existing organization without a comprehensive and convincing description of what it would look like and how it would operate. *Towards a New Union* did offer a comprehensive overview of principles and structure, but it was far from a founding document for an actual union. There was much left to envision and create, from a name and a new identity to a constitution that would codify the consensus recommendations of the Proposal Committee and address the dozens of structural and operational matters not yet considered. That is where the proposal to create six working groups came in, each with a separate mandate to frame and build the necessary components to bring the new union to life. In effect, delegates were asked to adopt the vision and a limited number of structural, leadership and financial decisions and refer the rest to the working groups.

Towards a New Union was rushed out the door to get to CAW locals in advance of the August convention in Toronto. The report was also posted on the New Union Project website, which had posted the results of every Proposal Committee meeting for members and observers to see.

There were no complaints about a lack of information when CAW delegates met in Toronto in the third week of August at a combined constitutional and collective bargaining convention. Leadership presentations by Lewenza and Coles and the Proposal Committee chairs Kennedy and Ménard set the stage for a two-hour debate. The resolution endorsed the report of the Proposal Committee and mandated that a founding convention of a new union would be organized in 2013. As expected, CAW members were ready to follow their leadership and take a leap into the future. The Proposal Committee resolution was unanimously accepted by the about 1,000 CAW delegates.[5]

It was also expected that the CEP convention, which was set for two months later in Quebec City, would not go so smoothly. With almost 1,500 delegates, the CEP convention was larger than the CAW convention agenda — a measure of both its greater number of small local unions and the tension and stakes for the smaller union. The agenda played out the same process as at the CAW convention: presentations from Kennedy and Ménard, a video highlighting the final report and final speeches from Coles and Lewenza before a floor debate on the resolution and a vote.

It was a given that the CEP vote would not be unanimous. Standing outside the consensus were groups of members in the B.C. pulp and paper sector, the Saskatchewan telecommunications and energy sector and Ontario's telecommunications sector. Endorsements from many large local unions were reassuring, but anything less than a decisive majority would be a serious blow to the project and possibly result in the CEP's withdrawal.

The politics of the convention were complicated further by a leadership challenge to Dave Coles. One of the fourteen elected officers, the communications sector administrative vice-president from Western Canada, was opposed to the New Union Project. Wendy Sol had declared her opposition to the new union and then declared her candidacy for president against Coles. Sol had been a supporter of Coles but could not bring herself to embrace the move to a new union. A former telephone operator in Manitoba, she was comfortable with the CEP's role as a mid-sized union and believed its distinct character and her own role would be wiped out by a larger CAW culture. Coles had appointed Sol as the designated officer working with the union's women's committee, where she had ensured that her apprehensions were reflected and where it was said that the union's equity work could be set back by the CAW's alleged male culture.

The Proposal Committee report had clearly connected with the CEP rank and file, as it had with the CAW, and no particular recommendation had emerged as a vote-determining issue. The intangible issue was trust and whether the decisive majority would be convinced to follow their leadership out of their existing union into a new identity. Not unexpectedly, the arguments of those opposed, expressed more in hospitality suites than on the floor of convention, portrayed the new union as a takeover by the larger CAW, which would impose its style of leadership on the CEP. The drama of the day led inexorably to the point when CAW leader Ken Lewenza would take the stage. Although a handful had seen or heard Lewenza in the media or at Federation of Labour conventions, the rest had no idea what to expect.

What they heard, as one veteran observer wrote, was "the union movement creed — justice for workers — with enough power and conviction to convince any of those wondering how to vote on the merger to vote yes."[6] Lewenza made the case for a renewed trade union movement with a "new tool box" because the old tools couldn't do the job anymore. But Lewenza wisely opted not to get into the details of how the new union would be different. No one really wanted to hear that from him; they wanted to know about him. The CAW president left the podium and nervously paced back and forth at the front of the stage as he delivered his testimonial and commitment to the union. He layered his personal story of how the union had been the mainstay of his life in Windsor. He described his personal development, overcoming of bigotries and education as a union activist and his family story of acquiring a home, raising a family and achieving a middle-class lifestyle and security. In a dramatic concluding flourish, he pulled out his wallet, displayed his various credit cards and raised one card up. "We all have too many cards," he said, "including ones that get us into debt up to our butt. But there is one card that matters most to me. It's my union card. Mine says CAW. But the important thing is, it's a union card. It's why I have a house, a car, and a job." It was a turning point that answered the rumour mill questions about the integrity of leadership that could be expected in a new union. Lewenza connected by speaking worker to worker and as a local leader like the great majority in the room, reminding the CEP delegates of their own stories and pride in their union.

There were over thirty speakers in the CEP debate that ensued, and several strong opposition speeches kept the suspense high. Leading the no side in the debate was the local president of the Toronto paper sector composite local, Ken Cole. Cole had been the rank-and-file chairperson of the Officers' Report Committee, a committee of sixteen members with the task of reviewing and reporting on the written reports of the president and other elected officers. My job at successive conventions was to work with the committee to produce a report that would set a constructive tone for convention. The report to the 2012 convention contained the expected balancing of praiseworthy achievements of the union with concerns and criticisms. However, on the new union proposal, it stressed the importance of the debate and stopped short of a recommendation. I was content with that given the passionate opposition of the committee chair.

Cole delivered an articulate appeal to maintain the CEP and argued that the goals of the New Union Project were larger than a single union could have and should be pursued instead through the broader labour movement. He pleaded with delegates to resolve the CEP's problems internally and to maintain its distinct character. Kim Ginter took the floor immediately to respond to Cole. Ginter pointed to the slow decline in membership and the stalemate in the CEP over organizational reforms and declared that it was time for change and that everyone knew it. "Ken Cole is a friend of mine," Ginter told the convention. "But Ken is wrong." Ginter's crusty, blunt edge with the CAW during the early stages of the New Union Project made him an unexpected adjunct to Lewenza to deliver an ardent appeal for the new union, but he had already made a personal decision to retire with the creation of the new union and believed deeply that it was the right course. "I had to be convinced, but when I was I knew we would make a stronger union for the members, and I was 100 per cent committed," he told me. Neither was his reference to Ken Cole as a friend just rhetoric. The two were and remain fast friends, and they had long arguments over the new union. "Ken told me he would speak against

Ken Lewenza addressing the CEP convention, October 15, 2012.

CEP Ontario Region Vice-President Kim Ginter speaking to the last CEP convention, August 30, 2013.

Celebrating New Union Project win at CEP convention, October 2012. Left to right: Marvin Pupeza, Dave Coles, Ken Lewenza, Gaétan Ménard, Peter Kennedy, Deb Tveit.

it," Kim recounted. "I told him to go ahead but that I would follow him to the microphone and be next after him. And I was."[7]

When the show-of-hands vote was taken, the motion had been endorsed by about 90 per cent of the CEP delegates.

In the CEP elections that followed a day later, Coles decisively defeated Wendy Sol. However, the margin was less than the new union vote would have indicated. From the perspective of the New Union Project, it was evident that the case for the new union had transcended the normal run of union politics and won the day on its own merit.

Media stories that week across Canada proclaimed that the two unions had now voted to establish a "super-union." That was the intention, and in principle, they had voted to do so. But the CAW and CEP conventions had not yet established a new union. It was just another milestone passed.

CHAPTER 3

A Union for Everyone

Three weeks after the CEP convention in Quebec City, the Proposal Committee secured the timetable for Phase 2 of the New Union Project by setting the date for the founding convention to open on August 30, 2013, and conclude on September 1, Labour Day 2013. As that was done, the extent of what else had to be done came into focus. The new entity would need an array of foundational documents and policies in place, as well as sufficient strategic and operational policies, for it to hit the ground running. The six working groups that had been proposed were quickly appointed with instructions to get their work under way immediately. The working groups would now add to the project a number of new voices from staff and local union activists.

This period of the New Union Project was no less political or risky than the first, but it now had multiple separate streams, each with significant goals and unresolved issues. An oversight body was needed to monitor working group progress, address problems and begin the negotiations on the latent issue of leadership. The "4×4" of the four national leaders brought together Lewenza, Coles, Kennedy and Ménard, with ongoing help from Stanford and me. In April 2013, it was extended to

Some of the project team: Fred Wilson, David Robertson, Patty Barrera and Jim Stanford in August 2012.

the "5×5," which added Michel Ouimet from the CEP and Jerry Dias from the CAW.

For Jim, me and the other members of the project team, this was in many ways the most creative period of the New Union Project that took leaders, staff and a broader section of members into deep dives around central issues of union renewal. The voyage of discovery around what could be new and different involved long hours and intense work as we sought out examples and advice from a range of labour activists and thinkers. Each member of the project team was assigned to work with one or more of the working groups, where they were called upon to facilitate creative and practical innovation in shaping policies and practices.

Project team member Duncan Brown presenting to the Unifor founding convention.

All the baseline policies, practices and strategies for a new union would have to be negotiated, taking into account the high-level decisions already made and the commitment that the new union would determine anew every aspect of the union's operations. In each case, the working groups would have to come to a consensus on taking

Project team member Jo-Ann
Hannah at the 2012 CAW Council.

the status quo from one of the organizations as a best practice or determining a whole new approach.

To fulfill the commitment of membership engagement at each stage and to minimize the chances of a founding convention fraught with controversies, another round of country-wide membership consultations was layered onto the work plan before finalizing documents. A staff conference was also added to make sure that staff were familiar with the developing proposals and in a position to answer membership questions.

In addition to the second round of membership meetings, three of the working groups — constitution, organizing and communications — were to establish rank-and-file "reference groups" that would hear more detailed reports and give feedback. The upshot for the working groups was that they would have about four months to be prepared to give substantial reports to membership meetings across the country in the spring. When all the consultations were complete, there would be only a few additional weeks before bringing final reports and documents to the Proposal Committee, which remained in place to ensure consistency, and then to the executive boards of each union for endorsement.

Two of the six working groups would carry particularly large workloads. The Communications Working Group would have the job of determining the name and communications strategy.[1] The choosing of a name involved unique research and analysis into the branding of a Canadian union — the first major union in Canada to leave behind traditional identities based on occupations in favour of a brand based on values and action.

The Constitution Working Group would have to draft a constitution ready for adoption that would put in place all the structures and governance measures needed for a seamless transition.[2] Several of the unresolved issues of membership would be determined in the process, as well as the drafting of a strike and defence policy and an anti-harassment policy.

New Union Project leaflet, distributed to membership meetings and local unions in 2012.

For most unions, the constitutional provisions and rules by which they operate have evolved over time, often with frequent updates and changes to integrate additional groups of members or to respond to the evolution of collective bargaining. Nevertheless, it is not uncommon to find that the basic constitutional provisions of unions were written decades earlier, dating in some cases to the Congress of Industrial Organizations organizing drives of the 1930s. The new union had set itself a different task of crafting a whole new constitution. The constitutions of the existing unions were given as starting and reference points but not end points.

In the former CAW, two full-time staff persons adjudicated elections, local union bylaws and other constitutional matters at the local level. Appeal procedures extended to an independent public review board, chaired by the long-time head of the Canadian Civil Liberties Association, Alan Borovoy. In the CEP, similar issues and provisions were a major function of the president's office and staff. Staffers involved in constitutional affairs have been heard to quip that they would be more than happy to debate the constitution with anyone who had read it. In the CEP and the CAW, as in many unions, there was no shortage of opinionated local union leaders or staff who had. A representative group of them now populated the Constitution Working Group and its extended Reference Group.

The other four working groups on organizing,[3] implementation,[4] staff relations[5] and convention[6] would also have to deliver practical answers on an organizing policy and strategy, the combining of existing systems, offices and staff into an integrated organizational system and the organizing of a founding convention. The jobs of over three hundred employees with three collective agreements and their apprehensions during a period of major change had to be addressed. Job security for all staff was a commitment made early in the process, but there had been little discussion so far on department structures and servicing models or how the goal of strategic decision making would be operationalized.

For the CEP, there was the matter of Article 18 in its constitution, which set out rules for any merger into a new organization. When the CEP was founded in 1992 as a merger of three unions, it was astute enough to consider that it could happen again and wrote constitutional language governing such a process. Those rules included that the constitution of the successor union must be circulated to all local unions in advance of a special convention that was mandated to make the final decision. This meant that the constitution and other founding documents for the September convention would have to be completed by early summer to be printed and circulated to the locals.

Among the unresolved constitutional matters, two stood out. One was the quintessential Canadian identity issue and a third rail of Canadian politics and of labour politics: the standing of Quebec. The early agreement in Quebec that was critical for the New Union Project was based on the shared view of the Quebec leadership of CAW and CEP that the new union would take the national question in the union to a higher stage. They saw the new union in Quebec as both increasing their influence in the Quebec labour movement and establishing a more mature relationship with the larger Canadian union.

The delicate but decisive issue for the Quebec region of the union was about identity and who would speak for the union in Quebec on Quebec matters. For the working group, it was hardly an abstract question. Michel Ouimet was the co-chair of the Constitution Working Group and was expected to become Quebec director of the new union by virtue of the CEP's larger membership in Quebec. Ouimet made it clear to me that the status quo from the CAW or CEP would not be acceptable to Quebec. But CAW and CEP English Canadian members alike made it equally clear that there would be no agreement to delegate authority to the Quebec leadership in a manner that would create a dual union with contradictory policies or strategies.

Only a small group knew there were large stakes in resolving the matter. "It's a big question what would have happened if we could not have reached that agreement," said Ouimet in reflection on the deliberations that ensued. "It could have been a deal breaker. To be frank, we were concerned about the role of Quebec in the new union, which would be more centralized than the CEP was. We needed stronger language, and we achieved that."

In both former unions, the Quebec regions already enjoyed considerable autonomy, reflecting the norm in most of the large unions after the Canadian Labour Congress protocols in 1994 that granted resources and organizational autonomy to the Quebec Federation of Labour (FTQ). Once described by Canadian labour icon Jean-Claude Parrot as the labour movement's "sovereignty association" agreement, the protocol also provided for FTQ appointees to fill some of the seats held by the Canadian Labour Congress at the global International Federation of Free Trade Unions and for the FTQ to fulfill the international obligations of the congress in francophone countries.

Although the Canadian Labour Congress had, at a high level, resolved its Quebec question, in most Canadian unions, Quebec autonomy had evolved without formal debates or declarations. There was no clear statement on the national status of Quebec in either the CAW or the CEP constitution. Instead, each constitution had recognized the special character of Quebec through recognition of the Quebec leader of the union, and in the case of the CAW through a separate Quebec council of local unions. The CAW's Quebec Council had a general mandate to "discuss agreements, organizational problems, provincial and federal legislation, and other issues of interest to local union members." In the CAW, the Quebec director was formally one of three "national officers" with the responsibility "to supervise organizational activities within Quebec." In the CEP, the vice-president of the Quebec region was also the executive vice-president of the national union. In constitutional terms, the powers of the CEP executive vice-president were similar to the extensive administrative and political role of other CEP vice-presidents in the CEP regional system.

The practice in both unions was that Quebec ran its own show on day-to-day operations and did so exclusively in French. On political matters, there were subtle parameters that recognized the Canadian leadership but, when appropriate, deferred to the Quebec leaders. The Quebec leadership of both founding unions expected these mandates and roles to be made fully consistent with the self-determination and national rights of Quebec.

The powerful glue that holds the Canada-Quebec trade union relationship together is collective bargaining. Industry and company bargaining groups linking Quebec and the rest of Canada had been stress tested in decades of pattern and co-ordinated bargaining in the auto, aerospace, transportation, forestry, telecommunications, energy, media and other sectors. For the most part, Quebec local leaders in both unions looked for and expected strong and effective leadership from the national president's office in collective bargaining. In bargaining and for many union services, Quebec had no interest in going it alone. When it came to Quebec politics and cultural issues, Quebec had a very different attitude.

Part of what Quebec needed was already set out by the Proposal

Committee. The national character of Quebec had been recognized in the statement of principles with the commitment that the structure of the union would reflect that recognition. The Quebec Council would be the primary legislative council for the union in Quebec and would elect its leadership and the Quebec director. The national union would be officially bilingual. The missing link for Ouimet was clarity that the leader of the union in Quebec would be the spokesperson and chief officer on Quebec national issues.

Ouimet and I struggled over the issue for several days before we came to an agreement on proposed language that cast the responsibilities of the Quebec director in a stronger way but without establishing a dual leadership. The proposal was that the Quebec director would "act under the direction of the National President on any matter concerning the National Union as a whole." However, "on matters related to the national character or distinctness of Quebec," the Quebec director would be the principal spokesperson and act on behalf of the national president.

The two weeks before the leadership of the two unions endorsed the proposal were tense. Like the agreement on regional directors, Quebec's status was affirmed with the understanding that the Quebec leader would be part of a "leadership team" together with the president, secretary-treasurer and other national executive board members. The line between Québécois and Canadian matters in this division of labour was not meant to be a wall separating Canada's two solitudes. As part of the leadership team, the Quebec director also has the primary responsibility for achieving the objectives of the national union and for implementing the programs and policies of the national union in Quebec. The "sovereignty association" relationship between Québécois and Canadian workers had been codified in the new union.

For the project team and both the Organizing and Constitution Working Groups, the other large and complex issue was the idea that the new union would be "a union for everyone." How would the new union fulfill the mandate of *Towards a New Union* and open its membership to precarious, temporary, contract, self-employed and freelance workers, whose conditions of work made traditional organizing impractical? The mandate went even further to extend membership to groups of workers in non-union workplaces, to workers who had joined the union in unsuccessful organizing drives and to students, young people and the unemployed. But if we thought the issue was therefore settled, we were soon disabused.

The idea of new members coming into the union without a collective agreement or even an identifiable employer was at the outset highly contentious. The first brainstorming session on what the status of these members would be took place in the Organizing Working Group. Jim Stanford was putting questions to the group: Would these members pay dues and join local unions, and could they vote on local union affairs? The room was not about to offer definitive answers, and I filled some of the space by suggesting that no one would join a union if they lacked basic membership rights. I pushed a button with Deb Tveit, who was sitting beside me. "What are you saying?" she retorted. "That someone from a place with no union will just come into the local and act like everyone else who pays the dues and have a contract? That is just crazy talk."

Deb was not opposed to the idea of non-traditional new union members. However, she saw things in the practical terms she understood from organizing her own workplace in Tillsonburg, Ontario, and working as a union organizer. And she was underscoring the truth of the matter. It was far from obvious how these workers would organize and how they would fit into the union. It was even less clear what rights and obligations would be given to members who may have little or no ability to pay normal union dues or be self-sustaining in their activities. There were almost no examples of how Canadian unions had successfully opened their doors to workers outside a bargaining context and certainly no precedent for the idea to do this for workers at large. We were flying by the seats of our pants, and it would take several months and a cumbersome process of identification, examination and exclusion to come up with a proposal that would have even a chance of success.

CAW Assistant to the President Deb Tveit in September 2013.

Our search for organizing frameworks that could offer inspiration took us first outside the labour movement, where remarkable activism was speaking loudly to us. The Occupy Wall Street protests of 2011 and 2012 that swept through US and Canadian cities were a large backdrop to the issues of union renewal and organizing. Occupy was noteworthy for its decentralized and informal organizational and political leadership, which at the same time appeared to be a problem for building a movement that could be sustained over the longer term. The larger lesson from Occupy was its remarkable success in changing the narrative on inequality and the lessons of the financial crisis. After years of disappointment in countering neo-liberal presumptions, Occupy was an ideological breakthrough showing that a class-based power analysis and a hard-hitting systemic critique of capitalism could have broad appeal.

Canadian inspiration also came from the 2012 "Carré Rouge" movement in Quebec, which saw a quarter of a million students participate in a university and college strike lasting for more than one hundred days. The student strike opposed tuition fee increases imposed by the Quebec Liberal government, which had broken a social compact over access to education in place since Quebec's Quiet Revolution in the 1960s and 1970s. Resistance to the tuition increases was mostly on campus until the Quebec government passed an extraordinary law banning any gathering of more than fifty people that was not preauthorized by police. Thousands of Quebecers then turned out to support the students in massive street demonstrations, with participants banging pots and pans. The mobilizations over the spring of 2012 became one of the largest acts of civil disobedience in Quebec history and became known as the "Maple Spring." The student strike was a major factor in the defeat of the Liberals in a fall election. The Parti Québécois government that came to power promptly halted the tuition increase.

We had a real-time vantage point on the student strike through Roxanne Dubois, CEP's newest staff person in its Ottawa headquarters, who was connected to the student leaders in Quebec from her role as the past chairperson of the Canadian Federation of Students. What was most interesting to us was how the students openly modelled themselves on unions, organizing into "locals" and identifying as "student unions." However, the student strike did not look or feel like a union operation, and it held out lessons for the labour movement on grassroots organizing and decision making. "The issue of blocking the tuition fee hike was debated on each campus in general assemblies," Dubois explained to me. "They allowed for open debate space where the outcome of general meetings would decide if the campus would go on strike. The strike was built campus by campus, without waging an air war but by talking to students and discussing best strategies." The instructive point for Dubois was not just that the student strategy and assembly model made for strong solidarity but that they also pointed to more transformational possibilities, she explained. "The slogan was 'Ensemble, bloquons la hausse': 'Together, let's block the increase.' The call was not reformist. It was a call to express student power over governments, administrators

CEP National Representative Roxanne Dubois at the Unifor founding convention. She became coordinator of Unifor's Community Chapter program.

and the right wing, who wished to make education only accessible to the wealthy and not a universal program."

Likely because of that inherent radicalism in the student strike, when Ken Lewenza and Dave Coles made plans for a solidarity visit to a student rally that summer, the president of the FTQ, Michel Arsenault, invoked Canadian Labour Congress protocols to tell Coles and Lewenza to stay home. The demonstration was organized by CLASSE, the most radical of the three student organizations that organized the strike. CLASSE's spokesperson, Gabriel Nadeau Dubois, had called for continuing actions in support of the student strike in spite of the injunctions against the protests, and he was later charged with contempt of court. His case was not resolved until 2016, when he was acquitted of the charges by the Supreme Court of Canada. However, in 2012, Arsenault did not want Coles and Lewenza at the CLASSE demonstrations, and his correspondence to Ken Georgetti was tersely passed on to both unions. Rather than make an issue of it with the FTQ, Coles and Lewenza did not attend, but Gaétan Ménard and Sylvain Martin attended the rally to ensure the new union's presence.

There was yet another rising from below that was pushing the boundaries of trade union orthodoxy. In November 2012, a series of fast-food worker strikes began in New York City when about one hundred mostly black, non-union workers from McDonald's, Burger King, Wendy's, Domino's, Papa John's, KFC and Pizza Hut walked off the job with the demand for a $15 minimum wage. In April 2013, on the anniversary of the assassination of Martin Luther King, Jr., a second fast-food strike doubled participation in New York City and began a wave of other actions over the following three months involving more than two thousand workers in Chicago, Detroit, St. Louis, Milwaukee, Seattle and Kansas City. By September 2014, the fast-food strike movement was able to organize actions in a hundred US cities, and in April 2015, ten thousand fast-food workers and low-income workers in retail, home care and airports walked out. The actions had the support of US unions, particularly the Service Employees International Union and the

United Food and Commercial Workers, but they also co-operated with black organizations and community groups to provide organizational capacity adjacent to trade union organizing departments.

The project team was struggling to fill in the gap between the rising social movements and the practical potential that we saw for the new union. Work was well under way compiling an extensive review of non-traditional trade union organizing and academic research on labour movement renewal. Our commitment to break down the barriers between the organized and the unorganized working class was just one of multiple expressions of the same idea elsewhere. There was much to learn from the creative sparks lighting up labour movements in several countries.[7]

Early in 2013, when the Organizing Group began in-depth debate over its options, thick binders on international experience and labour strategies had been circulated. Our reference point was our own modified *Wagner Act* model with its origins in the United States.

The 1935 *Wagner Act* was a particularly American approach to labour relations. Commonly known after its sponsor, Democratic New York Senator Robert Wagner, it was officially the *National Labor Relations Act*. The Wagner model provided for exclusive representation by a single union with majority support in a workplace. The focus on the workplace, known as enterprise bargaining, required bargaining beyond the workplace to be negotiated.

The limitations of the Wagner model for unions in the post industrial economy of the late twentieth century had been known for decades and US unions and academic advisors had been searching for solutions and alternatives. Much of the US thinking about new models of trade union organizing had been sparked by the work of US professors Robert Freeman and Joel Rogers, who published the book *What Workers Want* in 1999. Jim Stanford circulated sections of the book to the project team. The book decried the decline of worker representation in the US economy and argued for a model of workplace representation the authors termed "open source unionism." The courageous fast-food workers conducting co-ordinated strikes in 2012 in many ways appeared to be open-source networks of workers co-ordinating their actions at great distances across the United States.[8]

Another initiative emerging in the United States in late 2012 was the United Auto Workers (UAW) strategy to organize foreign auto manufacturers. Leveraging its connections to the German auto union, IG Metall, the UAW was proposing a German-style "works council" for the non-union Volkswagen plant in Chattanooga, Tennessee. It was the first of several attempts by the UAW to use non-traditional organizing in southern US auto plants owned by European auto companies.

In continental Europe, labour relations is markedly different. Trade unions are not required to organize a majority of workers before collective bargaining commences, and multiple unions are permitted in a single workplace.

Outside of Scandinavia, where unionization rates are higher, European union membership as a percentage of workers, or density, ranges between 10 and 35 per cent. However, labour and social legislation often extends the results of collective bargaining to other workers in the sector. European trade unions could be somewhat complacent about their slowly declining density because they maintained up to 80 per cent union "coverage" in key economic sectors.

Many European unions were breaking from business-as-usual strategies to reverse these trends. The Dutch union FNV Bondgenoten had organized precarious workers in the cleaning industry, echoing the US "Justice for Janitors" campaign, as well as domestic workers. The Swedish white collar union Unionen had used non-traditional organizing to reach out to students and young people outside the workforce. The German metal workers union IG Metall had mounted a large and partially successful organizing campaign in the growing wind energy sector.

The United Kingdom's system is closer to the North American *Wagner Act* model based on a majoritarian principle and the certification of a union with majority support as the exclusive bargaining agent. But unlike Canada, the United Kingdom has no Rand formula ensuring that if a union is certified, everyone will pay union dues. Duncan Brown and I were interested in the innovative approaches of one UK union in particular, Unite the Union. We met Tony Burke, assistant to Unite General Secretary Len McCluskey, during a visit to Toronto. Burke told us that Unite's organizing model included about five thousand workers in non-union workplaces in 2012. Individuals could join the union online and would be contacted by an organizer within twenty-four hours. If an organizing drive was not ready to commence in the shop, the worker would be placed in an existing local union. They would pay regular Unite dues but would have the services of Unite servicing representatives and other services of the union, from legal to education. However, the model would need significantly more individual members paying dues to become self-sustaining. Unite's model has evolved considerably since then, and in 2018, Unite began offering membership to workers in various membership categories, from low income to part time and full time.[9]

New Zealand was perhaps a more pertinent case study analogous to the de-unionization threatening the Canadian labour movement. The anti-union attacks in New Zealand began in the 1980s under a Labour government and were continued and deepened through the 1990s under the conservative National Party.[10] Over the next decade, the New Zealand labour movement fought back and began to use non-traditional organizing. In 2009, the New Zealand Council of Trade Unions launched a community membership initiative called "Together." Designed to campaign as a social movement, membership was at large and available online. Focusing on rights at work, solidarity and social issues, it emphasized values as a reason to join rather than a limited range of information services and consumer benefits.[11]

In the project team, we believed we had conducted a fairly exhaustive study of non-traditional organizing and representation. However, five years later, in January 2018, a later expression of the New Union Project learned of a small but more powerful example of "non-majority" unionism. Through Unifor's engagement with the United Electrical, Radio and Machine Workers (UE) in the North American

Solidarity Project, Unifor met UE's Local 150 in the right-to-work state of North Carolina. Local 150 had maintained a union for more than a thousand mostly black private and public sector workers without bargaining rights for over twenty years. Using petitions, newsletters, public actions and direct negotiations with employers, the local has played a key role in securing $15/hour minimum wages for state and municipal workers and a long list of other workplace gains. It is a cautionary note for researchers and reflective of the institutional and racial blinders in the labour movement that the experience of the left-wing UE, that had survived outside the American Federation of Labor-Congress of Industrial Organizations (AFL-CIO) since the Cold War purges of the 1940s, remained hidden to us. Meeting Local 150 in North Carolina had a powerful impact on the Unifor delegation and profoundly altered our understanding of what it means to form a union, within and outside the *Wagner Act* model.[12]

But not even US circumstances could be easily transposed into Canadian conditions. The US *Wagner Act* model is the closest to Canada's, but not the same. A key difference is the right of American workers to take "concerted action" through Section 7 of the *National Labor Relations Act*, regardless of whether they had secured formal bargaining rights. These protections explained why groups of fast-food workers could walk off the job in political protests and return to their jobs without being fired. In Canada, only certified unions had the right to concerted action, and then only in specific conditions, after an impasse in collective bargaining, a strike vote and often conciliation or other government-imposed processes.

As the project team attempted to draw conclusions from the various case studies we had assembled, it wasn't yet clear how fast-food workers or other unorganized workers in Canada could engage in legal collective actions or forms of minority unionism without losing their jobs. The broad themes and global labour movement successes and failures elsewhere could only be a backdrop for a Canadian strategy. To drill down on the real options for implementing new member categories in the new union, Canadian law and emerging organizational forms had to be examined. Towards these goals, the Organizing Working Group held two crucial sessions in January 2013. The first session was organized around seven presentations that took us into a deep dive on workers' rights, Canadian law and how non-union workers were finding representation.

Several of the presentations grounded the discussion around what was already being done. Both the CAW and CEP, like many other unions, had been representing workers in so-called non-traditional sectors for years. The Fish, Food and Allied Workers Union in Newfoundland and Atlantic Canada, a CAW division, was a large example. Its president, Earle McCurdy, described how the union, like its counterpart on the West Coast, the United Fishermen and Allied Workers' Union, represented wage workers in processing plants but also small boat fishers and crews. The grey lines between boat owners, working fishers and plant workers had been sorted out over years of organizing and bargaining. Although their forms of income differed, boat owners, fishers and plant workers had common interests negotiating fairness from the fish companies and in dealing with the federal regulators of their industry.

Another example of non-traditional members was a CAW group of about seven hundred owner-operator truck drivers in the Port of Vancouver driving for about a dozen transport companies grouped in the Vancouver Container Truckers' Association. The unionized owner-operator truckers negotiated agreements with the companies in spite of their grey zone as owner-operators and dependent contractors of the trucking association or CN. A few union truckers owned multiple trucks and had some employees.

The CEP brought to the table its experiences representing freelance media workers in the film industry and media. National Association of Broadcast Employees and Technicians-CEP Local 700-M in Toronto represented several thousand freelance film technicians, trades and labourers. The local negotiated collective agreements with film production companies and dispatched the freelancers on a project basis from its hiring hall. At the Organizing Working Group, Michael O'Reilly, president of the CEP's fledgling Canadian Freelance Union, sketched out its slow but steady efforts to advocate and provide services for self-employed writers, photographers, web designers and others. The union was providing assistance and services to its three hundred members but had not yet secured a bargaining relationship with any major media employer.

These cases were reassuring that the chasm between *Wagner Act* trade unionism and those outside it could be bridged and had been. But these were bridges from the mainland to the closest islands, building on long-standing labour bases with fishers and the film industry or extending existing organizational bases to contract sectors in trucking and media. To bring union membership to the ocean of unorganized workers in vast sectors of the new economy with negligible density would need more than a bridge.

The larger link to the unorganized working class began to make sense with the presentation to the Organizing Working Group by York University law professor David Doorey. Doorey had recently published an argument for "a worker voice beyond the Wagner model" that he called "Graduated Freedom of Association."[13] The thesis drew on the well-known critiques of the limits of Wagnerism but placed it strongly in a Canadian context. The Wagner model that is the basis of the federal *Canada Labour Code* and all provincial labour codes asserts a majoritarian principle that if a majority choose to unionize, the union becomes the exclusive bargaining agent for all workers. The model provides effective union security for unionized workplaces, but it is, as Doorey put it, "all or nothing." For 83 per cent of private sector workers, it was the latter.

Doorey's proposal was one of the first to respond to Supreme Court decisions in 2007 and 2011 affirming the collective rights of workers under the *Charter of Rights and Freedoms*.[14] As Doorey explained,

The SCC has found that Section 2(d) (freedom of
association) of the Charter *guarantees workers at*
least a right to make collective representations to their
employers through an organization of their choosing,
without reprisals and imposes a duty on employers
to consider those representations in good faith and
to engage in meaningful dialogue with the workers'
collective representatives. The SCC calls this bundle of
rights and freedoms "collective bargaining." Lawyers
continue to quarrel over the implications of this newly
recognized constitutional right to collective bargaining
but one outcome is evident and striking. Only a very
small proportion of Canadian workers in the private
sector are able to exercise their Charter *right to*
collective bargaining in practice.

What this meant for the new union's goal of opening its membership was that non-union workers could and should exercise their right to have a collective voice even if a union majority was not practical. Doorey argued that a fundamental break with the *Wagner Act* was not needed and that unions should continue to pursue the "thick rights" of full collective bargaining provided by labour legislation. But if Canadian unions were prepared to make the commitment, unions could begin earlier to assist workers to exercise the "thin rights" of freedom of association set out by the Supreme Court. Although the Canadian Wagner model did not provide the right to "concerted action," Doorey held the view that the court's decision and existing non-discrimination clauses in labour codes would give a measure of protection against retaliation if workers without a union certification joined and became active in unions or associations.

As the layers of the possibilities stacked up on the Organizing Working Group's table, other presenters challenged the group to imagine where this could take the new union and the new categories of members it sought to represent. A strong theme was the need for organizing centres and advocacy reaching out to the "precariat" of mostly young, racialized and immigrant workers plying low-wage and insecure jobs in the service economy.

"Do not let the legislative framework inhibit your organizing," Deena Ladd from Toronto's Workers' Action Centre put to the group. Economic restructuring had left contract workers, temporary agency workers, owner-operators, personal service workers and many misclassified workers outside the union and bargaining framework, and the task was to "organize and bring them back."

It was not difficult to see both the potential and the pitfalls and limits of advocacy and campaigning for members without a legal right to traditional bargaining. The Workers' Action Centre was well known for its minimum wage campaigns and the enforcement and improvement of employment standards regulations, often focusing on the cases of specific groups of workers or individuals. But it did not have the resources to provide general legal or advocacy services for large numbers of individual workers over workplace grievances and claims.[15]

One of the most common features of new member models was the offer to members to secure extended health benefits such as dental care or life insurance. Some unions had also introduced group purchasing plans offering discounts and union-branded credit cards with rebates. For the Organizing Working Group, the organizing advantage of these incentives was very unclear. In any event, they fell far short of the "mutual aid" programs that are credited with supporting the high union densities in Scandinavia and Europe. In Finland, Sweden and Denmark, the most important mutual aid programs run by unions were the almost universal government-subsidized supplementary unemployment insurance plans.[16]

Two further sessions of the Organizing Working Group, each involving a day of consultation with the Reference Group, sorted through the central issues that had emerged. Three key questions needed an answer. The first question involved the goals of granting membership to workers outside bargaining units. Would membership be an organizing tool for the purpose of seeding workplaces until a drive for certification could be mounted? Or could membership have its own goals regardless of whether a certification could be achieved? The second set of questions was about what kind of structures members without collective agreements would have and whether at-large memberships would be open to individuals who could join online. The final question was perhaps not the most important from an organizing perspective, but without doubt was the most disputed politically: would community members outside of traditional bargaining units have a voice and a vote on union matters?

The working group set out its answers in a white paper, *Broadening the Concept of Union Citizenship — Members in Community Chapters in the New Union*. Traditional bargaining units would remain the core of the union, the white paper assured, and the community members would be a pre-formation for organizing drives wherever possible. But traditional organizing was "not the only goal": the community members would also be organized to increase the overall membership of the union, to involve the new members in union activity and to use their collective strength to better their lives in the workplace and community. "Becoming a union member is not an individual act," the white paper asserted. There would not be members at large on the receiving end of what we called "1-888-unionism." New members would be organized in community chapters that would have a community of interest and a "common platform" for action.

In exceptional cases, the community chapters could be directly chartered by the national executive board of the union, but, generally, the chapters would be connected to sponsoring local unions. The local unions would determine the scope of involvement in union affairs depending on the specific conditions, including representation on the local union executive. However, at the outset, the community members would not have votes on collective bargaining matters or be able to stand for elected office. There was recognition that the organizing and actions of the workers and community activists who build the community chapters would shape their growth and development. "We will be flexible, creative and determined in building and supporting these Community Chapters," the white paper stated. "Through experimentation and experience, we will find models and settings that work better than others."

Following quickly on the white paper, the Constitution Working Group defined three categories of members in the new union: members in bargaining units, members in community chapters and members in retired workers chapters.

The popular understanding of citizenship in a democracy is that it confers equal rights to all. That is true to a point, but constitutions and laws in democracies also define different access to rights and freedoms, such as the age of majority, the distinction between permanent residents and citizens and residency requirements to access services. In a similar spirit and logic, the new union constitution did not create tiers of membership, but it did specify different rights and responsibilities for the three categories of members.

It was an unexpected turn that the debate over rights and responsibilities that ensued in the Constitution Working Group and its Reference Group was not about community chapters but instead focused on the retired workers chapters. The CAW had a long tradition of retiree members, especially in the automobile industry. Auto locals had retiree chapters with thousands of members, and collective agreement provisions provided for a dues payment to the union to partially fund its activities. The retirees had a vibrant role, regularly filling buses to participate in rallies and other major union events. The CEP culture was very different, with a few small retiree groups organized sporadically across the country.

In the Constitution Working Group, draft language by David Robertson and Lewis Gottheil proposed the CAW model that union members on retirement should have a constitutional right to organize a chapter of retired workers within the local union. Within the local, retirees would be represented on the executive by a designated position and prohibited from voting on collective bargaining matters. On other matters, including the right to vote for local union officers, the national constitution would treat them as any other member.

However, some in the CEP argued that retiree interests were not always aligned with the interests of active members and that local unions should have the right to determine if retirees were welcome — not just whether the retirees would have a voice and a vote but if there would be retiree chapters at all. The arguments were strongest from Quebec, where a group of angry retirees was suing their bankrupt forest company, White Birch, and the CEP because their pensions had been cut. A similar suit had been filed by some retirees from the former Fraser Papers in New Brunswick. The union was frustrated by the pensioners' actions because in bargaining with the largest forest company, AbitibiBowater, they had made protection of pensioners a top priority and agreed to significant concessions to prevent reductions in the pensions of 25,000 retirees. At White Birch, Fraser and some other companies, the CEP had also fought for pensioners but had less ability to maintain pensions with companies in *Companies' Creditors Arrangement Act* processes. There was now a pushback against granting unconditional membership rights to retirees.

The retiree issue had reached a stalemate in the Constitution Working Group, and as the debate continued and arguments were repeated, it became heated. From the CEP side of the table, Joe Gargiso reacted to suggestions that concerns over divergent retiree interests were exaggerated by countering that unreasonable conditions were being imposed on CEP locals that were dealing with retirees in the courts. Alex Keeney, a former president of CAW Local 200 in Windsor with hundreds of retiree members, let it be known that the issue was fundamental for the CAW and retiree members would never be left behind. Angela Adams snapped back that she was equally capable of drawing a line in the sand. With strong divisions in the room and only Dave Moffat and myself from the CEP supporting the retiree proposal, a cooling-off period was needed.

When the group resumed its work the following day, attitudes had softened and compromises came forward. Local unions that were having conflicts with retirees could delay the formation of retiree chapters for a period of time while current conflicts ebbed. However, after three years, retiree chapters would be unconstrained. I had confronted David Robertson over the sharp tenor of the exchanges, but he argued that the debate was necessary and the principle of retiree membership could not be smoothed over by facilitation. In retrospect, David was correct. The uncomfortable confrontation was important and useful for the new union. The retiree debate clarified the character of the new union and, together with the community chapter decisions, provided the membership basis of the union as a social movement. Conceivably, young people could join the union as students and maintain their membership through their working career and into retirement. The new union had made itself a union for everyone, potentially offering the solidarity of lifelong union citizenship.

The Constitution Working Group was in a race against time on a series of other structural issues that had to be completed to fill out the character of the new union. In particular, unfinished business regarding representation and rank-and-file democracy presented another culture clash to be resolved. The central representation issue was whether the union would operate on the basis of "representation by population" that would ensure that delegations to conferences and conventions would be proportional to membership so as to ensure that every decision reflected the majority of all members. The answer was not as straightforward as the question.

In both unions, the majority of members were in local unions of one hundred or more members. However, in the CAW, most members were in local unions with thousands of members. In the CEP, the majority of local unions were relatively small, with even smaller workplaces, and their combined membership was a significant minority of total members. The CEP structure was not based on a simple "rep-by-pop" formula and instead provided for a minimum participation of two delegates from small locals at conventions. If delegate ratios retained the minimum participation of the small locals as well as a rep-by-pop formula, it would require the very large, mostly CAW, locals to bring dozens of delegates, resulting in massive meetings. But the farther the ratio moved away from rep-by-pop, the greater the unfair balance would be between the two founding unions. The number of delegates at a council or convention from the many small CEP local unions would be disproportionately larger, with each delegate representing fewer members than a delegate from one of the large CAW local unions.

The Constitution Working Group had to dig deep to find a fair and optimum democratic balance of representation. A partial solution to recognize the rep-by-pop principles was that all elections would take place on a per capita basis, with all delegates casting votes proportionate to their memberships. Members could also require any resolution to have a per capita vote if the request for that vote was supported by a minimum of 20 per cent of delegates. But these were partial solutions because elections and special votes on controversial matters are exceptional events, with the work of the councils more often guided by consensus and a show of hands.

Another element to the analysis was the need for the new union to give space for activists in the union. It was not only representation between the large and small locals that needed balancing but also finding a solution to the under-representation of women, workers of colour, LGBTQ workers, young workers and disabled workers. A strict rep-by-pop formula limited diversity and equity because the largest locals were often found in resource sectors such as forestry and mining and in large-scale manufacturing sectors such as auto. The workforce in these sectors tended to be less diverse than in service sector jobs or than would be typical in smaller workplaces. In addition, activist members often have a focus on social issues, politics or areas of union life such as education, health, safety and the environment. They could often be overlooked in local union processes that would send local executive board members, bargaining teams and stewards to delegated events. If smaller locals sent only a single delegate to a council or convention, activists would be excluded. The working group understood that bringing more activists into the life of the councils would add content, passion and rank-and-file leadership.

Finally, there was the practical matter of size to consider. Resolving the representation balance by providing proportionate delegate entitlements to the large locals would result in conventions with thousands of delegates. Quite apart from the cost and availability of facilities for these huge meetings, questions were raised over whether democratic debates and grassroots participation would be possible at that scale.

As the clock ticked down on its timetable, the working group pored over multiple spreadsheets, delegate counts and analysis produced by CAW Research Director Bill Murnighan. As each possible formula was presented, it was critiqued from all sides, looking for the best combination of representation, equity and activism. The ultimate result was a consensus on a representative democracy model moderately weighted to smaller locals with enhanced provisions for equity and activist delegates. Overall size considerations prevented the new union from granting a minimum of two delegates from the smallest locals to the Canadian and regional councils, but they could send two or more using a provision for extra delegates from equity groups.

The architecture of the new union could now be seen more fully. The convention would be the largest meeting of members with an entitlement of over 2,000 delegates, the majority carrying per capita votes from large local unions. The Canadian Council in the second and third years of each three-year leadership mandate would have an entitlement of about 1,500 members and staff. The Quebec Council and regional councils would each engage hundreds of delegates, staff and members. Taken as a whole, the councils in Quebec and the regions would annually involve more than 2,000 potential participants. In addition, each council would have seven elected standing committees that would need union activists to succeed. The standing committees included the five equity group committees of women, workers of colour, LGBTQ workers, youth and disabled workers and two activist committees: a political action committee and a health, safety and environment committee.

The Canadian Council and regional councils would also depart from rep-by-pop to accommodate small locals and the commitment to equity and activism. All members of the thirty-five Quebec and regional standing committees were granted delegate status at the Canadian Council. In addition, the executive members of industry councils would be delegates to the Canadian Council, where the eleven representatives to the national executive board would be elected. The executive of the Retiree Council would comprise another ten delegates. The mix at the Canadian Council of local union delegates, standing committee activists and sector leaders was intended to create a union parliament with voices reflecting the broad work of the union.

The working group proposal fulfilled the promise of large rank-and-file councils. Delegate entitlement at the largest Ontario council could bring more than a thousand delegates to a meeting; the smallest membership group in Atlantic Canada would have about 200 delegates at a council meeting. British Columbia and the Prairies would also have more than 200 delegates, and a Quebec council could have over 400 voting delegates. The regional councils would be funded by a mandatory per capita payment by local unions for all members that would provide several hundred thousand dollars to the Atlantic, rising to about a million dollars for Ontario. There would be ample funds for campaigns and initiatives, with larger staff and department costs paid directly from the centre.

These decisions gave shape to the goal of a rank-and-file union in which major decisions would be made by hundreds of members in council meetings at the regional and national levels. The councils would be more than educational forums where members get together to share experience; the large gathering of members would elect leadership, adopt policy and be forums for accountability and actions around the important policy directions of the national union, from politics to servicing and bargaining.

The model was imperfect, but it was a fresh and credible union democracy with political activism, equity and sector bargaining strategies built into its design. The issue of large and small local unions would not be resolved at the union's founding; these issues would be considered in the promised "local union task force" to take place during the first mandate of the new union. But the debate over local union structures had already begun, breaking down myths and generalities into more nuanced truths.

There was a strong agreement that the patchwork of very small local unions was a weakness. These locals, with sometimes less than twenty members, lacked the resources for full participation in the union and were the most likely to be absent from council meetings or convention. But the working group had learned that the most significant complaints from members over poor representation and services arose most often from some of the largest locals, which were clearly not involving and engaging groups of members in isolated bargaining units. They also learned that some smaller local unions were very active in the national union and their community and had exceptionally high rates of membership participation.

The design of a union where major decisions are made by large numbers of members rather than by executives was a crucial part of our thinking to respond to the political threats swirling around Canadian unions. Unions are based on majoritarian principles, but real democracy and inclusion also demand attention to minorities within the union and the rights of individual members.

These were heady days of social conservatism, fuelled by the Harper majority in Ottawa and the virulent anti-labour rhetoric of Ontario Conservative leader Tim Hudak. The fact that Hudak and other Conservatives were able to put their demands in the forefront of Canadian politics and appear to be winning the debate was in itself a stunning setback for unions. Trade unions are legal entities, and the freedoms that were under attack are supported in various degrees by law in every jurisdiction in Canada and by international conventions at the International Labour Organization. To run against these underpinnings of free collective bargaining required a larger assault on the democratic legitimacy of unions. At the core of this ideological program is the assertion that trade unions suppress the individual rights of workers. From this base argument, the campaign against unions attacked union security, the collection of union dues and the spending of union funds in politics.

The anti-labour wing of the Conservative movement is a coalition of anti-labour construction, retail and hospitality employers, the Christian religious Right and right-wing libertarians. Each had a role in the coordinated offensive against unions that was coming to a head in 2012.

At the centre of the coalition was the non-union construction industry's "merit shop" committees. The merit shop term was developed by the US Associated Builders and Contractors in the 1950s to suggest a workplace organization where wages, conditions and promotions would be determined by each individual's merit and not by seniority or other terms of a contract. Eventually, the merit shop became synonymous with "open shop" or non-union. By 2008, there were merit shop associations in eight Canadian provinces.

Merit shop associations are devoted to reversing the postwar compromises to recognize unions and the union security provisions they describe as forced unionism imposed by the Rand formula and closed-shop union agreements. They also oppose card-based certification laws, alleging that union organizers intimidate individual workers to sign union cards. The merit shop fumes against the political role of unions and the spending of member dues on hot-button political and social causes such as abortion rights for women, LGBTQ rights or Palestinian rights.

The Christian Right is another integral part of the Conservative coalition focused on workers' rights and social issues. In 2011 and 2012, while Hudak was campaigning against "forced unionism" with his proposal to scrap the Rand formula, the anti-abortion Campaign Life Coalition had a parallel "defund abortion campaign" that railed against compulsory union dues that supported pro-life policies on abortion.[18]

The Canadian Federation of Independent Business and various retail and fast-food companies joined with merit shop in 2000 to form Labour-Watch, set up to campaign for anti-labour laws. It had operated on the fringes of Canadian affairs while it carved out increasing influence alongside the libertarian right wing in the base of the Conservative party. A decade later, LabourWatch was ready to hatch larger strategies. LabourWatch funded a September 2011 poll by Nanos Research that purported to find that 83 per cent of Canadians supported "mandatory public financial disclosure for both public and private sector unions." The research would later be dismissed as "horrendously biased" by Allan Gregg, chairman of Harris/Decima and former Conservative party pollster, and was criticized by the polling industry's oversight association. It was never intended to be anything more than a set-up. A few weeks later, the LabourWatch poll was cited by Conservative Member of Parliament Russ Hiebert as evidence of "a broad public consensus" in support of his legislation, which would become Bill C-377 to require mandatory publishing of union expenses.[19]

There was not much that the New Union Project could do in the short term to confront the coalition that had seized the policy agenda of the Conservative party and was driving legislative attacks federally and in many provinces. But it was clear to us that for the union to be strong and withstand the ongoing co-ordinated campaign against collective rights, the statutes we were drafting required a rebalancing of rights. In particular, it meant a fulsome setting out of the rights of members in the union and protections against abuses of power or arbitrary treatment of individuals.

Neither of the former CEP and CAW constitutions had a stand-alone section on the rights of members. Like most union statutes, it was considered that the constitution as a whole set out the rights of members, which were in turn balanced by obligations and offences usually listed in a section on disciplinary issues. The new union constitution would take a different approach. A provision on membership rights would recast the balance by setting out explicitly unqualified rights of members. Drafted by David Robertson during the Proposal Committee stage of the project, Article V provided a list of very specific membership rights, a bit reminiscent of Canada's *Charter of Rights and Freedoms* applied to a union context.

Those rights included the right to "share equally" in the governance of the union and to nominate and vote in free and fair elections. The constitution went further to ensure that any member could participate in decision-making debates and that free speech and the freedom to criticize union governance would be protected. Full participation also necessitated a harassment-free environment in the union. On a practical level, the rights of members required "fair and reasonable consideration of individual interests when collective decisions are made," including a review process for decisions that could adversely impact an individual or a minority.

On the flip side of the responsibilities of members, the new provisions are decidedly more general in nature, requiring only respect for the democratic decisions of the union and an obligation to support the union's collective actions in bargaining and in defence of jobs. Underscoring the shift in balance to the rights of members, the sections of the constitution concerning charges against and between members no longer included any list of "offences" subject to discipline.

Another rebalancing was set out in the *Code of Ethics and Democratic Practices*. The *Code*, which forms part of the constitution, was an update and rewriting of the CAW *Code of Ethics*. It asserts the rights of members to participation and free speech, due process, natural justice and the right to engage in the union free from harassment and discrimination.

Where the *Code* goes further than in previous union constitutions are provisions that take aim at the day-to-day abuses of authority, often out of sight of other members, where the concerns or complaints of individuals are ignored or arbitrarily denied. The *Code* is explicit in that it covers all aspects of union life and prohibits any "cover-up" of any abuse or the impeding of any investigation by a staff person or an officer.

Conflict of interest provisions were also inserted into the constitution through the *Code*. Unions have been slow in responding to higher expectations on conflict, with union leaders often heard repeating the baseless argument that "everything the union does is a conflict" because everyone in the union benefits from its actions. Collective benefits are not conflictual, but carrying out the work of the union in a way to specifically benefit a responsible national or local officer or staff person may well be a conflict of interest. The *Code* requires all national and local union officials and representatives to disclose any "significant personal interests" with regard to any decision they participate in or make. This could include personal relationships, expectation of profit, ownership or investments in a company or offers of gifts, employment or other personal gain.

Another issue affecting the reputation of unions is the practice of some unions to allow leaders and staff to combine separate union responsibilities to amass additional personal income. In some cases, union officials serve on pension boards or receive government appointments that include significant honorariums or salaries. Sometimes leaders can hold multiple positions within a union, labour central or labour movement institution that provide additional income. Although usually not a conflict of interest, these various roles can easily appear to be perks or privileges rather than extra work on behalf of members. The *Code* takes a strong, ethical position to disallow any national officer or staff person from having any other employment relationship or from accepting any other salary, honorarium or significant gift for carrying out union duties. The only exceptions are strictly personal endeavours such as awards and prizes, royalties or proceeds from books or works of art and personal investments.

These issues are not the winning arguments in organizing drives, nor are they repeated often in union debates. That is until an anti-union campaign purports to speak for union members claiming the union has failed to represent them or a union leader gains sudden media attention because of corruption or abusive behaviour. When this happens, union rhetoric about democracy is usually of little help. The only effective answer to the accusation of abuse of power is a quick, robust and effective countervailing redress by the union. Nothing less will stop the undermining of the trust members hold in their union. Union security in Canada by design requires the granting of membership to everyone in a bargaining unit, and unions are made up of every kind of person with the full range of human motivations. It is up to the union to establish a culture and democratic practices that act as an ethical screen for anyone seeking to represent and lead others.

Not least, a modern rebalancing of individual and collective rights also required specific attention to the massive social advances over identity and equality. The lived experience of individuals in a trade union differs dramatically according to gender, race, sexuality or other identities. To complete the balance between the union and its members, a larger debate unfolded over equity. How far should or could the new union go in proscribing equity and requiring structures within the union to be reflective of membership diversity?

Part of the response to these issues was an anti-harassment policy that combined and updated the existing policies in light of experience and the best current practices in the labour and social movements. The anti-harassment policy was entrenched in the constitution as a parallel process to address issues of sexism, racism, bullying and other forms of oppression. Members would have the choice of seeking redress either through the charges and trial provisions of the constitution or through the anti-harassment process that guaranteed confidentiality and expedited processes.

For the wider equity issues of recognition, representation and inclusion, the constitution declared an overarching principle and a commitment that the union would view all its work and practices through a gender and equity lens. The lens was intended to be a framework for evaluating structures, bylaws or decisions that come before the national executive board or other adjudicative bodies. But the constitution also asserted that the equity groups themselves would have full inclusion and would be "represented in the structures of the union at all levels." Without doubt, these provisions have profoundly affected the character of Unifor.

CHAPTER 4

Unifor

Winter was breaking across Canada in March 2013, and there was a spring in the step of the new union organizers. The intense working group sessions through the winter had delivered across the board, and the groups were ready to bring a number of blueprints to the Proposal Committee for review and then to pivotal meetings of the two national executive boards: the CAW on March 14 and the CEP on April 9. With leadership endorsement of these covenants, the new union would be ready to meet the membership in the second cross-country series of regional meetings in April and May.

The accomplishments were impressive: from the Constitution Working Group, a draft constitution, anti-harassment policy, strike fund policy and an inventory of existing union policies; from the Organizing Working Group, an organizing strategy and policy and the proposal for community chapters; from the Implementation Working Group, a timetable and organizational chart that set out departmental structures and offices, blending existing departments and creating a strategic planning role and capacity; from the Staff Relations Working Group, a report on a first round of meetings with the four staff unions; and from the Convention Working Group, logistics and a conceptual agenda for the founding convention now only five months down the road.

One working group working against the clock had been given a mandate that required a very different process and creative venture. The Communications Working Group had a different starting point because the new union was to have a new name, identity and brand. For these goals, it would serve no purpose to negotiate the best practices of past experience; the new identity had to be forged entirely out of the values and hopes driving the New Union Project. The Communications Working Group also brought a very different group of personalities. CAW co-chair Susan Spratt was the past director of the union in Western Canada. Her CEP co-chair, Peter Murdoch, was the CEP's media vice-president. The staff complement working on the identity and brand issues were a generation younger than their union leadership and Proposal Committee members. Shannon Devine was possibly the youngest communications director in the Canadian trade union movement and like many in the CAW tradition, she was the product of an auto industry union family. When CEP's Communications Director Michelle Walsh signalled her retirement, she was replaced on the working group by Roxanne Dubois.

A creative force backing up the Communications Working Group from the consulting group, Strategic Communications or Stratcom, added another blend of veteran and youthful intellectuals who would work closely with the project. The Stratcom squad added Matt Smith, David Kraft and Peter Bleyer. Bleyer, a former executive director of the Council of Canadians and an experienced trade union consultant and staffer, would play an important role in choosing a name. Another group of innovative consultants, Pivot Design, was brought in later to work on visual design.

The assembled communications team had few sentimental attachments to the past and was eager to break new ground. "We sought to create something truly new that speaks to us on the level of values we espouse as trade unionists and the hopes we have for our movement,"

Shannon Devine, CAW communications director and staff member of the Communications Working Group in 2013.

said Spratt and Murdoch about the goals the communications group set for itself.

There was no doubt that the identity of unions generally in Canada had taken a beating, with fewer numbers of Canadians having a positive view of what unions stand for and who they benefit. Research carried out by the Canadian Labour Congress had found that support for the view that unions had outlived their usefulness had spiked upwards from 32 per cent in 2006 to 51 per cent in 2012.[1] Another more favourable study showed that although a solid majority of 61 per cent of Canadians in 2012 thought unions did a good job protecting their members, the number dropped to just 46 per cent who would say that unions benefited the broader community.[2]

There are clearly many reasons explaining labour's decline in public approval, with no easy answers. The factors driving public opinion range from a lesser social and community role by unions to poor communications and ham-fisted bargaining strategies that alienated sections of the public. As pollster Allan Gregg would later tell the founding convention, public opinion about unions is largely a reaction to whether unions are perceived to be acting in the public interest. Likely the largest problem for unions is their growing isolation from large sections of the new working class in service sectors. Workers in those sectors often have almost no understanding of what unions do or how they operate and can be easy prey for demagogic blaming of unions when a plant closed and moved production to a low-wage region.

None of these issues could be resolved by a communications strategy, but it provided an informed starting point for the communications group and underscored the need for a far-reaching process that would go far beyond the inside views of union activists.

It was hardly a matter of just reducing the vision of the Proposal Committee to a name and a logo. That could only have resulted in a mirror image of the union leadership, not a common identifier for 300,000 workers and potentially millions of others in their communities. The development of an identity and a brand instead had to go down a path of broad-based consultations and investigation into how members and the public related to the existing unions and to the goals of the New Union Project. For many outside the labour movement, this resembled a classic branding exercise and did not seem all that remarkable. But for a contemporary trade union, it was nearly unique, especially given the scope of the exercise to produce an entirely new identity and brand.

In March 2013, the Communications Working Group was still in the throes of that investigation, examining the preliminary results from a membership questionnaire that had been circulated in January and a set of focus group sessions across the country in February. The January questionnaire was a first attempt at a rank-and-file engagement beyond the forums of members in local unions, special meetings, conferences and conventions. Should the new union be "strong and powerful," "grounded and principled," "energetic and enthusiastic" or "calm and composed?" Grounded and principled was the popular choice for the new union's character. From a list of about twenty values and principles, members in English Canada preferred a union that would be described as "accountable, democratic and progressive." In Quebec, the three most chosen value identifiers were "démocratique, équitable, intègre." Among three visual expressions of the new union, "young, hip and funky," "traditional, simple and serious" and "fresh, clean and modern," the latter dominated.

The popular descriptors were certainly not at odds with the New Union Project work to that point of identifying founding principles. Moreover, they offered considerable wisdom and guidance for the presentation of values that would connect with members. These members had an expectation of a union grounded strongly in principle and integrity. They were looking for a fresh and modern identity with progressive goals but still accountable and responsive to members.

The questionnaire scraped the surface of the new union, with 5,300 questionnaires returned — a probable reflection of the views of the most involved and aware union members. To get a perspective on the attitudes of less active and uninvolved members, focus group sessions were organized in Toronto, Vancouver, Winnipeg, Thunder Bay, Chicoutimi, Montreal and Halifax. The focus groups set out to take the pulse of both union members and community members outside the union. There would be two small group sessions of eight persons in each location, one group of union members and another set of individuals from the community without a connection to the new union. The union member focus groups were made up of randomly selected members, excluding anyone involved in local or national leadership bodies, with a mix of involved and uninvolved members. The community focus groups were balanced between two or three from union families and five to six from the non-union world, but excluding those with nothing positive or useful to say about unions and those who were overly enthusiastic about unions.

If not entirely a cold bath for the new union, the focus groups were certainly sobering and instructive of the outreach still to be done. The focus group report presented a blunt message:

> The new union is being launched at a time when the climate of opinion towards labour unions is unfavourable or equivocal, even among otherwise "progressive" individuals;

The vision or aspirations of the new union are viewed skeptically by union members and the public who see them as abstract and overreaching, and of little practical benefit;

The membership of the CEP and the CAW are unaware and uninvolved in the process of creating the new union. [3]

Overall, the opinions of members towards the new union ranged from neutral to favourable. For union members and the public, the rationale for creating a new union — stagnating wages, increased economic inequality, preserving social programs — was accepted as a credible explanation for the project. But there was widespread skepticism about the ambitious vision of the new union and a wariness of "bigness." Some said the new union seemed to be more of a political party than a union.

An interesting twist of expectations was that the public groups reacted more favourably than union members towards the prospect of the new union's strong community presence. Members were more likely to question the feasibility of the union extending its role strongly into the community. On the related but distinct question of politics and political action, union members generally appreciated the need for and purpose of political action to defend workers' rights. But both union members and community participants wanted to see political action that was not reduced to partisanship for a political party.

The community voices were also generally positive regarding the new union objective to "organize workers who currently have no access to union membership," although they doubted it could be accomplished and did not see themselves as prospective members. Almost all of the focus group participants viewed the pursuit of jobs, greater equality and economic progress for workers as legitimate mandates and strongly approved of a commitment by the new union to progress for all Canadians.

The matter of a name for the new union remained at a preliminary stage, and the questionnaire and focus groups did not yield a proposition. However, eight early ideas for names were floated by the focus groups, and the insight gathered helped provide a general direction to the name search. The generic but mundane "Canadian Workers Union" had appeal because of its clarity and inclusiveness. On the other end of the spectrum, "Uni21" was an interesting, youthful but somewhat incomprehensible suggestion. Although it was unappealing at first, when the name was discussed in the context of a "union for the twenty-first century," it gained support. Other prototype names were "One Voice," "Union Alliance," "Impact" and "Unify"; all garnered lukewarm responses.

There were only a few, but important, take-aways to give direction to the name search that the Communications Working Group could present to the Proposal Committee and executive boards in March. The name should be modern and not traditional. It should suggest that the union is protective and inclusive, and it should emphasize positivity and problem solving. But for the imminent regional meetings of local union leaders and members, the new union would remain nameless.

The larger conclusion from the survey and focus groups was that a major membership engagement strategy was needed, and this gave urgency to the regional meetings scheduled for April and May of 2013. The open meetings were for local union leaderships and members from either union in fifteen Canadian cities: Vancouver, Winnipeg, Thunder Bay, Ottawa, Windsor, Sarnia, London, Brampton, Oshawa, Edmonton, Regina, Halifax, Fredericton, Quebec City and Trois Rivières.

The regional meetings drew more than two thousand local leaders and activists with focused questions on constitutional and operational issues. In contrast to the focus groups' skepticism, the activist membership was by this time largely enthusiastic. The new union's ambitious goals and mission were almost entirely unquestioned and applauded at times. Membership questions focused strongly on issues such as delegate representation to conferences and conventions, the proposals for retiree chapters and some detailed local matters, such as the disposition of assets of local unions in the event of the closure and windup of a local union.

The regional meetings resulted in three changes to the draft constitution. Delegate formulas to convention and to the Canadian and regional councils were loosened to remove limits on "special delegates" with a voice and no vote from equity groups. The change would allow smaller locals greater representation but require them to allot the extra representation to women or other equity members. A second amendment on local union standing committees removed a mandatory requirement that every local must establish standing committees dealing with political action, health and safety, as well as separate equity committees for women, youth, Aboriginal workers and workers of colour, LGBTQ members and disabled members. All of these committees remained named in the constitution but were made optional at the local level. The third amendment modified the local dues structures, replacing a set formula with a minimum local dues rate considered to be the least required to service members and participate in union affairs. The hope and expectation was that the changes to the constitution would reassure local activists that their opinions counted and that the union would be responsive and accountable. But how deep was the message penetrating?

A larger slice of members was reached in two rounds of telephone town hall meetings. With members of both unions organized into time zones, "robocall" messages set up conference call participation on the following day, where members could join a conference call and listen in on a discussion led by CAW President Ken Lewenza and CEP President Dave Coles. Total participation in the town halls reached 26,375. Somewhat interactive, the town hall meetings allowed over sixty members to get air time with questions, concerns and discussion, although over 600 members were in queue. Soon after the founding of Unifor, 236,000 reliable direct mail addresses were assembled and an information questionnaire was sent out. The direct mail spiked responses to 16,475. The message coming back was not qualitatively different from that of the earlier, smaller questionnaire. Membership priorities for the new union were focused on collective bargaining power (61 per cent), with a particular emphasis on pensions and retirement security. This was not a surprising consensus given that 81 per cent of the respondents were in a cohort of forty-five years or older. However, a healthy 41 per cent identified public image and attitudes towards unions as a priority for the new union to address.[4]

The survey demographics added additional insight into what sections of the membership were paying attention to the new union process and were hopeful enough to respond. The working assumption of 33 per cent women in the membership was almost doubled in survey participation: 62 per cent of respondents were women, and overall one in four identified as a member of an equity-seeking group.

In *Towards a New Union*, the final report of the Proposal Committee projected that some 20,000 union members would be actively engaged, serving as local union executive members, bargaining committee members, members of local and regional committees from health and safety to equity groups, workplace stewards and delegates to conferences, councils and convention. Several tens of thousands more attended union meetings and stood behind these activists.

It seemed that the New Union Project had succeeded in connecting to and canvassing most of the aware and involved union members. The outreach had gone far beyond the activists into the hundreds of thousands that the focus groups had described as "unaware and uninvolved." Clearly, the informed consent of those thousands is a constant dilemma for union democracies. The new union efforts underscored the dual realities that unions are voluntary participatory democracies for those who engage and representative democracies for others. Of course, parallel tests of informed consent by stronger majorities are regularly provided by collective agreement ratification votes, surveys measuring satisfaction with union representation and ballots of members in union elections. But these engagements would have to wait as the new union moved to closure on the choosing of a name.

In the Stratcom team and the Communications Working Group, the pressure was on to produce a name, a logo and an overarching identity. May 9 was showtime for the Communications Working Group and the Stratcom team. Peter Murdoch, Susan Spratt, Shannon Devine, Roxanne Dubois and the Stratcom team of Matt Smith, Peter Bleyer, David Kraft and Ian Chalmers (Pivot Design) met with the 5×5 leadership to pitch their recommendation. The presenters began by reviewing the problems of a traditional name, and they reminded the 5×5 that it had already been agreed that the new union would be named without reference to occupations. Nor were there generic options that could be substituted. The "Canadian Workers Union" or any variation of it would be reduced to twin English and French acronyms, and the name must be a single word requiring no translation. Moreover, the diversity of the new union defied any simple description beyond that of a strong, united union. Among the hundreds of existing union brands that had been considered and proposals received from members, the Swedish "Unionen" struck the creative team as a strong, clean and modern name. They moved on to their proposal. The root of the word "union," "uni," had similar meanings in English and French, combining notions of unity and solidarity. Adding to it a sense of positive motion and force resulted in something entirely new: "Unifor." The name was particularly appealing in French, an amalgam of the words "unis" (united) and "fort" (strong). The metaphoric impact of the name was accentuated by the new logo: a bold red shield with a prominent U intended to evoke ideas of strength, armour and protection.

There was no immediate reaction from the table. The first reaction was genuine surprise. The communications group had pulled off an astounding accomplishment, utterly unthinkable in either union's recent past. Neither the leadership of the two unions nor anyone else in the New Union Project outside the confidentiality of the communications group had any prior tipoff or preparation for what they were seeing that morning.

No matter how many times it had been said that a name and identity would break convention, the initial reactions to "Unifor" were confused, especially over the made-up nature of the name. "I just don't know what it means," Ken Lewenza said honestly. Jerry Dias was more negative and dismissively flippant in his tone. But rather quickly, other voices around the table were positive, and the first "I like it" began a round of affirmations. As the new identity sunk in, the boldness of the visuals was clearly striking home. Gradually, the explanations and intentions of the proposal became clearer. The made-up name without any direct connection to language commonly used by union members was a stretch but also an invitation to think differently. "The name Unifor was chosen as a new word to represent a new concept of unionism," Stratcom argued. "Our new union will reach out and organize Canadians more widely than ever before. We aim to become a union FOR everyone. In this regard the new name was chosen to represent a new approach, a new story and new chapter in the history of the Canadian labour movement."

The argument that sealed the decision put the issue of a name in a different context. The name Unifor would have different reactions and interpretations, but the new union's identity and what Unifor would come to represent would be determined by the actions of the new union.

Moreover, the 5×5 was not given any options to choose among. The proposal came with the unanimous approval of the Communications Working Group, which was not really looking for unanimity at this stage. The founding convention was just three months away, and the recommendation was the result of an exhaustive process. The group had already determined that the name and its variations (*Unifor — the Union* and *Unifor — Canada* or *Unifor — Québec*) were unique and not protected by any copyright or trademark. Nothing short of a unanimous and total rejection of the working group's proposal could have altered the course.

The name and logo were kept under wraps until a similar presentation was made to a joint meeting of the CAW and CEP executive boards on May 29 and then to a group of about 150 members and staff who witnessed the unveiling at a livestreamed media event on May 30 in the

Essex Ballroom of the Toronto Sheraton. The responses were again a mix of immediate support and excitement and levels of confusion and questioning over the made-up name. In a series of communications to local unions over the previous weeks, members had been invited to tune in via a live-stream broadcast of the event. The public launch brought more strong and mixed reactions. It was clear at least that the goal of a bold identity that breaks with tradition was met.

Simultaneous with the public launch of the name and logo, the *Windsor Star* interviewed union members for opinions on the Unifor name and logo. "Unifor sounds like a multinational kind of company," said Mike LaPlante, a member of CAW Local 444 and line worker at Chrysler's Windsor Assembly Plant. "It doesn't sound like something (that) instills solidarity." Jerry Logan, CAW unit chair at TRW Automotive, had the reaction that the new union was hoping for: "You know, I grew up under the CAW banner. It's kind of a little bit of a change for us, but I think it symbolizes what we want to do as an organization, to include everybody. It might take some time to grow on me, but I think it's symbolic of what we want to do in the future . . . I think the logo is tremendous. I love the use of the shield: to serve and protect type thing."[5]

The name debate revealed the cultural barriers for a union to break with tradition, even when it sets out to do just that. It would take months before the controversy over Unifor would subside, but there was from the beginning a street-level grasp of its basic messaging, particularly its visual presentation, with the large U mounted on a red shield. Members immediately understood that it represented protection. But it also evoked another meaning that was not central to the original presentation. For many members, the U meant inclusion: a "union for U."

The communications group began the exhaustive job of branding the new union. Within days, clothing, documents and online graphics bore the Unifor colours and design, and an extensive effort was launched to explain the name and logo as the expression of the new union's values. Unifor's name and look were just in time to meet the practical deadlines of preparing a founding convention ninety days out.

Most of the pieces for the founding of Unifor were falling into place, with one large exception. At the beginning of June 2013, there was no agreement on leadership.

Leading a 300,000-member union would be "an exciting opportunity," but leadership discussions had not been held, the CAW's Ken Lewenza told the *Windsor Star* in early May. "We have a unity committee in place made up of CAW and CEP members and it will make recommendations in advance of the founding convention and I'm with them on this issue. The union will be bigger than who leads it. We've largely kept the issue of leadership out of our discussions, which is the way it should be," he said.[6]

There had been musings about who would lead the union, and some individuals had signalled personal decisions. Notably, Dave Coles, who was approaching retirement, had indicated he would not stand for office at the founding convention. However, Ken Lewenza, the presumed leader of the new union, had made a point of not speaking about his personal plans. From the first tentative meetings of the two sides a year earlier and through the Proposal Committee process, there had been no organized discussion or informal decisions made on leadership matters. The recommendations of the Proposal Committee had been made without consideration of the existing or future positions of any of the existing leaders or staff in either union. It is quite likely that the New Union Project would not have succeeded if its mission had been complicated and compromised by the needs or ambitions of leaders and senior staff.

The discussion on leadership started slowly and did not begin to come to conclusions until the final stretch before the founding convention. Inevitably, the political choices and ambitions of the central players would come into play, but those leadership choices were not the most important to the New Union Project. The more controversial issues to be resolved were instead the leadership selection process, the role of caucuses and open elections.

Leadership discussions began after both unions had endorsed the call for a new union at their 2012 conventions. These tentative discussions had begun in the 4×4 leadership meetings in February and March and had reached consensus that at the founding of the new union, the three officers should reflect the founding unions by having two officers from the CAW and one from the CEP. It was agreed that the rest of the national executive board and regional leaderships should also reflect a national and regional balance between the unions. There was recognition that the gender and regional balances set out in the new union proposal, as well as the "equity lens" in the draft constitution, were fundamental to the leadership choices.

One reason for the tentative discussion on leadership was Lewenza's own uncertainty about his personal future. Ken Lewenza was popular in the CAW and was the CAW leader whom CEP members had come to know best, especially for his performance at the CEP convention. He was the obvious choice for president, but he told the 4×4 that he was reflecting on his role. "I have to decide if it is time to go back to Windsor," he told us.

As the weeks progressed towards the founding convention, Lewenza's indecision was increasingly taken as affirmation that he would stand for president. But suddenly in mid-July, with just six weeks remaining to the founding, Lewenza stunned both unions with the announcement that he would not stand for the position of Unifor president. Lewenza later explained to the 5×5 that it was a matter of heart and the realization that the energy and potential of the new union also called for a new president. He believed that for the new union to consolidate and succeed, the president should be prepared to serve a second term, a commitment he was not ready to make. "What we are doing is bigger than we ever dreamed," said an emotional Lewenza. "I had to think about whether I was the person that could give this job what it needed everywhere across the country or if my heart would be in Windsor."

Jerry Dias also expected that Lewenza would lead the union and was as surprised as anyone else by the announcement. There had been an informal understanding in the CAW leadership that Jerry Dias was the leading choice to succeed Lewenza on his retirement. However, Dias had a strong bias against labour leaders presiding over their organizations into their mid-sixties and beyond, and he doubted the timing of succeeding Lewenza when he chose to step down. Not expecting Ken's decision, he was planning on taking his own early retirement when his pension numbers added up in a few years. All that changed suddenly.

Dias was a new figure to many, but he was steeped in CAW-UAW history. The son of a staff representative, he was the product of the UAW family education program as a teenager. He followed in his father's footsteps, becoming a steward at age twenty at Local 112, De Havilland Aircraft (now Bombardier). He became local president at age twenty-six and a few years later became a CAW national representative. He then became an assistant to the president soon after Buzz Hargrove succeeded Bob White as CAW president and quickly became one of the union's lead negotiators in the beleaguered manufacturing sector. Known inside the CAW as a militant and a self-described democratic socialist, he was not well known to CEP local union activists, and there were few opportunities in the last part of the summer to change that. Dias would have to make his mark at convention — a dynamic that would both build anticipation and underscore that the new union would break from the past.

The other national leadership positions, secretary-treasurer and Quebec director, had likewise largely been kept off the table to that point. However, an agreement had been reached on the principle of a "two and one" combination among the three national officers to be named, reflecting the proportionate sizes of the two founding unions.

Peter Kennedy, the CAW secretary-treasurer, had won the trust and support of CEP leaders through his role as co-chair of the Proposal Committee, and although nearing retirement, he made it clear that he wanted to stay on at least for the first term of office in the new union. He was the logical choice for secretary-treasurer by seniority and experience and because the "two and one" principle pointed to the CEP's Michel Ouimet becoming Quebec director.

These parameters complicated the situation for Gaétan Ménard, who believed his strong role in the New Union Project had earned consideration for the position of secretary-treasurer. The 5×5 appealed to Ménard to accept an offer to be part of the leadership as assistant to the officers. There was tacit understanding that he may well be a candidate for secretary-treasurer after the retirements of Peter Kennedy and Michel Ouimet, providing that an understanding with the Quebec Region could maintain the two and one principle. Ménard was unwilling to take an assistant role but eventually agreed to take the role of transition officer, a senior role with the responsibility of providing oversight to the integration of both unions into Unifor's new structures. Ménard's future in the union was altered suddenly by a series of family health issues that precluded a move from the Quebec Outaouais region to Metro Toronto. Among these was the aftermath of a dramatic situation in which Ménard's spouse, Josée, played a heroic role as an elementary school principal in facing down a gun-bearing intruder into her Buckingham school. Ménard left Unifor in 2014 to become a full-time vice-president of the Canadian Industrial Relations Board.

For the most part, these leadership questions were removed from the daily work of the New Union Project even after the 5×5 engaged the subject in the summer of 2013. Among staff and in the membership, leadership was an occasional topic of discussion but generally not a matter of contention. Union members tend to accept leadership choices, as long as the process is trusted. That factor presented a potentially larger problem that could derail Unifor.

The CAW leadership culture was rooted in its international history with the United Auto Workers and the Congress of Industrial Organizations, and its long-standing caucus system was integral to that culture. Historically, caucuses grew out of political orientations and the alliances that accompanied those trends to establish internal trade union unity. Labour politics in the 1930s and 1940s were shaped by many different political frameworks: socialist and communist, social democratic, liberal and anti-communist. Competition between political factions was exacerbated after the Cold War took root in the trade union movement in 1946 with the active intervention of government and security forces into the internal affairs of trade unions. During this period, Walter Reuther, president of the UAW from 1946 to 1970, shaped the UAW into a progressive force in American labour and politics that both resisted some aspects of the Cold War and internally addressed ideological factionalism through the creation of the "Administration Caucus." The goal of the caucus was to ensure a stable, representative leadership committed to a common political direction.

Over the years, the caucus system evolved in step with national politics in both the United States and Canada. In 1985, when the Canadian division of the UAW separated over profound political differences and trade union strategies, the Administration Caucus was not in question and was integrated into the life of the CAW. The caucus was open to all members and reflected the mainstream of union activists. At the national level and in the larger local unions, the caucus would typically endorse slates of candidates who were considered to provide a representative balance of locals, trades and occupations and minimum representation for women and minorities. It also had a role of resolving leadership conflicts by choosing between rivals before they faced off against each other at convention.

The CAW caucus system affirmed Canadian director Bob White as the first national president and later chose his assistant, Buzz Hargrove, to be his successor. Succession planning was a consensus role of the caucus, and it was expected that assistants were being prepared for potential officer roles. However, in 2008, when a successor to Hargrove had to be chosen, a critical vote in the caucus chose Ken Lewenza over an assistant, Hemi Mitic. Mitic was experienced, capable and, in his view, ready to step into the president's role. But among his peers, he lacked the progressive credentials and common touch that the union needed. They found that in Lewenza — the first time that a local union president bypassed staff and assistant roles to take the leadership, and the decision underscored the role of the Administration Caucus.

CEP leaders had little knowledge of the CAW history and leadership

Left to right: CAW forefather Bob White, his spouse Marilyn and Jim O'Neill, former CAW secretary-treasurer, August 29, 2013.

culture, but the idea of a slate of recommended candidates around an administration caucus was foreign to them. The CEP culture could not have been more different. The balance of leadership was determined by contested elections that were expected at every convention for both officer and rank-and-file executive board positions. In the CEP, there had never been a standing leadership caucus that engaged in succession planning. The CEP approach to leadership unity was expressed instead by a large number of officer positions that minimized competition. But there were strong reasons for them to consider a new approach to leadership.

National leadership in the CEP had been determined by the merger agreements to form the union in 1992 and later mergers, resulting in a large number of elected officers. An early commitment to reduce the number of officers was only partially carried out, and the CEP continued to elect fourteen officers. Three were national officers and the other eleven were regional officers elected across four regions. With the exception only of national president and secretary-treasurer, each of

Former CEP President Brian Payne at the last CEP convention.

the elected positions was designated for a person from the respective paper, energy and communications sector. The third national officer, the media vice-president, was reserved for a person from the media and graphical sectors. Over time, national leadership was determined by a mix of political alliances between regions, most often driven by the politics of pattern bargaining in the major pattern bargaining units that spanned the regions. Within these alliances, there was also no shortage of rivalries between regions, sectors and individuals. The rivalries could have abrupt consequences and leave behind resentments that would affect leadership decisions years later. Fred Pomeroy, the former president of the Communications Workers of Canada and the CEP's second president, unexpectedly announced his retirement months before the national convention in 2000. His early departure was prompted by the decision of disgruntled paper worker vice-presidents to nominate Western Vice-President Brian Payne as his successor. Pomeroy responded by quitting early, with few preparations in place for the 2000 convention, and Payne hurriedly relocated to Ottawa after being named by the executive board as acting president. He would eventually become CEP's

most successful and popular leader, but it required reaching out to the
other sectors and forging regional alliances.

Payne sought to reassure the telecommunications sector and its large
base in Quebec by supporting Quebec's nominee for national secretary-
treasurer, Rejean Bercier, a senior negotiator from the telecommunications sector. However, the leadership balance proposed by Payne was
unacceptable to a group of Ontario paper workers who were intent on
denying leadership roles to anyone associated with the "interest-based
bargaining" approach to bargaining with Bell Canada that Pomeroy and
the telecommunications leadership had supported. In their view the
bargaining model, which requires the union to focus on the interests of
the employer in the course of making demands, fostered a non-adver-
sarial relationship with management that compromised the militancy
of the union. Ontario nominated paper worker representative and
president of the Ontario NDP, André Foucault, for national secretary-
treasurer. Foucault emerged the winner by a few hundred votes out of
about 130,000 per capita votes cast. The high drama of the election was
elevated by a lengthy convention recess to resolve counting errors; the
culprit turned out to be a faulty calculator.

With Quebec rebuffed and two paper workers then leading the four
sectors of the union, it would take Payne some time and major strikes
in every sector before a strong solidarity was re-established among the
regions, sectors and the national union. To repair unity with Quebec,
Payne brokered an agreement on administrative issues and a new casting of the role of Quebec vice-president within the union as executive
vice-president of the national union. Quebec was appeased but would
nevertheless take the opportunity later to repay Ontario for its role in
the 2000 election by throwing its support to Western Vice-President
Dave Coles to become Brian Payne's successor in 2006 over Ontario
Vice-President Cecil Makowski.

In the absence of the New Union Project and with Dave Coles coming
to the end of his three terms and a year as national president, it was
fully expected that another round of CEP politics would have unfolded.

Some in the CEP leadership would argue that rank-and-file per capita membership votes ultimately decided these rivalries, as they should. But against the background of their political history, others were open to a different system that would produce better results and stronger leadership unity.

There was an appreciation in the 5×5 that on the subject of caucus politics, there was a large gap between the political cultures of the two organizations. The CAW understood that CEP local leaders would not easily embrace slate politics where a list of recommended candidates is presented for endorsement or the idea of an administration caucus, which sounded like a self-preserving shadow leadership. Conversely, CEP leaders accepted that CAW caucuses were not about to disband. By definition, union caucuses were outside formal constitutional structures and were in the democratic purview of members to form.

A more immediate concern for the CEP side was the obvious imbalance in membership between the two unions. Without guidance, an open election could easily result in the CAW capturing a greater share of leadership and influence than the relative share of the two unions. Throughout the New Union Project, the two unions had treated each other as equals, with all decisions made by consensus. That equality would come to an end with the creation of Unifor and across-the-board elections at convention, successive regional councils and the Canadian Council. The new union structure could not offer everyone a position commensurate with his or her current status or offer every sector the same representation. The only way forward was through a carefully constructed leadership team that would respect the founding balance of the two unions and the gender equity and regional balances built into the design. The new union would not have an administration caucus, with the perception of a self-perpetuating leadership. Unifor would instead create a founding leadership based on a proposed "unity team" of national officers, regional directors and executive board members.

In the cycle of leadership renewal in Unifor, a convention would elect the three national officers and three regional directors. Over the following year, regional councils would elect chairpersons who would serve on the executive board, and conferences of retiree, skilled trade and Aboriginal members and members of colour would elect their representation. One year after the convention, the Canadian Council would complete leadership renewal by electing eleven industry council representatives. The executive board would have a direct role here in recommending candidates, but for the explicit purpose of ensuring that the constitutional requirements for gender, equity and regional balances would be met. Even in this case, a check on a too-heavy hand of the executive board was the requirement that any recommendation for an industry council representative on the national executive board must also carry the endorsement of the respective industry council.

With these caveats, Unifor would build a political culture incorporating a caucus system. The informal political agreement by the joint leadership was to maintain the unity team for future leadership renewal beyond the founding convention but as an unofficial, non-constitutional mechanism open to all members. The unity team would provide a space for a broad group of union activists to have input into the representative balance of leadership aspirants.

For the founding convention, there would be a "slate" to ensure that the balances between the CAW and the CEP and on gender and region were met. It was a crucial proposition, especially for the smaller CEP, which had to demonstrate that its evolution into Unifor was not the takeover that some detractors alleged. In two regions of the new union, the former CEP was larger, and this was reflected in the nomination of Michel Ouimet as Quebec director, one of the three national officers, and Scott Doherty, who had been endorsed by CEP's Western region leadership and staff for the position of Western regional director. Three CEP women also took prominent positions as rank-and-file regional chairpersons on the B.C. Council, the Prairie Council and the Atlantic Council, and each of the four principal CEP sectors was guaranteed representation among the eleven industry council representatives for the term of the first executive board. In June, the CEP sectors held special meetings to endorse their choice as industry council representatives. When the unity team was complete, the smaller union had leadership representation equal to or greater than its proportionality in every sphere.

CAW leadership choices were more straightforward because of its existing national executive board structure, made up predominantly by industry representatives. However, Unifor's structure could not provide executive positions to all CAW industry representatives. CAW's larger numbers also carried a responsibility to ensure that the union was seen to meet its gender equity commitments, especially among the full-time regional directors to be elected at the founding convention. Ontario health care leader Katha Fortier was nominated for Ontario director, and Lana Payne, the popular president of the Newfoundland and Labrador Federation of Labour from the CAW's affiliate union, Fish, Food and Allied Workers, was convinced to take the nomination for Atlantic director. The unity team met or exceeded all the constitutional balances, advancing eleven women out of twenty-five national executive board members, sixteen former CAW and nine former CEP members, and thirteen out of twenty-five from Ontario.

In the last days of the New Union Project, a different mood set in. Almost two years of built-up tensions over the choices and decisions of the New Union Project gave way to an urgent focus on the single purpose of founding Unifor. There were no deal breakers left on the large issues that would define Unifor. The remaining decisions were over departmental structures, staff assignments, offices and the political and organizing plans that would launch a wave of recognition and organizing successes for the new union.

However, the shift in emphasis brought with it an even larger sense of urgency. With each passing day to Labour Day, the level of detail was growing across an expanding set of task lists, not just for a convention larger than any that the CAW or CEP had previously held. From launching a website to issuing email addresses, distributing union materials bearing the Unifor logo, arranging signage on buildings and organizing staff, office and financial systems, thousands of hours and decisions went into the operationalization of Unifor to hit the Canadian scene running on day one. The massive effort was being carried by dozens of support staff, IT technicians and representatives. Considerable organizational detail passed through the desk of Rita Lorie in Ken Lewenza's Toronto office and Nicole Brulé's office in the CEP's Ottawa headquarters. The energy was driven by a common determination that Unifor's founding could not be diminished by any mistake, delay or oversight.

There was speculation and hope that the founding of Unifor would attract wide attention through the labour movement and beyond and result in spontaneous engagement and organizing. There was talk of "launching the wave." In hindsight, the wave was an outward projection of the excitement at the centre of the New Union Project. There would be a wave, although not a tsunami flowing from the single impact of founding the union on the Labour Day weekend. Like all truly important organizing, it would result from vision and detailed organizational plans. Three more of those pieces were being finalized amid the convention preparations: a vision statement and plan to guide Unifor's first mandate, an organizing policy and the design of the new union's strategic planning process.

Unifor would emerge on the Labour Day weekend of 2013 with the mission, constitution and structure crafted over the previous two years. However, Unifor would begin with a clean slate and no active campaigns or initiatives apart from ongoing collective bargaining. The vision statement *A New Union for a Challenging World* was to fill the gap and provide a set of priorities, directions and guidance for the major tasks of the new union in its first years. Six priorities were set out, beginning with the organizational task of creating and populating the envisaged councils and structures of the new union. The new union would have to guarantee "seamless" collective bargaining and pattern bargaining structures with an aggressive agenda to expand wages, benefits and job security. New organizing was to be kickstarted by a conscious effort to root the new union in an "organizing culture."

Bold campaigns to protect labour rights and win social gains such as enhanced public pensions and expanded medicare were also on the new union's immediate agenda. The final priority, and the goal that would lead the union into its first controversies, was to build the labour movement, beginning with a large delegation to the 2014 Canadian Labour Congress convention.[7]

The centrepiece priority was the organizing plan and its companion policy, *Broadening Union Citizenship*, which set out the structures and processes for the community chapters. The organizing plan began with a self-critical recognition that in both former unions, organizing had been inconsistent and sporadic and significantly removed from the day-to-day life of union activists. Organizing had been hived off as the special responsibility of professional organizers, a decision the vision paper declared to be "a fundamental mistake."

Unifor's organizing policy intended to change that paradigm, starting with a higher level of resources. The organizing fund would receive 10 per cent of revenues — an estimated $10 million annually. An organizing fund of 10 per cent of revenues was not precedent setting for Canadian labour and was still short of the 20 to 25 per cent that some organizers maintain is necessary for reversing declines in union density. Nevertheless, Unifor's $10 million annual organizing budget would be the largest aggregate organizing fund ever established by a Canadian union.

The organizing policy was at pains to emphasize that however crucial a large organizing budget would be, organizing culture and strategy remained more important. The policy set out a series of provisions aimed at creating an organizing culture. Oaths of office would include personal commitments to organizing; organizing would be part of job descriptions for union staff; there would be organizing reports to every executive board and to all councils of the union; an annual organizing conference would be held; and neutrality agreements and recognition would be part of bargaining agendas. The funding would enable a well-resourced national organizing department with tools such as a national organizing database.

The organizing model set out in the policy drew on organizing experience over more than a decade throughout North America. "Ultimately workers must organize themselves," it stated in its commitment to "inside committees" of workers, wherever possible operating openly and asserting their right to organize in workplaces. A key part of the model, but one that was admittedly a challenge for Unifor as for most Canadian unions, was to ensure that organizers and organizing materials would reflect the diversity of changing workplaces, from race and ethnicity to language, gender and age.

If organizing was the first commitment of the new union to define itself, front and centre in the minds of leaders and delegates alike was how to make their new union and logo be seen, heard and read by millions of Canadians. The issues and campaigns set out for the founding convention would, in fact, define union activity for more than three years to come. These included commitment to equity struggles from gender, heritage, race, language, sexual identity, ability and age, presented as central to Unifor's work. A union campaign on trade issues to "see through the rhetoric and myths of free trade" was promised, particularly on the Canada-European Union Comprehensive Economic and Trade Agreement (CETA) and the newly proposed Trans-Pacific Partnership (TPP). Good jobs in the face of austerity and growing precarious work were another campaign priority, and a commitment to organize the "Good Jobs Summit" in the union's first year would become one of Unifor's first major public projects. In October 2014, over a thousand participants would turn out to the summit at the former Maple Leaf Gardens in Toronto, the Ryerson University Mattamy Athletic Centre.

The urgent and momentous matter in the vision document was the defence of workers' rights and a plan to counter the challenge to the Rand formula in Ontario and the federal Bill C-377 on union finances. Seen as a whole, the Conservative agenda on union rights added up to "a catalogue of anti-union policy-making, the like of which has not been seen in Canada since the modern majoritarian industrial relations system was invented during World War II."

The union's multidimensional pushback would be directed first at union members, many of whom had little understanding of the history or significance of the Rand formula. The imperative was for members to understand clearly that making union dues optional would inevitably cripple the ability of the union to negotiate good wages and benefits and hurt them in the pocketbook. Later to be called the "integrated campaign on labour rights," the massive education program was cast as no less than "a turning point in the history of collective bargaining — the moment when the tide was reversed and the legal and political basis of trade unionism was restored and stabilized for another generation to come." This mission would define the first years of Unifor, and remarkably, within just three years, the tide was reversed.

The final stages of the New Union Project laid out these plans for the new union, but another crucial component of *Towards a New Union* remained to be fulfilled. Unifor's objectives were premised on creating an organization that would breathe life into plans and targets and succeed. The moment of truth that had sparked Unifor was premised on the many labour movement organizational failures arising both from a lack of will and ability. We all knew that pointing fingers at others would ring hollow; the challenge for Unifor was to create a force that would act differently and produce results.

In labour movement struggles, every win, loss and draw is relative. Bargaining triumphs can change very little long term, whereas retreats and losses sometimes harden militancy and strengthen solidarity for bigger fights ahead. But when key struggles are significantly more often lost than won, or when campaigns are launched and then quietly dropped or when leadership mandates of three, five or ten years go by without tangible gains that build the union and the movement, a relative analysis hardly suffices. The point inherent in the making of Unifor was that relative failures must be confronted and failed models changed.

The New Union Project had provided a space for discussion about the common set of problems in union culture that explained why things go wrong, leading to disappointments and sometimes fiascos. Leadership distraction on day-to-day events and lack of preparation for challenges and emergencies that could have been expected are frequent underlying issues. The absence of preparation for key struggles or events is often shown by poor internal and external communications or underestimation of the resources needed to carry through a project or a fight. From a larger perspective, organizations lacking strategic focus tend to abandon difficult long-term objectives in practical terms. Immediate events and politics become daily priorities. For unions, this results in the normalization of unfulfilled organizing, political and social goals. Over time, the social goals of the movement become library items, and neither members nor leaders are concerned over the growing gaps between aspirations and actuality.

One of the goals emerging from the New Union Project was to introduce a strategic planning culture and process in Unifor to complement and support the elected leadership processes. Major policy and political decisions would be made by the rank-and-file national executive board, composed mainly of regional and industry council representatives, reflecting the membership diversity of the union. The board would meet for the better part of a week no less than three times a year. With hundreds of thousands of members spread across five regions and twenty economic sectors, the myriad of reports to every national executive board would be an expression of the regional, local and sectoral dynamism that the design of Unifor intended.

Unifor's strategic idea was to add to the leadership structure an internal mechanism that would focus leadership attention and resources on key issues, events and emergent situations in as close to real time as possible. It would counter the centrifugal forces inherent in a *union for everyone* by regularly refocusing leadership on foundational goals. This mechanism would not make major political decisions or set policy but would co-ordinate implementation of political decisions and ensure readiness for major events and struggles. In the 5×5 leadership meetings leading to the founding convention, the Strategic Planning Committee was conceived to be that mechanism, bringing together the national officers, regional directors, assistants and senior staff as needed. Most unions engage in some kind of strategic planning, as did Unifor's predecessors. But the intense and dedicated function of Unifor's Strategic Planning Committee was an order beyond anything practised in the former unions.

As all these last plans were laid, the centre of attention in the 5×5 leadership was the convention agenda and an intricate founding script whereby two unions would simultaneously agree to merge into a new organization and transfer their bargaining authority and assets to Unifor. Partly legal, partly political and significantly symbolic, the script was the work of Unifor's director of legal services, Lewis Gottheil.

In the background of the New Union Project, Gottheil had worked for months on anticipating and answering the legal and procedural questions that arise from forming an organization of the size and scope of Unifor. Bargaining rights are fundamental to the existence of a union and can be vulnerable whenever they reappear before labour boards. In 1999, when the Canadian retail division of the United Steelworkers had left the international union and was merging with the CAW, retail giant Cadillac Fairview attempted to use the merger as an opportunity to force a vote that would include an option to decertify the union. The union prevailed, with the Ontario Labour Relations Board ruling that a successor application is not an opportunity for a decertification attempt. On the other hand, evidence of membership support was necessary, and in the absence of visible membership endorsement, a vote could be ordered.

Informed by that history, throughout 2013, all reports on the new union to CAW and CEP bodies, the regional membership meetings and town hall telephone conferences were carefully recorded. As the convention approached, local unions and sector groups in both unions adopted explicit motions of endorsement of merging into Unifor. Both unions also had their distinct constitutional issues that were in play. The CAW constitution provided for mergers on the authorization of the national executive board, but with a large proviso: "as long as the action does not affect CAW-Canada's identity or standing in the trade union movement."

The last CAW convention, August 30, 2013.

The CAW would have to change that provision to enter into Unifor.

The CEP's constitution allowed for a merger into another identity but set out a distinct process whereby the national executive board was required to convene a special convention to authorize the transfer of rights and property to a new union. Two key prerequisites in the CEP process were that the constitution of the new organization needed to be circulated to all locals for discussion prior to the special convention and the new organization must protect and continue all local unions and their assets. The New Union Project had met these conditions, but a special convention had to be convened.

On August 30, 2013, each union would convene special conventions. The final CAW convention would take place at the Sheraton Centre in Toronto. The CAW convention would include an address from its president, Ken Lewenza, and adopt a constitutional resolution to amend its merger provisions that would allow for the creation of Unifor. The CEP would gather at the Metro Toronto Convention Centre, and after hearing the final address of President Dave Coles, it would conduct a vote pursuant to the merger provision in its constitution.

At 9:30 a.m. in the Sheraton Centre, the CAW delegates who had been

The last CEP convention, August 30, 2013.

elected to the last regular convention in August 2012 were reconvened, and the motions to alter their constitution and to proceed with the founding of Unifor were unanimously adopted. Simultaneously, at the Metro Toronto Convention Centre, the CEP convention opened, and at 11:00 a.m., after one speaker for and one against the motion to approve the new union, an electronic roll-call vote approved the formation of Unifor by a margin of 79.4 per cent.

At noon, both conventions were adjourned and delegates marched separately towards the corner of Yonge Street and Richmond Street, where Industry Canada's offices were located, the site of Unifor's first street rally in defence of jobs in the telecommunications sector. The two parades merged in a symbolic coming together on Yonge Street, fists in the air and spirits high.

On Saturday, August 31, delegates from both conventions assembled as one at the Metro Toronto Convention Centre to found Unifor. Peter Kennedy announced that there were more than 4,000 persons in the main hall and an adjoining overflow room. That total included about 2,500 delegates from the final CAW and CEP conventions and an almost equal amount of staff, guests and observers. Thousands more were connected by live stream. Ken Lewenza was the chair for the morning ses-

Dave Coles, Jerry Dias and Peter Kennedy as the two marches from the last convention of each union reach each other, August 30, 2013.

sion, and Dave Coles would chair the afternoon session of the first day.

At about 11:30 a.m., Lewis Gottheil came forward to explain the steps in the script to found the union. The delegates' first act was to sign a membership card in Unifor and become members of the new union. On cue, the thousands in the room retrieved forms from their kits and individually signed a membership application. Most signed a card that would confer voting rights as a Unifor delegate; a smaller number of retired officers, members and staff became founding members in their capacity as honorary delegates.

Gottheil then had delegates retrieve the draft constitution for one final overview and explanation of the New Union Project process that had already led to amendments to the draft constitution. It would be open to further amendments at the first regular convention, but the vote now was yes or no. A no vote would stop the process; a yes vote would establish the union and allow for a leadership to be elected.

At seven minutes past noon, Unifor's first per capita vote took place, with regular delegates using an electronic voting device coded to reflect the number of votes in the local union they represented. Some national

Dave Coles, Ken Lewenza, Gaétan Ménard and Jerry Dias embracing as the two union marches converged on Yonge Street, Toronto, August 30, 2013.

executive board members from the founding unions would cast single votes. The vote was held open for a minute, and the screens showed that the voting delegates represented a per capita strength of 276,842 members — 90 per cent of the new union's approximate 305,000 members. The screen then showed that the constitution was adopted by 96 per cent.

The new members had adopted their constitution and at that moment had formally created Unifor. In a symbolic gesture amid the celebration on the floor, delegates stood and peeled their CAW and CEP magnetic logos from their delegate badges, revealing the Unifor logo. Except for one final vote later in the day on behalf of their former unions, they were now all Unifor delegates.

At about 1:30 p.m., elections were held for each of the twenty-five national executive positions. Only one was contested when a rank-and-

Part of the street party leading into the founding convention of Unifor.

Members celebrating their new union.
Left to right: Michelle Kervin Palleschi,
Derek Barry, Cheryl Robinson, Kim Kent,
Caroline Haddad.

file member from Local 707 in Oakville, Lindsay Hinshelwood, challenged Jerry Dias for president. A second per capita vote was held, electing Dias with 82.5 per cent of the vote.

Following the swearing in of the executive board and Dias's inaugural president's address, the convention was ready for the final piece of the founding script. In their last act as CAW and CEP members, delegates were now asked to merge their unions, assets and bargaining rights into the organization they had just created. Once again, votes were held using electronic voting devices, but this time by calculating separate results for the two founding unions. The identical merger documents were adopted by 99.3 per cent in the case of the CAW on the basis of one delegate, one vote and 95.46 per cent in the case of the CEP, with weighted votes calculated on a per capita basis. At approximately 4:45 p.m., August 31, 2013, the founding unions ceased to exist.

Unifor's creation on August 31 was emotional and laced with anxious moments and momentous decisions. It revealed a tension between the new union's careful construction and mission and its commitment to rank-and-file democracy and dissent. These aspects of the first day put a stamp on the new union and established the characteristics of union culture and democracy that would stay a part of Unifor.

The very first election was contested, and, with the exception of acclamations and routine procedure, votes to create the union were overwhelming but not unanimous. Hinshelwood's candidacy was a reflection

Scott Doherty, first Western regional director, later to become assistant to the president.

of long-standing differences on the Left of the former CAW, although she was by no means representative of the range of minority dissent at the founding convention. That dissent also included a number of people, mostly from the CEP, committed to stronger political support for the NDP and a larger group that simply wanted to retain its smaller former union. Some of these undoubtedly cast a vote for Hinshelwood to send a message that they were not yet ready to put their trust in the new union leadership. A worker at the Oakville Ford plant, Hinshelwood identified with rank-and-file opposition to a form of two-tier wages negotiated during the auto crisis of 2008–2009 and the "auto bailout" of government support for the sector, which she also opposed. Her candidacy was featured in socialist publications, notably the Trotskyist *Socialist Action*, and the Socialist Project, which a number of former CAW staff were also associated with. For this wing of the Left, Unifor is seen as too close to industry and government and not consistently left wing or principled. Their viewpoints are disputed strongly by many others who proudly identify with the left tradition in Canadian labour.

There were also calls from the floor of the founding convention for Unifor to immediately put its promise of equity and diversity on display at the podium. It was an uncomfortable reality that those promises were hard to see in the faces of the outgoing leadership of the founding unions at the front of the room. It would not be the first equity debate in Unifor, although the union's commitment to these issues that would be shown in the first council meetings and since would produce a much different and more powerful milieu and dialogue that would unite the new union.

Left to right: Lana Payne, Atlantic regional director, and Katha Fortier, Ontario regional director, at the founding convention, with Randy Kitt, Angela Adams and Penny Fawcett.

Another pressure point of Unifor culture that made its presence known at the founding was a constant high emotional intensity and gruelling pace. The demands of recognition and ceremony to respectfully usher out the former proud unions and celebrate the historic events of the day made for a long and exhausting session. Keynote addresses and video greetings from a pantheon of Canadian social movements, public intellectuals and labour movement leaders added to the gravitas. Social democratic icon Stephen Lewis, Canadian social movement leader Maude Barlow, humorist and activist Mary Walsh and labour leaders from the Canadian Labour Congress, CUPE and United Steelworkers spoke to the significance of Unifor's creation. Two keynotes stood out: Canadian pollster and pundit Allan Gregg with a hopeful message of a Canadian public wishing the labour movement well and ready to provide fulsome support to unions when it perceived that unions were acting in the public interest, and author Naomi Klein, who put before the convention a challenge to make the fight on climate change and sustainability the centrepiece of a labour-led movement for fundamental social change.[8]

The most anticipated speech of the day was Jerry Dias's. It was a lengthy speech, as many of his future addresses would be, clocking in

Jerry Dias's address to the founding convention, August 31, 2013.

at one hour and fifteen minutes. But the new leader brought to the podium a long list of objectives and expectations to be met. Not least was the need to introduce himself to many who, he acknowledged, were just getting to know him.[9]

The personal story that Dias told was of the "classic blue collar, working class immigrant family." His parents were Guyanese immigrants. His father, Jerry, Sr., found work at the De Havilland Aircraft plant in Toronto. He preceded his son as president of United Auto Workers Local Union 112 and in the trajectory to union staff was appointed by UAW Canadian Director Bob White as a staff representative.

Dias's mother worked for an envelope manufacturer in Toronto and was a member of an old printing trades craft union, the Toronto Book-binders Union. That local would merge with others into the Graphic Communications International Union to eventually become part of CEP Local 591. "If my father was UAW-CAW, and my mother was CEP, I guess that makes me Unifor," he quipped.

Dias used his address to define himself and Unifor in three important ways. He began with the confession that his presence was conflicted because his heart was not in the convention hall but with his mother, who had been moved into a care home in Oshawa. He went on to underscore his personal involvement, and that of his son Jordan, with the Women's Centre of Halton and its work on the issue of violence against women. "Ending violence against women will be a priority for Unifor and it starts today," he declared. Over the next two years at consecutive Unifor councils across Canada, that issue would be front and centre.

Dias kept emphasizing equity issues, saying that Unifor "will be a union that takes its responsibility to fight discrimination and exclusion" and pledged the union to step up the struggle for equity, particularly LGBTQ rights in response to anti-gay legislation that had been adopted in the Russian legislature. Reflecting on the fiftieth anniversary of Martin Luther King, Jr.'s, "March on Washington for Jobs and Freedom," he spoke to King's "dual dream of racial and economic equality . . . freedom and jobs."

The second set of defining goals would change the world of work and defend trade union rights. He excoriated the "choices made by rampant capitalism — growing inequality, the petro-dollar and decline in manufacturing jobs." Pointing to precarious work and the "lousy jobs, lousy pay, lousy hours, no pensions, no benefits, and average wages no better than a generation ago," Dias declared, "Unifor is here because it is time to stop playing defence and start playing offence."

"Unless we rebuild union power, we won't get better results," he warned. Dias told the convention that Unifor was "born in the middle of an historic battle to defend labour rights." Drawing attention to the delegates from Local 200 at the Ford engine plant in Windsor, where the sit-down strike of 1945 had led to the now-threatened Rand formula, he vowed, "Unifor will define ourselves through our resistance and struggle . . . [W]e will do everything necessary to preserve the right to free collective bargaining."

The overarching theme in the Dias address was his summation of the New Union Project:

> We are faithful to our past. But we cannot be captives
> of the past and we start today to build a new history.
> What kind of a union do our members want? They want
> a modern, accountable, democratic, transparent union,
> and above all a progressive union. They want a union
> that fights for equality and inclusion, that communicates
> effectively and listens as well as it speaks . . . Unifor must

*be a fighting union defined by our willingness to identify
injustice wherever it is experienced and then leap into
action to correct those injustices . . . We will be judged
not by rhetoric but by our actions — as it should be. That
is why we are activists — because we want action.*

*Today we are building a new union with a vision
of true equality at its core . . . building a Union that
organizes everyday because if we can't organize
ourselves we can't organize others . . . building a union
that fights for Canadian democracy and pushes back
against greedy employers and corrupt politicians.
When they push us we will push back twice as hard . . .
building a union with the determination and capacity to
dream that a better world is possible.*

On September 1, the convention ended at Toronto's Nathan Phillips Square with Unifest, a free public concert to celebrate the founding of Unifor featuring artists The Stars, Blackie and the Rodeo Kings, Les Colocs and others. On September 2, the convention participants were joined by several thousand more Unifor members from local unions and workplaces in Greater Toronto to lead the annual Labour Day Parade.

CHAPTER 5

Canada's Union

Unifor exploded into Canadian labour politics on Labour Day weekend of 2013 and formally brought the New Union Project to a conclusion. But the founding left considerable unfinished business that would continue to define the new union. Unifor had declared its goals of changing the labour movement, changing politics and reversing the labour movement's decline. Although it was far from clear when or how it would clash with labour's status quo and incite political controversy, it would only be a matter of months before its inherently disruptive elements and attributes would emerge.

With Lewenza and Coles and four other former CEP officers taking their retirements at the founding convention and an executive board very different in composition from the former boards of each union, Unifor also burst on the scene with new faces and personalities. Attention now turned to Dias, who seized the space that had emerged to assert himself and unify the new leadership. He put aside the tough-guy persona that had carried him through multiple confrontations with employers over the previous decade, and a motivational, personal and humorous Dias was introduced to the membership and media, with his personal emphasis on social issues and violence against women.

I accompanied Jerry a few weeks after the founding on his first foray into the office of federal Conservative Labour Minister Kellie Leitch. Before the minister could say much, Dias told her bluntly that there was a contradiction between her role as minister of labour and her responsibility for the status of women. "How can you advance the status of women and at the same time support legislation to weaken unions?" he put to her. "Women in unions earn significantly more than women without unions." Minutes later, he told her that if Bill C-377 on union finances was made law, Unifor would defy the legislation.

Dias began his relationship with the new executive board by revealing the details of his meetings with Leitch as well as his first encounter with a group of major employers from the auto, transportation, energy and telecommunications sectors. Dias and Kennedy were at the Sheraton Gateway and came across a number of employer negotiators from different sectors that the new union was certified with. When they saw a number of them come out of the same room, Dias and Kennedy barrelled into the room and found forty or more industrial relations staff from major Unifor employers. As the Unifor leaders walked around the large meeting table jocularly shaking hands, the employer reps admitted it was indeed a summit on how to respond to the new union. Dias drew embarrassed laughter from the group with a suggestion that they could save their money and time by talking to the union directly instead of organizing secret meetings to guess at what Unifor would do. These were early signals to employers, politicians and the union of an assertive style of leadership and an aggressive role for the union that would be unconstrained by protocols and formalities.

Kennedy played an alternative role in shaping Unifor culture, with the deliberate use of language to break with past conventions and identities. His comments to the first Unifor National Executive Board meeting deliberately omitted any mention of the CAW or the CEP by name and instead referenced them only as "one of our predecessor unions."

At Unifor headquarters, the planning role recommended by the New Union Project was taken up by Unifor's new Strategic Planning Committee, conceived as one of the central characteristics of the new union. My role in Unifor was to be the director and organizer of the new planning body. It would meet every six weeks, co-facilitated by myself and Jim Stanford. At its first meeting, the committee took the new union's officers, regional directors, assistants and key department directors into a visioning exercise of what "defining moments" would show that the new union was realizing its founding missions. A dozen such moments were envisioned, some to complete the founding of the new union, such as establishing the regional councils and the industry councils and organizing the first community chapters. Organizing the Good Jobs Summit in the first year and defeating Harper's labour legislation and the sellout of Canadian ownership rules in the telecommunications industry were among the other early goals that the committee considered to be defining of the union's character and progress.[1]

It would not take long before the committee found itself debating whether it should add to the list of defining moments its goal of changing the labour movement. In March 2014, Unifor had to determine whether it would lead a campaign to end the fifteen-year presidency of Ken Georgetti and to elect Unifor member Hassan Yussuff. Yussuff, who had served as secretary-treasurer under Georgetti, was not prepared to continue to support him any longer. Not only Yussuff but also the two women officers of the congress, Barbara Byers and Marie Clarke Walker, were calling for change. They were fed up with Georgetti's presidential style, which excluded them from real leadership roles they had been elected to fulfill. In the case of Marie Clarke Walker, he had diminished her status by instructing her to work out of the Canadian Labour Congress's Toronto office. The widespread view of labour activists was that the congress had suffered under more than a decade of bureaucratic management that had left activism and idealism behind. It seemed the congress had the least influence that could be remembered, just as the movement faced its biggest challenge of the postwar era.

Dias was at first cautious. Unifor was established with every intention of engagement with the Canadian Labour Congress and co-operation with its major affiliates. Moreover, with the new union only months old and still preoccupied with creating its extensive system of councils in regions and industry sectors, its plate was very full. Nor was it at all clear that a challenge to the leadership of Georgetti would be successful. He appeared to have the unqualified support of the major affiliates, including the single largest congress affiliate, CUPE.

Dias had been initially prepared to support an alternative plan that would have seen CUPE President Paul Moist succeed Georgetti as Canadian Labour Congress president, and he had put that to Moist. But it soon became evident that there was a backroom arrangement between Georgetti, Moist and the international unions to re-elect Georgetti, who would subsequently retire midterm, with his successor — likely Moist — to be picked by the leadership of the affiliates rather than by a convention. With CUPE and all the major international unions complicit in the plan, their dominance of the congress's Executive Committee and their delegate count at a convention indicated they could carry it off. It was the kind of arrangement that summed up the disdain for democracy and activism Unifor wanted to break from. Not only had Dias been excluded from the deal, but it was also apparent that an additional purpose was to ensure that Unifor and Yussuff would not lead the Canadian Labour Congress.

The congress's leadership became one of the first major debates in the new Strategic Planning Committee and then in the national executive board. On several occasions, the internal debate focused on Unifor's mission to change the labour movement. Change and renewal in the labour movement were written into the purposes of Unifor, from its first projections in *A Moment of Truth* to "inspire, push and embarrass" labour centrals and, failing that, for the new union "to do the job itself." It was increasingly clear that Unifor could not endorse Georgetti's re-election. The choice for the new union was to take a pass on leadership issues, including the future of Yussuff, or to lead a challenge. When Dias finally said "Let's do this" at the committee, he affirmed a majority view already formed, and the national executive board was easily convinced.

Yussuff was as much a product of the former CAW as any of the CAW founders of Unifor. He had been a mechanic at an automotive parts manufacturer in Toronto and then a plant chairperson and staff representative. He served in the CAW national office as director of its human rights department. His spouse, Jenny Ahn, was a well-known CAW staff representative who became Unifor's first director of political action and later an assistant to the president. Like Dias's family, Yussuff had emigrated from Guyana. He had publicly and repeatedly credited to his union his personal development from immigrant worker to national labour leader.

The problem that Yussuff faced at the outset was his own lengthy period since 2002 as a Canadian Labour Congress officer during the Georgetti period. His campaign would have to counter that fact with a program for change, echoing the themes of democracy, social unionism and political strategies that had been framed by the New Union Project. The larger problem was the role of CUPE and the international unions in

Canadian Labour Congress President Hassan Yussuff at Unifor's second national convention, August 25, 2016, in Ottawa.

the Georgetti camp. By a standard count of delegate strength, the election was theirs to lose. For Yussuff to prevail, the campaign would have to forge a majority of individual delegates for change against the superior institutional delegate count held by the Georgetti camp. The Unifor-Yussuff campaign began with a smaller coalition of teachers' unions, the Public Service Alliance, postal workers and the Service Employees International Union. John Cartwright, Toronto Labour Council president, chaired the campaign committee, with the task of reaching out and into other union delegations with appeals to women, youth, equity groups and progressives. Also important were the Yussuff campaign's informal relationship with the parallel candidacies of Barbara Byers and Marie Clarke Walker against Georgetti nominees and the votes of left-wing activists grouped around the campaign of Hassan Husseini.

The May 2014 convention was the largest labour convention in Canadian history, with over five thousand delegates. Credit for Yussuff's stunning victory by sixty-four votes was claimed by any number of activist groups that the coalition embraced. In the votes that followed for the remaining officers, the Georgetti slate was decisively defeated. Barbara Byers was elected secretary-treasurer, and Marie Clarke Walker and Donald Lafleur were easily elected as congress vice-presidents.

Yussuff's victory marked the first defeat of an incumbent Canadian Labour Congress president in modern labour history and the election of the first worker of colour to the leadership of the movement. It also framed the emergence of Unifor as a major and polarizing catalyst in the labour movement. Dias described the victory as the moment that Unifor came together as a united force after its founding convention.

The win was followed by the building of a similar coalition to elect a centre-left leadership in the B.C. Federation of Labour in a contest that was widely seen as a replay of the Canadian Labour Congress election. And soon after in Ontario, Unifor and the United Steelworkers reconciled to be the principal players in the "FedForward" coalition to restore unity to the fractured Ontario Federation of Labour. The unity candidate for the federation's president was Unifor's Chris Buckley, whose lengthy record of trade union accomplishments included serving as a member of the Proposal Committee during the New Union Project. Soon after these events, Unifor would find itself embroiled in debate and controversy over labour's role in politics and its relationship with the NDP.

Politics was the exceptional matter that from early in Unifor's life set it apart and underscored its role as an agent for change in the Canadian labour movement. Unifor did not set out with a plan in its first year to organize political altercations in the labour movement and the NDP, nor had the union yet set out a comprehensive political analysis or strategy. But neither could Unifor avoid lunging into politics to face down the threats to trade union freedoms. Across the political spectrum and especially in labour and social democratic politics, Unifor's political pragmatism and access to government were confusing and seemed to be at odds with the union's strong left-wing policies and militancy. Among some Canadian unions formally affiliated with the NDP, Unifor's strategies provoked anger over a perceived lack of support for the organic relationship between labour and the NDP. It was no coincidence that the main axis of that response was the unions resentful of both Unifor's perceived takeover of the Canadian Labour Congress and its strategic voting strategies in the Ontario election.

As it was with the Canadian Labour Congress campaign, Unifor's political role was rooted in the New Union Project, but neither its actions and choices nor its impact on the movement was predetermined. To the contrary, Unifor's political policy had been deliberately delayed one year, to be considered thoughtfully at its first Canadian Council in September 2014. Fast-moving events and the thrusting of Unifor onto the Canadian political scene would not allow it the luxury of a year of reflection to define its politics. The experiences of the new union in that year shaped its outlook and the larger policy that would emerge.

The Montreal Canadian Labour Congress convention that elected Yussuff coincided with the opening of the 2014 Ontario provincial election, destined to be a decisive political showdown over trade union rights. The minority Liberal government of the new premier, Kathleen Wynne, faced re-election, and in the weeks preceding Unifor's founding, Wynne had been battered in by-elections despite her personal popularity. The by-election results projected a potential Conservative majority government and an NDP opposition.

More important than the fortunes of Premier Wynne was the campaign by Conservative leader Tim Hudak to rewrite the Ontario *Labour Relations Act* and remove the Rand formula, and perhaps go all the way to the right-to-work laws recently passed in Michigan and Wisconsin. Three weeks after Unifor's founding, the Ontario Progressive Conservatives met in convention and adopted a white paper on "flexible labour markets," with a proposal to end Ontario's legislated Rand formula. Hudak's plans were soon publicly revealed in a leaked memo that outlined the daily Conservative campaign plan for an expected provincial election. On day seven of the campaign plan, Hudak was scheduled to appear at a non-union factory in Windsor to announce his "worker choice" policy, which would end the Rand formula.[2]

As Hudak was increasingly strident in making the trade union movement his proxy adversary in Ontario politics, Unifor was biding its time while it organized membership outreach to inform members about the threat to union security. The union recommitted to the "Working Families Coalition," made up primarily of building trades and teachers' unions, which was preparing a well-funded campaign against Hudak. Dias reached out to former Ontario premier Bill Davis and encouraged him to speak publicly against Hudak's anti-labour program, which Davis did. Unifor also forged direct relationships with the Wynne government, which was prepared to make Hudak's labour policies central election issues.

From Unifor's perspective, the labour movement needed time to mobilize, and the best course of action was for the Ontario NDP to continue to support Wynne's minority government. In meetings with Ontario NDP leader Andrea Horwath, Dias appealed to her not to provoke an early election, but the meetings with Horwath were brief. The

Ontario NDP leader hailed from Hamilton, where she and the United Steelworkers were partisan opponents of the strategic voting strategies that the CAW had employed in the federal election only months before. Horwath viewed Dias and the new union with suspicion. She believed that scandals over the decommissioning of natural gas power plants had put the Wynne government on the defensive and that the Ontario NDP would be poised to make gains in an election. Matters would come to a head in the spring of 2014 with the presentation of the Liberal budget. If the Ontario NDP supported the budget, an early showdown with the Conservatives could be averted. The key was for the Liberals to present a genuinely progressive budget that labour and the NDP could support. Dias and the Ontario leadership of Unifor met Wynne and Labour minister Yasir Naqvi on multiple occasions to discuss social and economic policy and minimum wages in Ontario.

In February 2014, a by-election in Niagara Falls was seen as a test for the developing political situation. Although the vacant seat had been held by a Liberal, Unifor opted to throw its support to the NDP candidate, Wayne Gates, a Niagara city councillor and president of Unifor Local 199. The riding was adjacent to Hudak's constituency, and Gates's candidacy was seen as highlighting the central issue of trade union rights. It was Unifor's first major electoral commitment involving dozens of union organizers and an inflammatory public challenge by Dias to debate Hudak "anytime or anywhere." Gates won the by-election, and the union celebrated.

The May 2014 Liberal budget was widely described as progressive, borrowing heavily from the NDP playbook and more. The budget flouted austerity and massively increased deficit spending to $12.5 billion, including a $2 billion transportation infrastructure program and a $2.5 billion jobs program over ten years. The major social proposal in the budget was an Ontario pension plan that would supplement Canada Pension Plan (CPP) benefits for 3 million Ontario workers. The budget also included pledges for increased social spending on a range of issues, including a $4 per hour wage increase for personal support workers in

Left to right: Katha Fortier, Wayne Gates and Unifor political director Rolly Kiehne, on steps of Queen's Park in July 2014 soon after Gates's election as MPP for Niagara.

health care. On minimum wages, the budget added an annual indexing to the modest increase in minimum wages to $11 an hour that had been passed earlier in the year.

The decision by Andrea Horwath to vote against the budget and trigger an election on June 11, 2014, was a turning point for Unifor leadership. Horwath's decision was interpreted as highly cynical, putting the interests of the trade union movement at risk for questionable short-term political gains. By the time of the budget, Wynne and her government's popularity had risen on the basis of her populist policies, and the Ontario NDP was well back of the Liberals and the Conservatives.

There had been debate in Unifor about whether to use the term "strategic voting" to describe its electoral strategy in Ontario. The sensitivity to the term and the common argument of NDP leaders that strategic voting meant the abandonment of principles and long-term goals in favour of a lesser evil was well known. The union remained committed to throwing its support to every Ontario NDP incumbent and others in a position to win. However, the breach with Horwath and the issues at play in Ontario soon eclipsed the concerns over the optics of strategic voting. It was clear that the defeat of Hudak and the re-election of the Wynne government did represent the best long-term interest of the trade union movement.

The campaign that ensued reinforced Unifor's direction. Hudak continued to focus his political attack on workers, at one point proposing to fire a hundred thousand Ontario public servants. The NDP positioned itself as a centrist, suggesting that a review of public spending was needed to end waste and questioning the viability of the Ontario pension proposal. Halfway through the campaign, Horwath called for a $12 minimum wage, although without indexing. The proposal was seen by activists as a reluctant measure and not a significant improvement on what the Liberals were already doing. Horwath's positions divided the NDP, generating a rare open letter from more than thirty NDP campaign veterans expressing alarm over the direction of the party.

Unifor's influence was felt in the Ontario labour movement, which had united around an energetic anti-Hudak campaign organized by the Ontario Federation of Labour and culminating in a call on union members to vote strategically. This unprecedented shift in labour strategy by a central labour body in Canada was also punctuated by Yussuff's victory at the convention in May, which resulted in the Canadian Labour Congress immediately offering its support to the federation's campaign. Unifor was central to the labour campaign, contributing heavily to the Working Families campaign and sending campaigners and resources to support NDP members of provincial Parliament and selected Liberals in key ridings. Jim Stanford struck a blow on the Hudak campaign by revealing that his claim to create a million jobs exaggerated by eight times the potential job creation from his policies.

The election of Wynne's majority government was widely credited to two interrelated factors: her strategy of outflanking the NDP on the left and the labour movement's anti-Hudak campaign. Hudak resigned on election night, putting an ignominious end to his promise to undo the Rand formula in Ontario. The outcome changed Ontario politics

Ontario Premier Kathleen Wynne at Unifor Good Jobs Summit October 4, 2014, Ryerson University Mattamy Centre, Maple Leaf Gardens, Toronto.

on several levels. His replacement as interim leader of the Progressive Conservatives, Jim Wilson, attempted to put distance between the party and Hudak with the comment that the Tories must stop attacking people if they ever hope to form a government again.[3] For the next four years, Ontario's Progressive Conservatives stepped back from their anti-labour stance, and at times the party appeared to be returning to its more moderate roots during the Bill Davis era. However the suggestion of a moderate Conservative party in Ontario was short lived and came to a crashing end with the takeover of the party by right-wing populist Doug Ford in 2018.[4]

The Ontario election would also continue to reverberate in labour movement political debates. For Unifor, the result consolidated its growing political influence. The union would soon have strong disagreements with the Wynne government, particularly over health care funding and the privatization of Hydro One. But the union had also established an ongoing presence and connection to the Wynne Liberals that was critical to a historic review and reform of Ontario labour law in 2016–2017.

Andrea Horwath was a survivor of the 2014 campaign, although it took almost all of the subsequent four years and voter fatigue with fifteen years of Liberal government for the Ontario NDP to mount a serious challenge for government in the 2018 election. The lesson for the Ontario NDP from 2014 was to run on a much bolder progressive program and it was rewarded by forming the Official Opposition.

The politics of Ontario did not necessarily determine relationships with the federal NDP in 2014 but similar stark choices for the labour movement and federal NDP decisions were combining to push along the new union's developing independent political action strategy. At the federal level, the labour movement faced no less perilous circumstances. In the fall of 2013, Canada's federal Parliament had resumed after a summer prorogation, and sweeping anti-labour laws were high on the government's agenda.

The Conservative's flagship anti-labour legislation, Bill C-377, attacked union finances, requiring the publication of all expenses of $5,000 or more. The obvious intention of the law was to undermine political spending by unions, but it would at the same time reveal all trade union business to employers and political enemies. The bill had been defeated in the Senate, but the prorogation of Parliament had rendered the Senate action void; it would now be returned to the Senate prior to a proclamation into law. The second Conservative initiative on labour rights was Bill C-525. It had been introduced before the prorogation, eliminating over seventy years of card check organizing and imposing compulsory certification votes in the federal sector. It came with a twist that made it even more radical: requiring that a successful certification vote would require a majority of eligible voters, not actual voters. Moreover, Bill C-525 proposed that to defeat a decertification vote would also require a majority of eligible voters to vote against the decertification. The super-majority provisions that would effectively un-elect most members of Parliament if applied to general elections were later removed from the bill, but there was no doubt that C-525 was envisaged as a dagger pointed at the heart of unions. In addition to these measures, the fall session of Parliament also brought down an omnibus budget implementation bill, Bill C-4, which included changes to the safety provisions of the *Canada Labour Code* that would diminish the right to refuse unsafe work and impose new essential services laws restricting the right to strike in the public service.

The definitive mood in the Unifor leadership was apprehension, fear and urgency to push back against the tide. Harper was exercising his majority ruthlessly, and the NDP Opposition in the federal Parliament had few cards to play. In the Ken Georgetti presidency of the Canadian Labour Congress, there was an assessment that Harper held the upper hand in his fight with unions and that traditional protest and defiance would only play into his hands. Internally, Unifor's Strategic Planning Committee saw the union in a race against time and was focused on its "integrated labour rights campaign" aimed at reaching hundreds of thousands of members in one-on-one meetings over union rights and the political threats to their union security. If the Rand formula were outlawed, it could mean that the union would have to reorganize its membership and gather authorizations for alternative dues payment mechanisms. The union was working overtime to inform and prepare the membership for the worst outcome.

Alongside the internal strategy, Unifor launched a counterattack on Ottawa. Ninety days after its formation, close to one hundred Unifor leaders and activists from federal jurisdiction local unions mounted the union's first lobby on Ottawa. The lobby featured a reception attended by members of Parliament and senators on Parliament Hill, notably including Leitch, and a meeting with the lobby group representing federally regulated employers in the transportation and communications sectors, FETCO. The union protested employer complicity in Harper's legislation and demanded, unsuccessfully, that the telecommunications, media, airline and railroad companies join in demanding the withdrawal of Harper's bills.

Driven by Dias's personality and style, the union was making its presence felt in Ottawa, almost immediately appearing before Parliamentary and Senate hearings. In Leitch's offices, Dias now upped the ante by inviting the government to intervene in Unifor federal bargaining in airlines, railroads or the St. Lawrence Seaway and promised that the union would defy those orders.[5]

In the Canadian Senate, the leading voice against Bill C-377 was Conservative Senator Hugh Segal. On December 7, Segal made a high-profile keynote address before eight hundred delegates at the union's first Ontario Council meeting that highlighted the deep divisions between Conservatives that still existed on labour and social issues.

Although most of the labour movement planned and executed its federal politics in close co-ordination with the offices of Tom Mulcair, Dias was finding every way possible to confront Conservatives and to make Unifor's influence felt even in the hostile turf of Conservative-dominated Ottawa. The lesson was not lost that politics, like organizing or bargaining, demanded boldness and strong, direct engagement. Simply working with traditional allies in the NDP was entirely insufficient.

But Unifor had not disregarded the NDP or its federal leader, Tom Mulcair. In his address to the Unifor founding convention, Dias had included a place of honour for the memory of Jack Layton and had provocatively endorsed the yet-unannounced Olivia Chow for mayor of Toronto. One of his first public speeches was to the B.C. NDP convention in early November, where he offered full support and assistance to the party in preparing for the coming election. He had also been to Mulcair's offices to try to develop a working relationship. However, Mulcair was a different kind of NDP leader than Jack Layton, and, as with Horwath, the early meetings with him were tense. There was agreement to co-operate and share resources, but Unifor's aggressive independent political action was clearly not well received by the NDP leader. On the Unifor side, there was already disappointment over the NDP's calculated neutrality on CETA, despite its clear negative impacts on the telecommunications, dairy and auto industries. Those differences were exacerbated later when Mulcair whipped the NDP caucus, which included several former Unifor members, to vote in favour of the Canada-Korea Free Trade Agreement.

Relations with the federal Liberal Party and its new leader, Justin Trudeau, were amicable, especially given the Liberal opposition to the

Harper labour laws in Parliament and the Senate. Trudeau had already surprised many by his ability and rise in popularity, but the federal Liberal Party was still the third party in Canadian politics and far from central to Unifor's political strategy.

Relations with the NDP soon spilled over into Unifor's internal politics over the future of its local union representing the federal NDP staff in Ottawa and constituency offices across the country. The issue of "staff unions" representing full-time workers in other unions and the somewhat similar context for the staff of the NDP had troubled Unifor's leadership from the outset. Many of these union and political workers had long-standing connections to Unifor's predecessor unions, and those relationships had not been particularly controversial. But Unifor's explicit purpose to change politics and the labour movement altered the equation. Debate and dissent were not at issue, but the union's necessity to unite around its decisions could not be undermined by conflicting loyalties to other organizations. In early 2014, the Unifor National Executive Board attempted to clarify those relationships through the policy that members working for other labour movement organizations must be guided foremost by Unifor's policies, constitution and caucus decisions.[6]

With emotions running high after the Canadian Labour Congress convention and the Ontario election, the NDP staff local made it clear that they could not coexist in a parent union that did not affiliate unconditionally to the NDP. A mutual agreement was reached in the summer of 2014 for the NDP staff local to leave Unifor. Although some media reports characterized the parting of the ways as a rupture in Unifor-NDP relations, it had a very different meaning inside Unifor. The debate around the separation was never principally about the NDP; the decision represented the need for the union to have an independent political policy determined by its own debates and decisions that could not be predetermined by the NDP or any other political affiliation.

A lot of political water had flowed under bridges by the time that Unifor's first Canadian Council convened in Vancouver on September

13, 2014. Differing political estimations that may have provoked sharp differences two years earlier had been eroded by the shared experiences of the new union's desperate struggle against labour's adversaries. There was one overarching political goal that united Unifor members: "After a decade of Conservative minority and majority rule, it is time to take our country back and to restore labour rights and social progress," said the resolution on the federal election. "There is no more important task before us than to ensure the defeat of the Harper government."

The political strategy for the federal election was built on the strategic voting strategy used in the Ontario election and proposed a detailed and balanced electoral tactic that set out the primary goal of defeating the Harper government. However, the strategy also gave a nod to the "historic opportunity" for the NDP Official Opposition to become Canada's first social democratic government.[7]

From Unifor's perspective, the electoral strategy offered Tom Mulcair and the federal NDP the basis of a shared strategy. Mulcair was invited to address the Canadian Council, and his staff was briefed in advance. But it was soon clear that the NDP leader was not particularly interested in Unifor's federal election strategy or the analysis of social democratic and labour movement politics that had been debated on the floor just prior to his speech. Mulcair arrived at the Unifor council with a different mission.

Mulcair walked into the convention hall to receive a warm reception as any NDP leader of the opposition could expect at a large trade union meeting. But there was little warmth radiating back from the NDP leader, who seemed tense and abrupt. Nor did he appear to pick up on the generous introduction from Dias, who told Unifor delegates that Mulcair had been described as the best Opposition leader ever in Canada and that he was best-qualified to be the next prime minister also.

Mulcair's speech was tightly scripted and unremarkable. The highlight was a call for a $15 federal minimum wage, an easy crowd pleaser. But there was little else to connect to the 1,100 people in the room and nothing to underscore a bond or relationship with the largest private

Dias, centre, with Libby Davies, right, Tom Mulcair, at the podium, at the Unifor Canadian Council September 13, 2014, Vancouver.

sector union in the country. It could have been left as simply an opportunity lost, but the NDP leader had calculated to end his address with a shot across Unifor's bow, ridiculing the idea of strategic voting as "no strategy at all." If spontaneous approval was expected, it was a horrible miscalculation of the room. Dias, Kennedy and the regional leaders flanking Mulcair were palpably angry. It was left to member of Parliament and deputy leader Libby Davies — a Unifor favourite — to seize the podium and rescue the disaster with a solidarity message.

The smoke and noise from Mulcair's bomb obscured what had been a significant move by Unifor in its relationship with the NDP. Since the high-profile expulsion of former CAW President Buzz Hargrove from the Ontario NDP in 2006, the CAW nationally had suspended its official participation in the party. The CEP affiliation to the federal party had effectively come to an end with the New Union Project, with the matter referred to the Canadian Council meeting. The policy document adopted just prior to Mulcair's speech was a significant rapprochement that recognized the historic relationship of the labour movement to the party and made a decision to participate in "the labour movement's relationship with the NDP." The Unifor decision meant that it would attend NDP federal conventions, and, through the Canadian Labour

Congress caucus, Unifor members would be part of the "labour members" to serve on the party's federal council. The opening to the party was ignored by Mulcair and his team.

Unifor's promised political policy and strategy that came before the Canadian Council, *Politics for Workers: Unifor's Political Project*, painted a much larger canvas than its relationship with the NDP.[8] The document was highly nuanced and did not offer anything as simple or straightforward as either an endorsement or a rejection of a political affiliation. It said nothing about the political prehistories of the founding unions and instead reflected on the political realities of that time and the need for the union to begin its own labour-based "political project."[9]

The idea of a political project had been first generated in a report to the national executive board following Unifor's first international delegation. A group of leaders and staff had travelled to Brazil to get a firsthand look at labour politics in that country and the unique relationship between the CUT labour central and the Brazilian Workers' Party. It is another stunning lesson in the precariousness of party politics that less than a decade later, Lula Da Silva, the metal worker and union leader who became president of Brazil, would be in jail. The country that in Porto Alegre reshaped the global Left through the social forum movements, would elect an extreme right-wing government widely described as neo-fascist.

Later in the year, a visit to Canada and to the Unifor National Executive Board, by Irvin Jim, general secretary of the National Union of Metalworkers of South Africa, also had an impact on the idea. The union, a stalwart of the coalition of the African National Congress, the South African Communist Party and the Congress of South African Trade Unions, had just taken the remarkable step of withdrawing its unconditional political support to the national congress and the party over the government of South Africa's support for privatization and failure to address mass poverty.

The global picture for labour politics sketched out in *Politics for Workers* was bleak. In spite of the havoc wrought and the near-collapse of global capitalism in the 2008 financial crisis, the main trend in global political results had been setbacks and losses for traditionally pro-labour parties and an increase in the power of conservative, right-wing and extreme right-wing parties. In contrast to historic losses for social democratic parties was a rising tide of popular movements from the Arab Spring to Occupy, Indignados (Spain) and the Carré Rouge student protests in Quebec. Notable also were the successes at that time of Latin American left-wing political parties, including former guerrilla insurgents.

The idea of a Unifor political project was informed by those global events but galvanized by the grim Canadian political scene in 2014. Canadian politics seemed to have been taken over by a "deeply ideological, strongly organized national Conservative movement." The Conservatives had massive organizational capacity that had allowed Stephen Harper "to effectively use wedge politics to form pluralities and majorities in parliament for almost a decade without majority public support."

The dominance of the Conservative party had been partly explained by the collapse of the Liberal Party of Canada. The Liberals suddenly appeared poised for a comeback based on the personality and family brand of Justin Trudeau. But *Politics for Workers* warned: "The character of a resurgent Liberal Party remains very unclear. The Party has adopted a number of progressive policy resolutions on subjects like national child care and a national transit strategy, but the party has also gone out of its way to show it is pro-business on issues of taxes, oil pipelines, deregulation and foreign ownership of telecommunications."

Much of this could be found in the analysis of other unions, with the predictable conclusion that the NDP was qualitatively different. At this point, the Unifor analysis went in its own direction, welcoming the federal NDP's "historic opportunity" but also the "deeply blunted expectations" of what an NDP victory could mean for labour. Unifor was clearly reluctant to endorse the notion that the union and the party are a single movement. The Canadian Labour Congress was a cofounder with the Co-operative Commonwealth Federation of the

NDP in 1961, but in the decades since, as the politics of the NDP moved substantially away from those roots, the role of the trade union movement within the party was curtailed. The drift apart had by the time of Unifor's emergence resulted in sharp differences over policy choices and electoral strategies. In spite of the affection for Jack Layton, his controversial decision to force the 2010 federal election was a recent case in point. The election resulted not only in the "orange wave" breakthrough for the NDP but also the dangerous and extreme Harper majority. Moreover, the decision by Horwath to force the Ontario election was fresh and raw. "Unifor cautioned against provoking elections federally and in Ontario and warned against the consequences of electing the Harper Conservatives and the Hudak Conservatives in Ontario," *Politics for Workers* laid out. "However the NDP chose instead to risk the interests of labour in a partisan competition with Liberals over incremental gains. This disagreement will continue with the NDP, or any party, if the worst outcome for labour is accepted as the better outcome for the party."[10]

These matters of principle and strategy ran deep. Beyond the debate with NDP leaders lay a political culture of partisan politics in Canada that seemed to block a pathway to progressive change. Citing medicare and pensions as examples, Unifor argued that "progressive social change requires the involvement and commitment of more than any one party to achieve. While coalition politics is commonplace in most democracies, Canadian political culture lacks an understanding and acceptance of this important part of democratic change."[11]

The 2015 federal election proved again that political choices and campaigns matter. Arguably, the election was Mulcair's to lose — as he did by allowing Trudeau to outflank him on the left and present the more populist and expansive agenda for change.

Unifor implemented every aspect of its electoral strategy without constraint. It allocated the great majority of its financial resources in the pre-writ period and was among the first Canadian unions to support the multimillion-dollar "Engage Canada" campaign that identified and attacked vulnerable Conservative constituencies. The pre-writ period came to a sudden halt with the early election call on August 2. Conservatives close to the Prime Minister's Office confided in Dias that the decision to call the longest election in Canadian history was motivated in part to shut down Unifor's campaign. During the eleven-week campaign, thousands of Unifor members were mobilized in dozens of priority ridings. Unifor was among the leading registered third parties that spent an additional $6 million during the post-writ campaign period — an amount five times greater than in the previous federal election.

Jubilation and relief were primary among the mix of emotions I felt on October 19, 2015 when Stephen Harper resigned as Conservative leader on election night. It marked the end of a frightening era which for four years had weighed down our spirits with a constant apprehension of ruinous assaults on the trade union movement as well as against progressive non-governmental organizations and civil society groups in need of government funding or charity status. By the end of their reign, liberal democracy itself was the target of their anti-immigrant bigotry and Islamophobia campaign tactics. The elation that was felt when Harper was defeated was from the lifting of that weight, and not for the Liberal red tide that had swept the country even more forcefully than the 2011 orange wave. But I was no different than other Unifor members and a great majority of Canadians in feeling hopeful that we would begin to recognize our country again.

I had spent election day in Toronto attempting to elect NDP candidate Linda McQuaig in Toronto-Centre, which instead elected the country's next finance minister, Bill Morneau. This election night brought me to a Danforth Street pub where NDP supporters were crestfallen after failing to elect anyone in the city of Toronto. Four years before, my fears were bulldozed over by the NDP's celebration; this time my relief was smothered by the dejection that dominated the night.

Unifor's election night statement welcomed the defeat of the Harper government and tried to bridge the chasm of the Liberal win and the NDP's disappointment. "Tonight's election results offer Canadians an opportunity to rebuild our country," Dias said. "The Liberals have indicated they want to transform the country and Parliament. Now they can. The new government must bring a new spirit of collaboration to Ottawa and work with the NDP so Canadians can benefit from the best ideas, which are often born of cooperation."

In December 2015, before the first session of the new Parliament, the Trudeau government ordered Revenue Canada to cease activity on Bill C-377. In January 2016, as the first session began, the government introduced legislation to repeal Bills C-377 and C-525.

In February 2016, Unifor members returned to Parliament Hill and found a very different political reception. This time, the lobby included meetings with the prime minister and his senior staff and eighteen federal ministries. Looking back to its "moment of truth" five years earlier and the existential threat that seemed just ahead, few would have predicted this turn of fortune. The labour movement was suddenly positioned to go from defensive struggles to commanding unprecedented influence and going on the offensive to breathe life and meaning into newly won constitutional rights.

The defeat of labour's most significant political adversaries in 2014 and 2015 also brought a brief period of tranquility in Canadian labour politics. The step back from the abyss gave breathing room for the young union to turn inward and make preparations for its second convention in Ottawa in 2016. The theme of the second convention, "It's Time," reflected a shift from defensive strategies to progress on multiple fronts. Still on a bounce from auto industry bargaining that had seen the union negotiate $1.5 billion dollars in new investment, an aggressive bargaining strategy was brought to convention promising political bargaining in major sectors. The strategy also pledged to raise the floor for union members and non-union workers in low-income sectors such as retail and hospitality. The convention called for a campaign on trade issues around an agenda for "fair trade." On social issues, Unifor devoted a large part of its Ottawa convention to truth and reconciliation for Aboriginal peoples. It presented its Nelson Mandela Award for human

Unifor Secretary-Treasurer Bob Orr thanking Justin Trudeau after his address to Unifor's second national convention in Ottawa, August 24, 2016.

rights to Justice Murray Sinclair, the chair of the Truth and Reconciliation Commission, and gave its Activist of the Year Award to Cindy Blackstock, the dynamic campaigner who had embarrassed the federal government and secured court orders to end the social and educational discrimination against Aboriginal youth.

Unifor's agenda was extensive, and its growing leadership role in the labour movement looked certain. But by early 2017, another set of issues once again set Unifor apart and challenged labour movement rules and customs. A clash of principles over rank-and-file democracy and international trusteeships and the emergence of Unifor's latent nationalist role as the singular large Canadian union in the private sector resulted in polarizing conflicts with the major Canadian Labour Congress affiliates.

The immediate issues revolved around the actions of two international unions to place local unions in Ontario under trusteeship and to remove their elected leadership. When a Canadian union puts a local union under trusteeship, the normal constitution and bylaws are suspended and all organizational and financial decisions are made by an

Convention 2016

Dias, Cindy Blackstock and First Nations youth group, Jordan's Principle, at Unifor's second convention, Ottawa, August 24, 2016.

appointed trustee. When the parent body is an American union with its executive offices in the United States, authority is transferred a step further to another country. US unions and their international leaders have no standing in the Canadian labour movement and no accountability to any labour body in Canada. Canadian workers affected by a trusteeship have limited options and must turn to the courts for redress. Historically, Canadian courts have viewed the relationship of Canadian locals to their US parent bodies as a matter of contract law defined by the constitution of the union. But in recent years, Canadian judges have taken a dim view of the abuse of these powers to usurp the democratic rights of Canadian members. That was the case in Unifor's stand-off with Amalgamated Transit Union (ATU) Local 113 when the international president, Larry Hanley, imposed a trusteeship on transit workers in Greater Toronto from his office in Silver Springs, Maryland.

Bob Kinnear had been president of ATU Local 113 for more than a decade, but he now wanted out of the union, which he maintained had no regard for Canadian autonomy. Kinnear had recently run for the position of Canadian international vice-president with the support of the Canadian caucus but was defeated by the majority of American delegates, who elected a rival that the Amalgamated Transit Union International favoured. Kinnear brought his case to Dias and Unifor a few weeks prior to making an application to the Canadian Labour Congress for "justification" to change affiliation under Article IV of the congress's constitution. Unifor told Kinnear that under congress rules, he would have to use the provisions in Article IV of the constitu-

Unifor members at Jobs Justice Climate action, Toronto, July 6, 2015.

tion to secure a vote on changing affiliation. These provisions both prohibited raiding between affiliates and allowed for members to request a Canadian Labour Congress investigation into their affiliation to a parent union and justification for a possible change in affiliation. The Article IV process could have eventually resulted in a congress-run process that would grant Amalgamated Transit Union members the option of changing affiliation. In that event, both Unifor and Kinnear expected that Unifor, which already was a major transportation and bus driver union, would be on the ballot. However, ATU International President Larry Hanley responded immediately to the news of the application by putting the local under trusteeship and dismissing Kinnear from office. The local executive was also removed, with a number of them later reinstated after signing loyalty oaths.

At the Canadian Labour Congress, Yussuff told Hanley and the Amalgamated Transit Union that if it wanted to use a trusteeship to prevent the local from exercising its rights under the congress's constitution, it would also forfeit the protection of the constitution against raiding. Yussuff's decision enraged the US unions operating in Canada, which saw Unifor's involvement as a raid against the Amalgamated Transit Union and a precursor of others to come against US unions. Unifor did not launch a raid against the Amalgamated Transit Union by signing cards that would force a labour board representation vote. But neither was Dias at arms' length from the ATU trusteeship. Dias and Kinnear held a joint media conference in which Dias condemned the usurping of local democracy and transfer of

International Women's Day march, Toronto, March 8, 2015. Left to right holding banner: Jackie McIntosh, Denise McMorris, Katha Fortier, Kellie Scanlan, Jenny Ahn, Josephine Petcher.

authority to the US union. Unifor also paid the legal fees of Kinnear, who sought an injunction against the trusteeship.

A report by a Canadian Labour Congress investigator did not support the charge that Unifor had raided the Amalgamated Transit Union but found that Dias had violated the rules by not informing the ATU International when Kinnear had approached him for support. "As I explained to the Investigator we did not notify the International for the obvious reasons that the trusteeship demonstrated," Dias commented after the release of the report. "I also acknowledged the financial support we provided Bob Kinnear to take legal actions. Without the support of Unifor, the judgement of Ontario Supreme Court Judge Penny overruling the trusteeship and reinstating Kinnear would not have been possible." Penny's decision was a short-lived but total vindication for Kinnear and Unifor. "It is not contested that Mr. Hanley's sole reason for imposing a trusteeship was because of Mr. Kinnear's request filed with the CLC to investigate possible dis-affiliation and this litigation," the judge ruled. "I find that the international has used the trusteeship to silence opposition and to spread misinformation to the members. It is clear that the purpose of the trusteeship is to quell dissent."[12]

Kinnear eventually resigned his position as president of the ATU local and withdrew his application to the Canadian Labour Congress, ending the Amalgamated Transit Union affair. But the politics reverberated inside Unifor and in the congress. The United Steelworkers led a campaign inside the congress to have Yussuff censored and Unifor condemned and penalized for its alleged raiding.

As the 2017 Toronto Canadian Labour Congress convention approached, it was unclear whether the unions supporting the Amalgamated Transit Union would challenge Yussuff for president. A candidate against Yussuff did not materialize, but the contests for secretary-treasurer to replace the retiring Barbara Byers and for the two vice-presidents were interpreted as proxy fights intended to rein in the leadership of Yussuff over the role of Unifor. With over one thousand Unifor delegates in attendance at the convention, the Yussuff team once again swept all the contested positions. However, the Amalgamated Transit Union episode and the convention had widened and hardened the divisions in the congress. During the Amalgamated Transit Union controversy, rhetoric in the labour movement was revved up to hyperbolic levels with ATU's Hanley attacking Dias personally, calling him a "cancer on the movement" and a "corporate sellout." In one comment, Hanley compared Unifor to the Nazi Party.[13] When CUPE and the US-based unions gave unqualified support to Hanley and the trusteeship, Dias and the Unifor leadership were further estranged.

Within months, the tinderbox of relationships in the Canadian Labour Congress would be put to a second and more consequential stress test. A second international trusteeship was imposed on UNITE HERE Local 75, representing Toronto hotel workers. The local had internal divisions, and some on the executive board had requested the trusteeship. But the elected local leadership also had support and organized large meetings of members to oppose an imminent trusteeship. Local 75 President Lis Pimentel sought support from Canadian Labour Congress unions and, after being rebuffed at the United Steelworkers' Canadian offices, took her case to Unifor.

UNITE HERE Local 75 meeting opposing trusteeship on January 9, 2018, Toronto. Many of these workers would establish Unifor Local 7575.

With the Amalgamated Transit Union experience still burning, neither Pimentel nor Dias saw any realistic remedy in the congress's Article IV processes. The International unions and other large Canadian affiliates had made it more than clear that they did not support the use of Article IV to facilitate the right of large bargaining units or whole locals to change affiliation. The Canadian Labour Congress executive would not challenge the trusteeship of the Toronto hotel workers, and it was too late for Pimentel and her group to launch a justification process, which would have no expeditious result. One of the outcomes of the convention had been a decision to review Article IV, but the congress executive had established a review committee that excluded Unifor.

However, a number of Local 75's bargaining units had two weeks remaining in their "open period" during which Ontario labour law provided for changing affiliation if enough members signed cards to force a representation vote. Article IV could not save the elected leadership of Pimental and her supporters, but it continued to prohibit raiding of one affiliate by another. Dias and the Unifor leadership knew that if they came to the defence of the UNITE HERE local, they would be charged and suspended from Canadian Labour Congress membership.

In January 2018, the Canadian labour movement was shaken by the decision of Unifor to suspend its affiliation to the Canadian Labour Congress. Dias's letter to Hassan Yussuff expressed his frustrations:

> *The inability of the CLC to deal with now two instances of U.S.-based unions interfering in elections and imposing trusteeship on Canadian local unions leaves Unifor at odds with many in the Canadian labour movement.*
>
> *Article 26 of the CLC constitution insists on Canadian components of U.S.-based unions having autonomy, but when the rubber hits the road, CLC lacks the ability to ensure U.S.-based unions have legitimate elections of Canadian leadership and as a result American-based unions are able to impose their will on Canadian locals. Unifor submits that contrary to the requirement of the CLC constitution, several U.S.-based unions do not have legitimate Canadian operations with autonomy from American interference.*
>
> *Unifor is routinely vilified by others for our principled position on these issues and our attempts to raise them are met with accusations and assertions that are without merit. For these reasons, Unifor's National Executive Board voted to cease affiliation to the CLC effective immediately.*

Over the ensuing two weeks, about a thousand hotel workers in four bargaining units joined Unifor's new Local 7575. Hundreds more would join later, representing only a portion of the large UNITE HERE local. Critics of Unifor pointed to the support for the international union in spite of the trusteeship. For Unifor, principles of democracy and Canadian autonomy were not determined by numbers. Local 7575 was welcomed into Unifor, and its enthusiastic members began the process of building a democratic, activist local union.

Unifor's withdrawal from the Canadian Labour Congress was wrenching for the young union, forcing a return to basic principles and a re-examination of its role. Its dispute with the Canadian Labour Congress unions was all the more distressful when Hassan Yussuff condemned Unifor's withdrawal from the congress and its raid against UNITE HERE. Yussuff's turn mirrored the strong backlash against Unifor from the major congress unions. There was no criticism of the international trusteeship by the congress or any other union; instead, the congress vilified Unifor. The nearly unanimous stand of the congress unions was in spite of Unifor's repeated claims that its actions were in defence of workers deprived of democratic rights and that it has no intention of using a raiding strategy to build its membership.

There are strong arguments for deterring raiding. It creates conflicts between unions that lessen solidarity, and it can divert resources away from organizing unorganized workers into internecine struggles to "reorganize" the organized. However, these concerns have to be balanced against the wishes of workers to belong to the union of their choice, and without that balance, workers are reduced to the status of assets or property. Raiding has long been a telltale manifestation of a thin layer of solidarity between unions and at the same time a symptom of an unresolved contradiction in Canada's labour movement. Raiding, especially involving relatively small numbers of workers, can be highly predatory. It can also signal important issues for workers and a desire for change.

The first decade of the 2000s was full of large-scale raids that created the political will for a new deal on managing both predatory raids and the desire for change. The International Brotherhood of Carpenters raided the Labourers International Union in Ontario, leading to their suspension from the Canadian Labour Congress. In Alberta, the Alberta Union of Provincial Employees embarked on a wide-scale raiding strategy, particularly against CUPE, and was suspended from its parent body, the National Union of Provincial Government Employees, and from the congress. The BC Nurses' Union was also removed over its successful organizing of licensed practical nurses who had been members of the B.C. Hospital Employees' Union. The International Teamsters organized a number of raids, notably against the National Union of Provincial

Government Employees in 2010, which led to the union's withdrawal from the congress in protest. The Teamsters also had a short but intense raiding war with the CAW; this dispute resulted in a protocol between the two unions that formed the basis of the 2011 Canadian Labour Congress protocol to amend Article IV of the constitution. The agreement sought to limit the destructive pattern of organizing strategies based on raiding but also provided a pathway for workers to change affiliations through a "justification" process.

The ability to change from one union to another is legally recognized in every labour code; it is as much a condition of freedom of association as is the right to organize. However, the Canadian Labour Congress had done its best to make exercising those rights illegal under its constitution. The position of the congress had been that any involvement of one union in the decision of workers in another to change affiliation is a raid. The logic of that view is that unhappy workers should decertify their union altogether before joining another. The justification provisions of Article IV were intended to provide another pathway, although in the view of Unifor, it had clearly failed to do that.

The trusteeships imposed on the Amalgamated Transit Union and UNITE HERE ran head-on into foundational principles and meaning for Unifor of what was wrong with the labour movement. Unifor leaders and activists could often be heard stating, "We are not a dues collection agency" or "Workers are not chattel." Although Unifor does have constitutional provisions to impose trusteeships, the provisions have not been used and are reserved for extreme situations or criminal activity. The strong consensus is that administrative measures cannot be used to resolve political issues or to stop members from leaving the union. To the contrary, its commitment to voluntary membership was underscored by the willingness to part company with dues-paying members of the NDP and some staff unions before its second convention.

It cannot be denied that Unifor's support for workers under US trusteeships held out the potential of several thousand additional members at the expense of the US unions. But these conflicts were not part of the union's organizing strategy. Whatever membership gains were involved paled in cost-benefit terms to the effort and costs to win these struggles, piled on top of the large-scale resources already expended on the efforts to elect Yussuff and to strengthen provincial labour federations and labour councils.

The larger, overarching context leading to Unifor's actions is rooted deep in its character as the singular, large Canadian union in the private sector. The Canadian character of the new union was a decisive factor that brought the CAW and the CEP together and separated them from US-based unions. In January 2012, CEP President Dave Coles and I travelled to Pittsburgh for a meeting with United Steelworkers International President Leo Gerard, Canadian Director Ken Neumann and International Vice-President Jon Geenen. The purpose of the meeting was to propose that the Canadian steelworkers join the discussions getting under way in the New Union Project. Gerard, himself a Canadian, rejected the proposal out of hand and said that the Canadian union would never break its ties with the International. Coles and I argued that if a new Canadian union emerged, it could be a partner with the United Steelworkers and the UK Unite "Workers United" project to act together in bargaining and politics across borders. We appealed to the United Steelworkers leaders to appreciate that the new union must be entirely Canadian to give legitimacy to the unprecedented economic and political influence it would wield. This powerful new union would change the Canadian labour movement for the better, we argued, and the Canadian members should be a part of it. Gerard's answer was amicable but a firm no.

Look inside Unifor, and it isn't hard to find its nationalist roots. Unifor's family tree expands to include as many as eighty-four separate former trade unions, the vast majority of which are former members of US unions. These include the tens of thousands of Unifor members in its largest industrial sectors: the CAW, which separated from the UAW in 1985, and two of the founding unions of the CEP: the Canadian Paperworkers, which left the United Paperworkers International Union in 1974, and the Energy and Chemical Workers, which broke from the

US Oil, Chemical and Atomic Workers Union in 1980. Unifor's media workers are almost all breakaways from US unions, including the National Association of Broadcast Employees and Technicians in 1974, the Vancouver and Southern Ontario Newspaper Guilds, which left the Communications Workers of America in 1994, and graphical workers, which left the International Typographical Union and the Graphic Communications International soon after.

Another core component of Unifor has its roots in the Confederation of Canadian Unions formed in 1969 to fight for an independent Canadian trade union movement. These include the Canadian Textile and Chemical Union founded by the famous labour organizer Madeleine Parent and Western miners and smelter workers in the Canadian Association of Industrial, Mechanical and Allied Workers and the Canadian Association of Smelter and Allied Workers, which left the United Steelworkers. These Confederation of Canadian Unions members migrated to the CAW between 1992 and 1994. They were joined in 2000 by bus drivers and transit workers in Vancouver and Victoria who had left the Amalgamated Transit Union in 1982 to form the confederation-affiliated Independent Canadian Transit Union.

The Fish, Food and Allied Workers Union decision to join the CAW involved a trusteeship, court cases, Canadian Labour Congress complaints and a high-profile conflict with the US United Food and Commercial Union in 1987. In 1999, another large group of workers, members of the United Steelworkers–affiliated Retail Wholesale Union, also decided to join the CAW, forming the union's retail division. A year later, the CAW health care division was created by the overwhelming votes of 30,000 Ontario health care workers to leave the Service Employees International Union, a conflict that resulted in the suspension of the CAW from the congress.

It is no exaggeration to say that the broad sweep of the "Canadian union movement" that challenged the domination of the Canadian trade union movement by US-based unions is today found within Unifor. The new union's response to the international trusteeships was hardly surprising.

In 2015, 69.7 per cent of Canadian union members were affiliated to Canadian national unions. That fact is often cited as evidence that an independent Canadian labour movement was achieved decades ago. But the degree to which the Canadian labour movement has been patriated is a matter of contention. The majority status of Canadian national unions is overwhelmingly due to the emergence and expansion of Canada's public sector unions, which are now a majority of total members and are almost entirely Canadian. In the private sector, so-called international unions continue to constitute a majority of unions and members.

Apart from Unifor, there is a very short list of Canadian unions with a large number of members in the private sector. In English Canada, the only other Canadian union with more than 50,000 private sector members is the dubious Christian Labour Association of Canada. The union is notorious for its low-wage agreements in health care and services, sometimes using labour law provisions allowing unions to negotiate terms and conditions less than provincial employment standards law. These top-down agreements, combined with so-called Christian values and opposition to adversarial unionism, have led it to be seen by most Canadian trade unionists as a union of convenience for employers. However, its largest group of members is based in Alberta's construction sector, where it provided an alternative to US construction unions. While the US building trades are one of the last adherents of "craft unionism," the construction locals of the labour association have provisions close to the building trades in total compensation and "wall-to-wall" certifications covering all trades in a single agreement.

The next tier of Canadian unions dealing directly with the corporate sector drops to about 22,000 members in the Alliance of Canadian Cinema, Television and Radio Artists and more than 5,000 members in two or three more unions.[14] There is a somewhat different situation in Quebec, with its distinct trade union structure and history. About 200,000 workers in the private sector are members of FTQ Construction, the three major private sector federations of the Confederation of National Unions and the Congress of Democratic Trade Unions.

In contrast to Unifor and this modest Canadian roster, more than a million Canadian trade unionists in the private sector remain as members of US-based unions, and almost 90 per cent of those are in large unions with 30,000 or more members. Therein lies the basis for continuing episodic conflict such as has shaped Canadian trade union development for a hundred years. These conflicts arose from the different political and strategic goals of workers in the US and Canadian contexts, as they still do.

From the 1919 Winnipeg General Strike, which forced the strikers to break from their US parent bodies that stood opposed to the strike, to the upstart Workers Unity League, which led Depression-era struggles, to the contrary strategies on concession bargaining in the 1980s and 1990s, to trade disputes and growing cultural and political differences between Canadian and American society in the twenty-first century, workers have over and over again broken from US-based unions in the course of their own struggles. To chart their own course, it demanded a concurrent fight for an independent Canadian trade union movement.

The ever-present tension over the role of US unions in Canada led to the decision by the Canadian Labour Congress in 1974 to adopt a constitutional set of "minimum standards of Canadian autonomy" (Article 26). Unchanged since then, the standards are unevenly applied and rarely, if ever, enforced. The provisions were intended to require US-based unions to provide Canadian members with the right to elect Canadian officers who speak for the union in Canada, to set policies on national affairs and to have separate affiliation to global union structures.

The compromise with the international unions did little to slow down the Canadian union movement, which gained momentum in the 1980s with yet another wave of workers leaving these unions, notably the CAW and Quebec construction workers. In Quebec, the provincial FTQ established FTQ Construction to accommodate electricians and other local unions that were leaving the American Federation of Labor-Congress of Industrial Organizations' (AFL-CIO's) building trades unions. At the same time in English Canada, these unions were estranged by the congress's support for the NDP and the policies of social unionism and environmentalism that the mainstream of the labour movement was moving towards. All this was too much for the international building trades unions, which in 1982 withdrew their more than 200,000 members from the Canadian Labour Congress to establish the rival Canadian Federation of Labour. A decade later, many AFL-CIO building trades unions drifted back into the congress, although the differences that had sparked the split remained largely unresolved. In 2004, about 8,000 carpenters in British Columbia and Alberta left the International Brotherhood of Carpenters to form an independent Canadian union, the Canadian Mechanical and Allied Workers Union, which at its outset was allied and affiliated to the CEP.

Breakaways from US unions ebbed after the early 2000s. In part, the rise of globalism took an edge away from nationalist struggles. The decline in private sector union density and the infrequency of labour disputes that would bring differing national bargaining strategies into focus were likely more determining.

The conflicts with international unions in 2017 and 2018 and the extraordinary decision to leave the Canadian Labour Congress did not arise directly from the New Union Project. However, without doubt, the preconditions for these events were in the making of Unifor. The mission of the union as an adaptive force for change in the labour movement and its foundational view of rank-and-file democracy were the starting points for taking on the quarrels with US unions when most Canadian unions saw those matters as the internal affairs of another organization.

In 2011, at the outset of the New Union Project, both the CAW and the CEP were signatories to the Canadian Labour Congress protocols and were focused squarely on issues of union density and renewal. Unifor saw its role as changing the labour movement within the congress. Membership in the congress was written into the constitution, and although it provided for a suspension of membership by the national executive board, it made such an action subject to a subsequent approval by a convention or Canadian council of all local unions.

In August 2018, Unifor members at the next Canadian Council meeting did vote on the executive board's decision to withdraw from the Canadian Labour Congress. Although there were speeches to the floor for and against the resolution to support the national executive board decision, the affirmative vote was nearly unanimous, with only a few hands against. However, the resolution also called on the leadership to "continue to seek a fair and meaningful resolution to this dispute with the Canadian Labour Congress and its affiliates."

Unifor's break with the Canadian Labour Congress was only the latest of the intermittent ruptures that have shaped the development of the Canadian labour movement. "Change never happens without challenge," the union explained to its membership and the movement the day after its withdrawal from the congress, adding,

> *Unifor's leadership believes strongly that in order to make things better for workers there is a need to advance this issue now, and by doing this Unifor's leadership hopes that there will be a stronger labour movement in Canada. The CLC must establish a solution that will create a fair process to allow Canadian workers to change their union affiliation, including leaving undemocratic U.S.-based unions, and to prevent, bullying and intimidation of workers should they choose to leave. While Article IV of the CLC Constitution outlines a democratic process for workers to change unions, it is not enforced, which means it is not working for workers. We must fix that.*[15]

The conflicts with the Canadian Labour Congress and US unions were driven by a mix of interrelated issues of democracy, identity and autonomy and damaged relationships. As in most matters, the course of events was also a reaction to the personalities and leadership that led to crucial decisions. Nevertheless, five years after its founding, the continuing break with the congress seemed to underscore the different path that the new union had chosen. Unifor's goal of changing the labour movement could not take place simply through the forums of the Canadian Labour Congress. The ongoing quest for a different solidarity and union renewal would require new relationships and new forums.

In 2017, Unifor and the independent US union, the United Electrical, Radio and Machine Workers (UE), announced an unlikely initiative that was intended to present an alternative narrative on cross-border solidarity and internationalism. The co-operation agreement between the two unions was announced as "bringing together two unions in two countries with one purpose: to demonstrate that true solidarity is based on equality and rank and file democracy."[16] The UE's internationalism and its appreciation of Canadian national self-determination were hardly coincidental to the new relationship. Its former Canadian membership had been entirely autonomous for decades after the war, and when it decided to join the CAW in the 1990s, the US leadership wished the union well.

There was a larger meaning, however, to this unusual connection that touched on the idealism of the New Union Project. When the UE attended Unifor's second convention in Ottawa in 2016 and then sought closer ties to Unifor because it saw its reflection in the larger Canadian union, Unifor's leadership was immediately attracted to the UE's feisty and principled militancy. The independent UE has a legendary history and big ideas that make it distinct in the American labour movement. It emerged from World War II as a 600,000–strong, avowedly left-wing Congress of Industrial Organizations union with Communist leaders, which made it a target for persecution by the McCarthy-era House Un-American Activities Committee (HUAC) which after 1945 held public hearings to expose alleged Communist influence in US government and civil society. UE was raided mercilessly by Red-baiting AFL-CIO unions, and by 1960 only 10 per cent of its members remained. But the UE refused to co-operate with HUAC and to join others in swearing Cold War loyalty oaths and instead put in its constitution that no member would be discriminated against because of political beliefs. The UE never rejoined the AFL-CIO and rebuilt its base in the public sector and small manufacturing, including several innovative minority unions. It is widely respected today by American progressives for its brand of left-wing, rank-and-file democracy and militancy. In 2016, it made its first endorsement in a US primary in its eighty years when it came out for Bernie Sanders. There are parallels between the union and Sanders, the septuagenarian who is trusted by millions of young activists because of a lifetime of principled activism and his proud identification as a socialist. The UE has a similar appeal. As *Harper's Magazine* put it in September 2018, "The UE was calling for racial equality before the civil rights movement; for ending gender discrimination before the second wave of the feminist movement; and for equal pay for comparable work before such a concept was widely understood . . . As far back as its 1947 convention, the UE was demanding that Wall Street be driven out of Washington."[17]

The co-operation agreement between the two unions envisaged member-to-member exchanges and mutual assistance in campaigns and organizing and a larger project to "research and discuss the prospects for a North American Solidarity Project to establish a continental labour alliance based on democratic, militant and social unionism, and true internationalism between American and Canadian workers." The North American Solidarity Project would soon expand to include other progressive US unions that shared the social union values of UE and Unifor and the need for union renewal.[18]

In November 2018, 150 labour activists and scholars gathered at Unifor's Family Education Centre in Port Elgin for a North American Solidarity Project conference. Apart from the Canadian Federation of Nurses Unions, other Canadian unions declined or ignored the invitation, still angry over Unifor's conflicts with US unions. However, about a hundred US trade unionists from UE, the Utility Workers Union of America, National Nurses United and LEO, the lecturers' union at the

University of Michigan, were present. Four major independent Mexican unions travelled to Port Elgin, including Sindicato Electricistas (Electrical Workers), Sindicato de Telefonistas (telephone workers), STUNAM (university workers) and SITIAVW (Volkswagen autoworkers), as well as the Mexican non-governmental organization CILAS. United Voice, an Australian union engaged in its own new union project, came for the discussion on union renewal issues. About a dozen labour studies scholars from the United States and Canada were speakers and participants.

The Port Elgin conference brought together what was once again an improbable group, lacking any traditional labour movement definition based on industry, sector or geography. The attendees were instead defined by social values and an agreement that the labour movement is in urgent need of change and renewal. The conference statement set out foundational principles for a new style of unionism:

> Our commitment to independent labour politics and social unionism is one of action: where our unions are the counter-balancing force that can lead the fight for the world we want to live in.
>
> We believe that empowering rank and file workers must be the core mission to organize successfully and achieve workplace democracy and fairness at work. Workers need unions more than ever and unions must change to connect and represent their needs and interests with militant action and not complacency.
>
> We believe that it is time for unions to present a bold vision for social change and union renewal that unites the working class. We have done it before, and we must do it again.[19]

Unifor would spend its fifth year outside the Canadian Labour Congress, although its engagement in politics, social justice campaigns, community projects and strike solidarity was hardly affected. Dias's profile soared higher from his role as the sole trade unionist from Canada, the United States and Mexico at the centre of the NAFTA renegotiation talks.

Unifor's fifth birthday could not have the celebratory atmosphere of its third. By 2018, there was a return to political anxiety and alarm in the trade union movement arising from the rise of right-wing populism in the United States, the election of Trump and the spectre of a new authoritarianism. Canada's apparent separate direction was then abruptly interrupted in June 2018 with the election of the Doug Ford Conservative government in Ontario, ending fifteen years of Liberal governance. Ford's victory rode a wave of right-wing populism with disturbing echoes of Donald Trump and other "alt-right" movements.[20]

As it was with Hudak in 2014, Ontario was again ground zero for workers' rights. The immediate impact of the Conservative victory on low-income workers and for workers' rights generally was devastating. Although Ford offered no policy on workers' rights during the election other than preventing the rise of the minimum wage to $15, before six months had passed, the government repealed almost every improvement in employment standards and labour law that had been won a year earlier. Lost was a scheduled $1 per hour increase in the minimum wage and a wide range of improvements to employment standards aimed at addressing the worst abuses of precarious work — ending discrimination against part-time workers, notice requirements in shift scheduling and paid sick days and outlawing demands for a doctor's letter on a sick day, enhanced emergency leave days, new regulations for temporary work agencies that prohibit paying agency workers less than other employees doing the same work and more.

New and hard-won trade union rights were equally pummelled. Card-based certification in precarious sectors, new organizing rules to provide employee lists during organizing drives, new rules for remedial certifications and strife fines when employers are guilty of unfair labour practices, successorship provisions for contract employees in publicly funded services, the right of employees to return to their jobs after a six-month strike and provisions allowing the labour board to review bargaining units and allow multi-employer or sectoral bargaining were all wiped out.

The deeply discouraging take-away from Bill 47 in Ontario was the abject contempt it showed for democratic governance, fact-based decision making and modernity. Bill 47 was given the ridiculous and perverse name *Making Ontario Open for Business Act* to reverse legislation enacted after the two-year *Changing Workplaces Review* carried out by business and labour advisors — the first serious review of Ontario labour standards and laws in twenty-five years. The shameless repeal of the review's recommendations was executed after a five-hour sham consultation period and with not a single reference to the extensive research or policy analysis upon which the previous legislation was carefully layered.[21]

The Ford government's swift and brazen attack on workers at the behest of the Chamber of Commerce and retail and hospitality employers was unvarnished class warfare. "Let's be clear, rich corporations are the only ones who stand to benefit from Bill 47, while the lowest wage earners will be forced back into poverty," the co-ordinator of Ontario's "Fight for $15" said when the law passed.[22]

With its animus to workers' rights well exposed, it may well be one step forward and two or more steps backward before the Ford government can be reined in or replaced. And there are fault lines in labour's political defence that speak loudly to the call for independent labour politics voiced at the solidarity project conference.

The mainstream labour movement has a political model dating to the postwar consensus and its social contracts. In this period, labour forged its attachments to social democratic, Christian democratic and liberal parties that were associated with the growth of the welfare state, unions and collective bargaining. The neo-liberal era ushered in by Reagan, Thatcher and Mulroney irrevocably broke the social contract so powerfully that the pro-worker parties of the postwar consensus, including most of Europe's social democratic parties and the Democratic Party in the US, soon were themselves identified with the policies of free trade, globalization and deregulation. Mainstream unions across the Western world soldiered on with the same political model and relationships from the previous era.

As of 2019, the rise of right-wing populism was challenging the political context of the last thirty years. Right-wing populism differs from the politics of the neo-liberal and globalization era because of its overt nationalism and coddling of racism and bigotries and because although it is financed and controlled by corporate elites, its social base resides in the working class. America's Trump, Brazil's Bolsonaro, France's Le Pen, the Philippines' Duarte and Ontario's Ford had a common calling card: the liberal and social democratic elites have left workers behind, and we are now your champions. That was the message from the alt-right nationalist Steve Bannon to an audience at the University of Toronto, delivered only a week before the trouncing of workers' rights in Ontario. "Ordinary people have long been shut out by political and capitalist elites who have done them immense harm . . . This is about the little guy versus the elites," Bannon said. "The little guy identifies with that, whether it's in Hungary, whether it's in Italy, whether it's in Brazil, whether it's in the United States."[23] Bannon's messaging was a political strategy, not a true reflection of what he represented. Bannon was a Goldman Sach's investment banker and Hollywood producer before becoming executive chairperson of Breitbart News, the self proclaimed voice of the "alt right" in the US. He was chief strategist for Donald Trump in 2016–2017 and in 2018 Bannon launched a project to unite far-right political parties in Europe.

As a third wave of new politics in the postwar period challenged labour movements at their base, the political strategies of most unions were still scarcely different than they were in 1960. The contracting out of politics to parties that had long since ceased placing workers' rights at the centre of their agendas, and that, with only a few exceptions, were globally at historically low levels of popular support had made workers' rights highly vulnerable to attacks and without the political strength to modernize and adapt to a new economy. There was no easy answer short of a radical politicalization of the labour movement, which presented the union itself as a political reference point for its members and workers generally.

The union movement not only had to fill a political space, but an ideological void also. Within the conservative coalition, populism had been given over to the alt-right, whereas workers' rights and labour law had been handed to the libertarians, who also ascended to new heights of influence and dominated conservative policy making. There is no more powerful example than the US Supreme Court decision to strike down union security provisions in the public sector. The ominous *Janus v. AFSCME* decision was a forceful application of libertarian individualism striking down the collective rights of union members.

In 2018, the *Janus* decision rendered mandatory union dues in public sector workplaces unconstitutional. The court struck down the ability of public sector unions to collect union dues from everyone in a bargaining unit by declaring this to be a violation of the "freedom of speech" (in this case, the First Amendment of the US Constitution) of those individuals who may disagree with the idea of unionism or the political positions of the union. The 5–4 majority decision stated that an "impingement on First Amendment rights occurs when public employees are required to provide financial support for a union that takes many positions during collective bargaining that have powerful political and civic consequences." The far-reaching implications of this judgment to make the right of free association secondary and subordinate to another right — the right to free speech — were powerfully elaborated by the dissenting opinion in *Janus*. "Speech is everywhere — a part of every human activity (employment, health care, securities trading, you name it). For that reason, almost all economic and regulatory policy affects or touches speech," the dissenting opinion replied, with the result that "black-robed rulers (are) overriding citizens" and preventing the American people from making democratic choices on workplace governance.[2] The full consequences of the *Janus* decision will only be known when further court decisions interpret it and after union organizing and resistance struggles adapt. However, as National Nurses United Director of Field Operations David Johnson explained to me in our North American Solidarity Project meetings, "Everything we do now as a union from organizing to education to bargaining assumes we will have to work within a complete right-to-work environment in the United States."

There was no *Janus* case before the Supreme Court of Canada in 2018, and its recent decisions pointed in an opposite direction. However, the logic and even the fine print of the argument were the same as those pursued in Canada by LabourWatch, merit shop and the conservative Right. Lose one election, and a Canadian *Janus* can be expected to materialize. This glaring threat underscored the need for independent labour politics that in the short term can help secure political majorities to block extreme right-wing governments, and in the longer term forge a non-partisan consensus on trade union rights as constitutionally protected human rights.

The problem was that the unrelenting conservative assault on workers' rights was based on the weakness of unions and the slow decline of collective bargaining institutions. A strategy to hold the line on trade union rights from election to election would continue to provide a three- or four-year reprieve at best until these underlying issues changed. Here unions faced their greatest challenge of modernity — a challenge that overwhelmed politics.

Ontario illustrates the case: to maintain the current union density in that province, unions have to more than double the number of new members organized every year. Put another way, unless unions change the way they organize to achieve extraordinary successes, they can quickly fall to levels of unionization that question their relevance. Look closer at this problem and another quagmire comes into focus. Outdated union models shaped half a century ago or longer when manufacturing and resources were dominant and the public sector was expanding are ill-equipped to keep pace with the growth of the new economy.[25]

This new economy had been reshaping the world of work for almost a generation. The shocking result was that a majority of the workforce was labouring in sectors of the economy that rendered them "practically ineligible for unionization," as the advisors to Ontario's *Changing Workplaces Review* concluded. This majority working outside unions' sphere of relevance were workers in small workplaces of nineteen or fewer employees, which amounted to 30 per cent of all workers in the province in 2015. Add to those another 25 per cent or more of the workforce working in "non-standard employment" that is temporary, contract, seasonal, self-employment, freelance or a combination of these.

These workplaces and workers were, for the most part, alien spaces to union organizing and bargaining. But if unions are not organizing small workplaces, it is questionable where they will organize. The 30 per cent of Ontario workers in small workplaces make up 87 per cent of all workplaces in the province. It is the same in British Columbia, where 88 per cent of workplaces have nineteen or fewer employees.[26]

The growing numbers of non-standard workers opened up an even wider divide between unions and workplace realities. These workers were, by definition, without a regular or permanent employer. There were some, of course, who may choose temporary or contract work and who may be well paid for their temporary services. Some non-standard workers, such as construction workers or actors, may be unionized. But the vast majority were not and were far more likely to fall through the cracks of employment standards regulations. The single largest group of non-standard workers were found in retail services, but the highest incidence of non-standard work was in the arts, entertainment and recreation. Large numbers find work through temporary help agencies, a grey zone of work where the agency is the employer, but the client provides the work. The overall picture was one of growing precariousness and inequality.[27]

Talk to union organizers and they are likely to tell you they are focused on the many thousands of workers with standard employment in larger workplaces that can be organized. This is true, to a point. But employment in the service sector in Canada is four times larger than employment in the goods-producing sectors. And the unionization rate in the private service sector is very low. Union density in Canada's retail sector is about 12 per cent, but take away unionized grocery stores and that rate would fall dramatically. In hotels and restaurants, union density is 6.7 per cent. Here we also find the world of work in virtually union-proof franchise operations, which account for up to 35 per cent of sales in restaurants and 45 per cent in retail.[28]

It is no coincidence that many of the large employers that fund the anti-union campaigns of the Canadian Federation of Independent Business, Chambers of Commerce and LabourWatch are in the retail, restaurant, accommodation and hospitality industries. They defend their hostility to unions by pointing to labour costs as a larger share of business costs than in manufacturing, often the largest single cost. Low-wage employers do not deserve sympathy; exploitation is their chosen business model, and it is not by any means the only possible one. But there are also objective reasons that drive the race to the bottom for workers. These businesses exist in a world of low-wage competition, rooted not only in their subjective disregard for the rights of others. Unions must examine those conditions if they have any hope of taking wages out of competition.

It is not just the hostility of employers but also the organization of work itself that has outflanked organized labour. In the cutthroat world of retail sales and low-wage competition, lead employers have shifted employment and workplace responsibility to subordinates. The subordinate employers are subcontractors performing outsourced work, franchise owners or small suppliers dependent on the price setting and just-in-time supply conditions of the large buyers. These are the "fissured workplaces" — a term coined by US professor David Weil — where lead employers effectively impose the terms and conditions of employment on workers in their production orbit or supply chain while divorcing themselves from any responsibility or liability for those same conditions.[29]

Classic examples of fissured workplaces are building or janitor services. Weil's research exposed how the market for janitorial services in large US cities made the widespread violations of employment standards and outright wage theft the probable and expected outcome. Similar trends are found in Canada: a 2016 inspection blitz by the Ontario Ministry of Labour at precarious workplaces in Greater Toronto found that 78 per cent of over three hundred employers were violating employment standards. Some were subcontractors in building services and security, but others included mainstream retail services such as GoodLife Fitness.[30]

Unifor has also encountered the parallel practice of "contract flipping," which uses low-bid outsourcing to dispose of workers and their union whenever low-wage service workers make modest gains with a subcontractor. Building service workers in Vancouver, parking lot workers at Toronto's Pearson Airport and school bus drivers in Ontario were victims of contract flipping, with the next group of contract workers or sometimes the same workers having to start over again at minimum-wage levels.

Workers in fast-food franchises are another everyday example where everything from work assignments and hours of work to the clothing and general appearance of workers are determined by the franchise, as well as product pricing, which sets the upper limits on wages. Big-box retail pricing and their demands for standards and just-in-time delivery of products often have the same effect on wages and working conditions in their supply chain.

These are all circumstances that steer unions away from attempting to organize and negotiate in these sectors where labour costs have been ratcheted down and built into business models. Organizing successes usually come at considerable cost and entail questionable opportunities. Often the service enterprise has few fixed capital costs and can respond to unionization simply by closing and relocating. Even if negotiations proceed, the union is well aware of the competitive realities and is reluctant to take on a fight that would put the jobs of its members in jeopardy. The result is that most large unions have thousands of members at or near the minimum wage — not the beacon of hope for workers that the so-called union advantage is supposed to herald.

Unions can and do complain that the system is increasingly rigged against workers, but the truth is that labour should not be surprised or intimidated by the excesses of capitalism. Capitalism and its unending reorganization of production in the pursuit of profits are why unions are needed. If unions find themselves relegated to a narrower and narrower slice of the working class hanging on to standard employment, they must look inward at their own broken models of organizing, representation and political action.

Union renewal will be necessarily disruptive and controversial. It is not a matter of regaining lost strength. Unions have to build power in new circumstances where workplaces, technologies and economies demand new approaches to organizing, servicing and bargaining. It begins with the self-realization that the decline of union density will continue until unions begin to speak and act on behalf of the majority of workers, and to do that, unions must change.

Without doubt, the most disruptive change will be to the business union model that underpins even the most progressive of unions in the *Wagner Act* system. It is a highly transactional paradigm that demands that in return for membership and representation, workers are able to pay the price of maintaining the existing professional organizing and servicing. Of course, unions are nothing but the strength of informed and mobilized members combined with organizers, negotiators, researchers, campaigners and leaders. But the blend of these strengths was far from balanced or sustainable in the normal union operation of 2019.

The conundrum is plain: a union organizer could spend several weeks or months organizing a group of workers, and a servicing representative could spend another several weeks or months concluding a first agreement and future agreements, on average every three years. Along the way, there are significant legal bills, as well as ancillary research, actuarial and communications support, education and still more services. The dues for an entire year for fifteen workers earning $15 per hour would not cover the cost of just one full-time union staffer for a month. If the numbers are small, unions can carry the costs of groups such as these, as they presently do. But if the numbers grow to be more representative of the larger working class, the system will collapse, and everyone knows it. That is why the servicing model drives the organizing model.

How can unions reorganize to include large numbers of modest- and low-income workers and still focus the power of workers backed up by the best research and support possible? The answers have been debated for a generation and are not mysterious.

Economies of scale will be increasingly important to share resources with and for members who most need assistance. These needed economies of scale can only be met in one of two ways. One road forward is through fewer unions and less competition between them. A parallel road is a much greater level of co-operation between unions that allows a free sharing of resources to workers needing representation. Either route is far outside the boundaries of transactional solidarity, which is strictly limited to the institutional interests of separate unions.

To make it possible to take wages out of competition in the services sector, unions must demand reforms to the *Wagner Act* enterprise bargaining system. To match the power of lead employers, we need forms of broader-based bargaining, such as multi-employer pattern bargaining, sectoral bargaining or extension of union standards to all workers in a sector. These ideas have also been understood for decades, but only a few unions have given any effort or resources to achieving labour law reforms that would alter the current model. And even when there are windows of opportunity to pursue forms of broader-based bargaining, it is sadly predictable that some large union will run interference, fearing some complication for its perceived interest.

These larger solutions must be combined with internal reforms. If unions want to truly engage in social unionism, they must operate more like social movements, with more of the daily work of the union carried out by empowered members. This involves the shifting of resources from their overwhelming concentration on bargaining and legal services to member education and mobilization. Every union knows that the best union representatives come from the membership and remain connected to their base. Union renewal won't be possible unless there is confidence that members have the ability to represent themselves when the union provides education and support.

Union renewal must ultimately lead to a reversal of its driving forces. Organizing has to drive servicing. That means much larger organizing resources even for a union such as Unifor, with its unprecedented organizing fund. And it means that organizing every new member has intrinsic value regardless of the bargaining and servicing context. Not every group of members will achieve a standard collective agreement in the short term, and other members will need representation and solidarity for non-standard employment outside the world of labour board certifications and traditional collective bargaining.

A simple glance at the evolving structure of the working class in diverse, non-standard relationships and the changing economic reorganization of both production and the service economy points to a self-evident conclusion that there cannot be a single representative union model for a labour movement of the majority. New forms of worker representation must respond to the needs of workers in their actual circumstances. Traditional. Sectoral. Majority and minority. Employees, contractors, the self-employed and worker co-ops. If the goal is to organize workers, all kinds of representational models will emerge and be tested in a democratic experimentalism. Instead of simply reinforcing the "best practices" of past achievements, successful unions will constantly innovate and experiment.

This view of organizing will also change the character of organizing. The primary goal cannot just be a majority sign-up or a vote. In the United States, thoughtful unions have already abandoned the primary goal of a National Labor Relations Board union election that unions rarely win and instead have the goal of establishing a collective voice for workers that can win recognition from employers. When the goalposts shift, so, too, does the playbook for the organizing drive. In this game, the most important organizing investment that the union can make is to inspire, train and support a committed core of workers who will carry the union through the organizing drive and long after, regardless of the immediate outcome. Unifor is already halfway to this paradigm shift with its provisions for members without collective agreements. It is time now to apply the principle to every organizing drive.

All these solutions require something more and fundamental. Trade union unity has to become a non-transactional solidarity based on values. True social unionism proceeds from a vision of working people as a class, not production units or bargaining units. It sees workers in all their equity dimensions and never shirks from challenging discrimination or exclusion. It establishes union security on the basis of rank-and-file democracy, where union affiliation is voluntary, where members have the right to dissent and where collective and individual rights are protected.

These are values that were debated for two years in the New Union Project and continue to motivate Unifor's actions. Unifor sees its conflicts with the Canadian Labour Congress and some US unions in 2017 and 2018 as part of this debate. Its relationships with its partners in the North American Solidarity Project are a response to the same issues, but based on shared values rather than disagreements.

There is an urgency to this moment that cautions against endless reports, conferences and debates; unions cannot afford to forestall change until an elusive consensus is won. The current relative stability of union density, which is somewhat unique to Canada, is constantly undermined by economic forces and highly dependent on political decisions. At best, there is an opportunity to marshal the considerable resources and organizational bases that the labour movement retains to shape a different future from the trajectory of the global labour movement to this point.

It is very unclear where in Canada or the United States political leadership may come from to champion workers' rights and lead the way to the changes needed in labour legislation for collective bargaining institutions to succeed in the twenty-first century. Where are the politicians who will stake their career on making it possible for the 80 per cent of Canadian private sector workers without unions to exercise their *Charter* right to organize and engage in free collective bargaining? When will unions stop bartering their support to politicians who minimize or ignore workers' rights?

Nor is it clear whether the mainstream of the union movement is prepared to make the changes needed to stop and reverse labour's decline. Recent experience suggests that the current generation of union leaders is very unlikely to be convinced that the status quo cannot hold. They may not lead change, but that will not prevent disruptive change imposed from above by economic and political change and demanded from below by workers and activists who are compelled to take the future of the movement into their own hands.

These were the very questions that led to the bold notion of a new kind of union with a new mission. On its fifth anniversary, Unifor stands out in the Canadian labour movement as a force for change and renewal, and it is forging unity within and outside the labour movement based on its shared values.

The New Union Project created Unifor, but in doing so, it brought to life a social movement and an ongoing working class project for a new world of work and justice.

Looking Back on *A Moment of Truth*: An International Perspective

Jim Stanford

Public debate regarding the New Union Project began in 2011 with the publication of *A Moment of Truth for Canadian Labour*. This short paper introduced the idea of forming a new Canadian union, beginning with a review of the important economic, political and structural threats facing the Canadian trade union movement. These included the long-term erosion of union density (union membership as a share of total employment), the aggressive anti-union actions of both employers and many governments (especially, at that time, the Harper government in Ottawa), the constraints on union progress posed by globalization and hypercompetitive private markets and the failure of Canadian unions and labour centrals to rise to these challenges with more ambitious, effective and democratic campaigns and structures. Most dire of all, the threat of US-style right-to-work laws — which had recently been proposed by Conservative parties in Saskatchewan and Ontario — hung over the union movement's head like a guillotine. The paper noted that Canadian private sector density had already fallen to the same level it had been in the United States in 1981, when Ronald Reagan smashed the air traffic controllers' union, unleashing an era of all-out union bashing that continues to this day in America. We concluded the paper bluntly: "If unions do not change, and quickly, we will steadily follow U.S. unions into continuing decline."[1]

Leaders of Unifor's two founding unions had already started considering whether the formation of a new union could help the movement address those threats, modernize its practices and lift its game. To this end, *A Moment of Truth* presented a preliminary inventory of the essential characteristics and preconditions that had to be met if a new union were to make a measurable difference in responding to these threats. The key features of more effective unionism identified in the paper included the following:

- Being able to bring together and represent workers at multiple levels, including their workplaces (through bargaining units), their communities (through amalgamated local unions) and their industries (through sector-wide union bodies) and around their other interests and concerns (through specialized councils and committees on gender, race, ability, LGBTQ issues, young workers, health and safety, environmental issues and more).

- Finding ways to leverage the capacities that come with size (including financial and organizational resources, profile, and bargaining clout) but in ways that preserve the capacity of individual workers to feel at home in their union. The paper recognized that "bigger can be better": a larger union can undertake more ambitious and powerful campaigns. But the point of forming a new union could not solely be to grow: the new union had to undertake a bigger transformation of union practice, structure and culture. Defining the new union with reference to its core values and a commitment to thorough social change rather than according to the specific industries in which its members were employed. Ultimately, what the members of a new union would have in common is a shared vision of building and wielding collective power, in the interests of themselves and of all workers. This "basis of unity" immediately implied that a new union's identity and name would never consist of a long acronym reflecting a basket of economic sectors (as had been the case in many previous union amalgamations).

A Moment of Truth anticipated the core themes that would later be fleshed out in detail through the two-year process that led to the creation of Unifor. Subsequent reports and recommendations from the Proposal Committee and then from the various working groups established to prepare the launch of the new union described Unifor's vision, structure, practices and politics in detail — through extensive dialogue, research and membership input. But the core seeds were already planted in *A Moment of Truth*: Canadian workers needed a more modern, democratic, effective union to lead the fight for equality and social justice. Given the profound threats facing the future of Canadian unions, a "business-as-usual" approach clearly wouldn't cut it.

I resigned from my role as economist with Unifor in 2016 for family reasons and since then have worked in Australia for a progressive labour research institute (the Centre for Future Work). Through that work, as well as through my earlier experience in global labour research and advocacy, I have developed an international perspective on the challenges facing workers and unions everywhere and how workers' organizations are facing up to those challenges. From that vantage point, it is useful to review the progress of Canada's labour movement in the years since the formation of Unifor. It is clear that despite the continued attacks on unions in Canada, the continued negative impact of globalization and financialization and the continuing internal problems that have dogged many unions and labour centrals, the Canadian labour movement has nevertheless chalked up some crucial and unique victories since the publication of *A Moment of Truth*. It would be folly, of course, to ascribe all of that progress to the New Union Project and the formation of Unifor: the movement's victories reflect the efforts of other unions, social movements, electoral campaigns and the beliefs and hard work of many thousands of individual activists. But it is absolutely clear that this progress could not have happened without Unifor and without the energy, profile and spirit of innovation that the formation of the new union unleashed.

Stepping Up to the Challenge

At its founding convention, Unifor passed an action plan that committed the new union to ambitious and innovative efforts in all areas of its work: organizing more members, strengthening bargaining and workplace representation, enhancing inclusion and equity within the union, spurring reform and activism in the broader labour movement and projecting a strong, inspiring voice into broader community and political dialogues.[2] Amid those efforts, several key successes clearly stand out as representative of the ability of Unifor — and, in concert, the broader labour movement — to advance the struggle for workers' interests. Often these victories may not be fully evident or appreciated within the movement at the time. Activists are understandably preoccupied with preparing for the next battle, and often we are disappointed that we couldn't achieve even more. But some of the achievements of the Canadian labour movement since Unifor's formation in 2013 — every one of which required Unifor's commitment, participation and leadership — clearly constitute "defining moments" of what a modern, democratic and activist labour movement can achieve. I will review what I think are some of the most important and globally significant milestones, but, of course, this can only be a partial catalogue of the incredible activism that has been achieved since the formation of the new union.

In my judgment, the resounding electoral defeat of Tim Hudak's Conservative party in Ontario in 2014 was a critical political milestone for Unifor, the implications of which continue to reverberate in Canadian politics. Hudak was the first mainstream Conservative leader in Canada to advocate US "right-to-work" laws,[3] aiming to smash the postwar trade-off (embodied in the famous Rand formula) that recognized unions as legitimate bargaining agents and allowed collective dues payment systems and other union security provisions (ratified by members through their collective agreements).[4] Hudak's proposal posed a dangerous threat to the existence of meaningful trade unionism in Canada. He invoked tired economic arguments against unions (including the need to remain "competitive" with newly right-to-work Michigan, for example). His victory in Canada's industrial heartland would have emboldened business forces across the country to target all union security provisions for extinction and move to the full harmonization of labour laws with the United States.

Even before Unifor was founded, its two founding unions made the fight to stop Hudak and preserve the Rand formula a centrepiece of the New Union Project. Community and workplace meetings, which were organized to discuss the progress of the New Union Project, also featured research presentations and organizing sessions to build the campaign to defend the Rand formula. The issue was highlighted in all provinces, not just Ontario, in recognition that the threat was not limited to one province. Ultimately, we knew we had to reinforce general public support and social consensus around the role of effective unions in building a fair society. In this concrete way, from its very conception, the New Union Project was integrally connected to the fight for the future of Canadian unions.

The Ontario 2014 election took place less than one year after Unifor's formation and was an early test of the new union's ability to mobilize focused political activism — in the name of the union, rather than being submerged within a partisan electoral campaign. Sensing the political winds, Hudak deleted his proposal to abolish the Rand formula from his party's official election platform. But no one was fooled: he had already revealed his deep conviction that unionism as we know it should be destroyed. Unifor threw impressive resources at all levels into the campaign to stop Hudak, including leadership time and attention, communications materials, research and grassroots organizing and door-knocking capacity.[5] Other unions (led by the Ontario Federation of Labour), joined by community and anti-poverty movements, also campaigned energetically against the Conservatives. Despite challenging an aging Liberal government (that had been in power for eleven years), Hudak lost the election badly, and his vociferous anti-union positions were widely agreed to have hurt him badly. By crushing Hudak's flirtation with right-to-work laws so decisively, Ontario's labour movement sent a message to all Conservatives in Canada: challenging the right of unions to exist is a recipe for electoral defeat. In this regard, the 2014 Ontario election was a decisive moment in national politics.

Slightly over a year later, the labour movement faced an equally critical test of its ability to carry the argument for workers' rights to the broader public — and to do so in a modern, effective, inclusive manner. The federal election of October 2015 was a referendum on the extractivist, business-led vision of Stephen Harper's Conservatives. After two minority terms (when their agenda was constrained by political math in the House of Commons), a majority Conservative government was elected in 2011. It put the pedal to the metal with a full-on, no-apologies plan to remake Canada, including trying to destroy all barriers to business dominance (notably the union movement) in its way. Harper's numerous anti-labour bills were clearly part of a bigger, long-term plan to weaken the economic and institutional counterweight provided by the union movement.[6] The union movement, and Unifor in particular, mobilized an unprecedented effort to expose the anti-worker bias of the Conservative government and to encourage Canadians to replace the government. Like the Ontario election campaign in 2014, this campaign was run in the name of the union movement itself (not a political party). Harper was defeated decisively, replaced by a majority Liberal government under Justin Trudeau.

The Liberals, of course, are clearly a business-friendly political party, and few unionists were under any illusion that big gains would be delivered to workers and their unions on a silver platter. But what was perhaps even more encouraging than the electoral defeat of the Harper Conservatives itself was the labour movement's determination and success in extracting incremental improvements from this new federal government. Two of those victories, from my perspective as an international observer, are globally significant. The first was the successful culmination of a long-standing labour campaign to expand the Canada Pension Plan (CPP). Defined-benefit public pension systems have been under attack for decades, with a powerful coalition of financial interests and fiscal conservatives pushing hard (backed by organizations such as the International Monetary Fund and the Organisation for Economic Co-operation and Development, or OECD) to replace them with financialized, individualized, defined-contribution plans (such as individual RRSPs). Canada is one of the only countries in the world where the provision of defined-benefit public pensions has been improved, not cut back. The united effort of Canadian unions, led by the Canadian Labour Congress's tireless lobbying efforts, with Unifor playing a critical role, was decisive. The electoral defeat of Tim Hudak, in which Unifor played such an important role, was also crucial on this issue: the decision of the Ontario Liberal government to form its own provincial pension plan, if agreement for national CPP expansion was not forthcoming, tipped the scales in favour of expanding the national plan.

The Trudeau government's decision to fully reverse or abandon Harper's anti-union labour laws (including Bills C-377 and C-525) is also globally significant. In most countries, labour law has followed a "ratchet effect" during the neo-liberal era. When right-wing parties come to power, they pursue a pro-business agenda unapologetically, and many regressive changes are made to labour law. When nominally left-wing or centre-left parties come to power, they tend to invoke language about the need for "balance" and governing for "all the people"; at most, they incrementally modify a few of the right-wing changes while leaving the overall (business-friendly) structure of the system in place.

This ratchet pattern is clearly visible over time in many jurisdictions, including the United States, the United Kingdom, Australia and some Canadian provinces. This time, however, the new federal government fully reversed the previous government's anti-union changes. This commitment did not reflect any especially "principled" behaviour by federal Liberal leaders; like any other politicians (including those on the Left), their main concern is getting re-elected. That the Liberals acted so firmly on those issues is testament to the renewed political influence of the labour movement. By playing such a crucial role in defeating Harper (with a flexible and non-partisan campaign) and being willing and able to continue to mobilize public opinion and activist campaigns to support crucial demands (such as CPP expansion), Canada's labour movement extracted historic concessions from a government that couldn't necessarily be counted on. I am not aware of another international example where a far-reaching anti-union bill such as C-525 was immediately and completely reversed by a subsequent government. And that reversal is already paying dividends for workers' efforts to organize in the federal jurisdiction, such as underpinning recent historic union victories at notoriously anti-union WestJet.[7]

Of course, debates in Canada continue to rage, and much anger has been directed at the federal Liberal government by progressives on a range of issues. Those struggles must continue, and no one should be surprised about the ultimately pro-business nature of that government. But the Canadian labour movement's success in extracting such important and globally unique concessions from a government with a strong business orientation reflects our improved capacity to organize, communicate and campaign. We should take pride in and inspiration from those victories, at the same time as rededicating ourselves to the next chapters of the struggle. And in all arenas — organizing new members, fighting at the bargaining table and campaigning for the hearts and minds of all Canadians — Unifor's efforts have been at the cutting edge of this historic progress.

Canada's Labour Movement in International Perspective

There is even empirical evidence that Canada's labour movement has performed better than its peers in most other industrial countries in the years since *A Moment of Truth* and the New Union Project were launched. Again, this relative success is not solely due to Unifor, but it clearly would not have occurred without Unifor. I will present several statistical indicators attesting to the important progress that Canada's workers' movement has made since Unifor was conceived.

Let us consider first the all-important challenge of preserving the union movement's membership base and halting (and hopefully reversing) the long decline in union density, which was addressed prominently in *A Moment of Truth*. Figure 1 illustrates the trends in Canadian union membership (as a proportion of paid employment), both in the overall economy and the private sector. Overall density has stabilized in the last three years at just above 30 per cent of total employment, halting a gradual decline (amounting to over 3 percentage points) that occurred from 1997 (when Statistics Canada began publishing this data series) through 2014. Unfortunately, private sector density has continued to erode since 2014, but at a slower rate than previously: down by less than half of 1 percentage point (to 16.4 per cent in 2017). That's a slower decline than occurred in the fifteen years prior to 2014 (when private sector density declined by a cumulative 4.5 percentage points), but still worrying. It's too early to tell whether the stabilization of union density in Canada marks a lasting change in the dynamics of union membership: the mathematics of sustaining union density in a growing labour market require an approximate doubling of new member organizing compared to the pace of recent years. But it is certainly clear that the union movement is doing a better job of maintaining membership, and Unifor's organizing of twenty thousand new members since 2013 (with important breakthroughs in health care, gaming and transportation) is an important part of that success.

Figure 1: Union Membership Density, Canada, 1997–2017

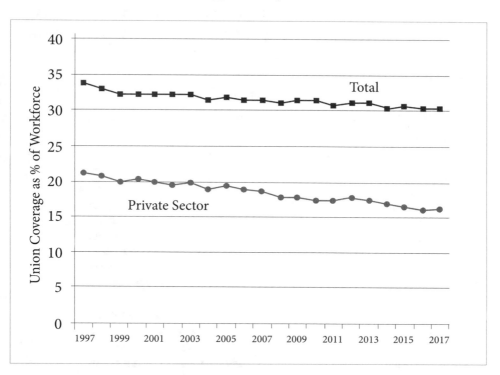

Source: Author's calculations from Statistics Canada, Table 14-10-0132-01.

The stabilization of union density in Canada in recent years looks even more noteworthy when considered in an international context. Union membership has been under pressure everywhere, for the same reasons as in Canada: global and competitive pressures, anti-union shifts in labour law, aggressive resistance from employers and changes in the nature of work and workplaces. Since 2011, however, when the New Union Project began, density has been more stable in Canada than in almost any other industrial country. Figure 2 shows the change in union density (for the total workforce, both public and private) in several OECD economies (based on OECD data, available only up to 2016). The decline in Canadian density (of around one-half percentage point of employment since 2011) is smaller than in most of our peer countries.

Only Korea (where density grew slightly) and France (where density was very low to start with[8]) fared better than Canada in preserving the proportion of workers belonging to unions. Relative to other countries, therefore, it is clear that Canada's labour movement has been doing something right.

Figure 2: Change in Union Density, OECD Countries, 2011 to 2016

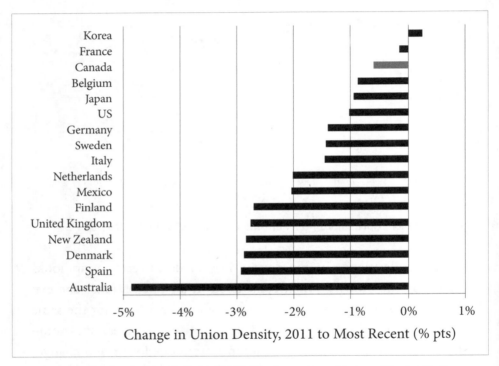

Change in Union Density, 2011 to Most Recent (% pts)

Source: Author's calculations from OECD Employment and Labour Market Statistics, www.oecd-ilibrary.org/employment/data/oecd-employment-and-labour-market-statistics_lfs-data-en.

Effective union power requires being able to mobilize members, including in work stoppages, when required to support bargaining demands and other issues. Here, too, Canada ranks as a "hot spot" of international trade union activity. Strikes are far less frequent in Canada than in previous decades (strike activity peaked in the militant 1970s and has declined dramatically since then). But strikes are still far more common in Canada than in most other industrial countries. Figure 3 indicates that strike frequency, measured by average days lost in work stoppages per thousand workers from 2011 through 2016, was third highest in Canada among all OECD countries with comparable data. France and Belgium were the only two places where work stoppages were more common. Of course, strikes only occur when they are necessary to back workers' demands; when unions are very strong, strikes may be rare (because the unions are able to win demands without striking).[9] But the Canadian experience certainly indicates that Canadian workers are willing and able to withdraw their labour when required to defend past gains and make progress. Again, Unifor has played an important role in sustaining the strike capacity of Canadian workers, with several important work stoppages (in industries including auto, trucking, health care, gaming and mining) during its first years of existence. Also notable has been Unifor's capacity (in disputes at Compass Minerals, Port Arthur Health Centre and the Port of Vancouver) to use creative, ambitious tactics and confidently mobilize the solidarity of the whole (larger) union to resolve work stoppages in its members' favour.

Figure 3: Work Stoppages, Selected OECD Countries, 2011–2016

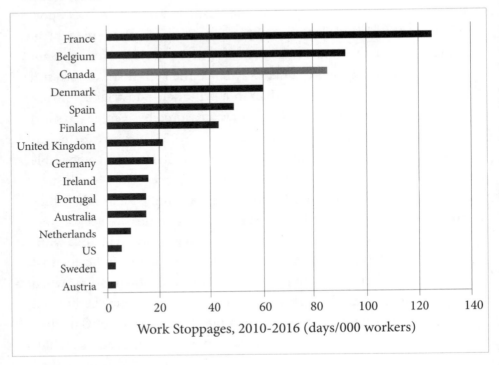

Source: Author's calculations from Statistics Canada, Table 14-10-0350-01, "Work Stoppages in Canada"; United States Bureau of Labour Statistics, "Work stoppages involving 1,000 or more workers, 1947-2017," February 9, 2018, www.bls.gov/news. release/wkstp.t01.htm; Australian Bureau of Statistics, Catalogue 6321.0.55.001, "Industrial Disputes," September 2018, Table 2b; and European Trade Union Institute, "Strikes: Map of Europe," 2000-2017, www.etui.org/Services/Strikes-Map-of-Europe.

The influence of trade unionism is felt not only through collective bargaining at specific workplaces but also more broadly through political and policy decisions by government, as well as in general trends in income distribution. In this regard, two further statistical indications confirm that Canada's labour movement has been relatively successful in comparison with the experience of other industrial countries. The fight to increase minimum wages has gained momentum around the world in the years since the global financial crisis. A growing consensus among economists and policy makers confirms that stronger minimum wages are effective in lifting wages despite deflationary macroeconomic and competitive forces; moreover, the old knee-jerk arguments that higher minimum wages will destroy jobs have been broadly discredited. Canada has been at the forefront of the international movement to lift minimum wages, led by successful campaigns for $14 minimum wages in Ontario and Alberta (soon to be followed by British Columbia and, hopefully, other provinces). Strengthening the minimum wage has been a top advocacy priority for Unifor since it was founded; in fact, the very first official government submission by the new union was a brief presented to an Ontario committee on September 6, 2013 (days after Unifor's creation), arguing for a $14 minimum wage.[10] Unifor also made comprehensive and very innovative submissions to the Ontario's government's subsequent *Changing Workplaces Review*. That submission not only supported the call for an even-higher minimum wage (now aiming for $15) but also provided influential suggestions for a thorough revitalization of labour laws to respond to the growth of precarious work, franchising and other negative trends.[11]

Figure 4 indicates the direction of change in minimum wages in several industrial countries. The figure measures the minimum wage in each country relative to the median wage paid across that country's labour market. This ratio, often called the "bite" of the minimum wage, is a good way to measure the level of the minimum wage relative to the overall prevailing level of wages across the labour market. Figure 4 shows the change in the minimum wage bite in each country from 2011 to 2016 (the latest year for which the OECD has consistent data). In several countries, the minimum wage has been eroded relative to the overall median; this decline has been most dramatic in the United States, where the minimum wage has been frozen in nominal terms (and hence declined in real and relative terms) since 2009. In contrast, between 2011 and 2016, the minimum wage in Canada grew by almost 2 percentage points relative to the median as most provinces boosted their minimums to $11 per hour or higher. However, the most important victories in Canada on the minimum wage have occurred in the last year (after the OECD data ends), with the increases (to $14) announced in Ontario, Alberta and soon British Columbia. Taking those significant increases into account, the minimum wage bite in Canada will have increased by almost 6 percentage points since 2011 — the biggest jump of any OECD country.

Figure 4: Change in Minimum Wage "Bite," OECD Countries

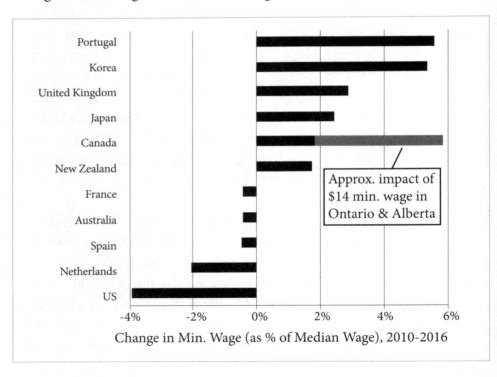

Source: Author's calculations from OECD Employment and Labour Market Statistics, www.oecd-ilibrary.org/employment/data/oecd-employment-and-labour-market-statistics_lfs-data-en.

The effect of stable trade union membership, relatively strong strike activity and rising minimum wages has contributed to a partial but important shift in the distribution of national income in Canada over the past decade. The postwar "golden age" of full employment and generous social programs peaked in the mid-1970s. At that point, business leaders and the wealthy began to push back with a whole set of conservative, business-friendly policies — what we now call "neo-liberalism." These policies included high interest rates and anti-inflation monetary policy, free trade agreements, fiscal cutbacks and privatization and, of course, far-reaching attacks on labour standards and unions. In the wake of that onslaught, the distribution of national income shifted notably from labour towards capital (including both business profits and the personal incomes of the richest 1 per cent of Canadians, who ultimately control most businesses). From the mid-1970s until the onset of the global financial crisis in 2008, workers' share of Canadian GDP (including wages, salaries and employer social contributions such as CPP and Employment Insurance premiums) declined by about 5 percentage points, and the profit share expanded correspondingly. That decline reduced workers' compensation by over $110 billion in today's terms. The erosion of the overall labour share of GDP paralleled (and exacerbated) growing inequality between Canadian households: since rich households own a vastly disproportionate share of wealth (that's what makes them rich!), they have benefited most from the growing share of national output allocated to profits and other forms of investment income (see Figure 5).

Figure 5: Labour Share of GDP, Canada, 1970–2018

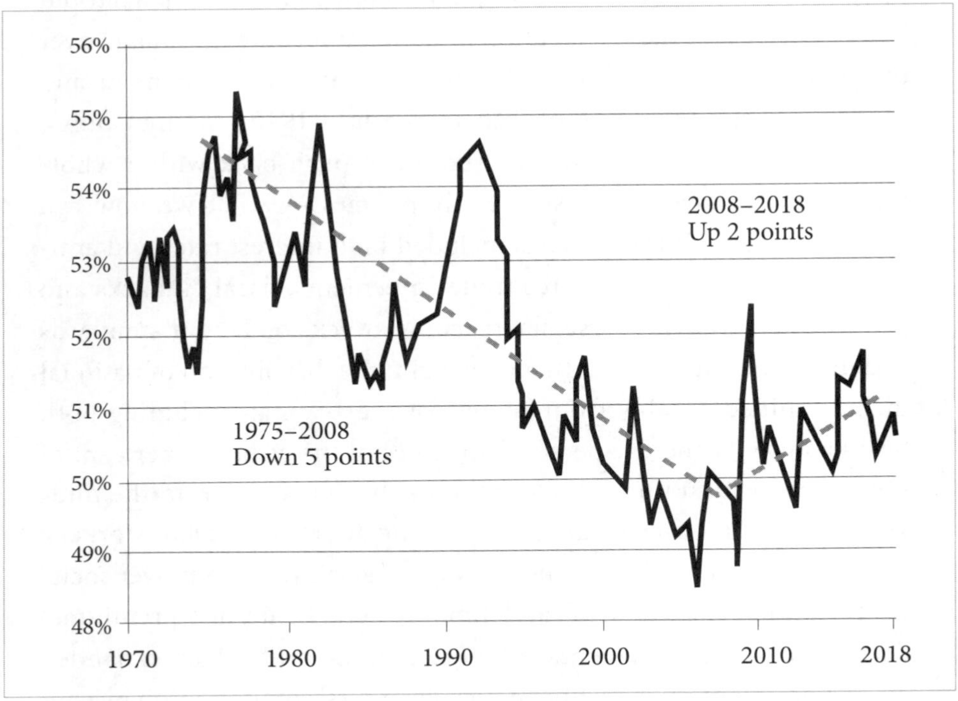

Source: *Author's calculations from Statistics Canada Table 36-10-0103-01. Includes wages, salaries and employer social contributions.*

Since the global financial crisis, however, an important and some-what surprising shift in income distribution back in favour of work-ers has become visible. The labour share of GDP has regained about 2 percentage points of its earlier loss under neo-liberalism. There are many complex factors that help to explain this reversal, including mac-roeconomic cycles, fluctuations in resource prices and the general shift to services production (which tends to be more labour intensive). But the relatively robust performance of Canadian unions, both in bargain-ing with employers and in strengthening labour-friendly policies (such as minimum wages), has certainly contributed to that important trend. Continued labour activism — in workplaces, in the political arena and in the battle of ideas that rages in our society every day — will be essential to defend and extend those gains. Canadian business leaders are already pushing back hard, complaining of "uncompetitive" taxes, wages and regulations. Nevertheless, Canada's experience according to this indicator once again confirms that our labour movement ranks high compared to other industrial countries. In most countries, the labour share of GDP has continued to decline since the global financial crisis. Indeed, the increase in workers' share of Canada's GDP in recent years ranks among the largest positive changes in any industrial country (exceeded only by gains in the workers' share of GDP in Korea, Norway, Switzerland and Iceland).

Together, this review of the state of labour and distributional struggles in Canada, comparing it to the experience of other countries, paints a cautiously optimistic picture. Canadian workers have been relatively successful in preserving their organizational and institutional power (including relatively high and stable rates of unionization). Perhaps more importantly, Canadian workers have been active in *wielding* that power — both through industrial conflict and political advocacy — to defend and even improve their share of the overall economic pie. In the years since the leaders of the CEP and the CAW identified the existential threat posed to the workers' movement in Canada, there has been an encouraging resurgence of union activism, with several important (if partial) victories to show for it. The progress that Canadian workers and their unions have made in the last several years reaffirms that fighting back makes a difference, and the energy, innovation and scale represented by Unifor's formation has been essential to that success. However, the long-term economic and political pressures that underpin the continuing decline in private sector unionization and that are redefining the world of work in other worrisome ways (such as the shift to precarious work and digital "gigs") still threaten the labour movement's future trajectory. There is still no room for "business as usual," even in this somewhat more optimistic reading of the current balance of economic and political forces in Canada. The labour movement must keep finding ways to become relevant and effective for millions of workers in precarious, temporary and non-standard jobs; it must dramatically improve its presence and activity with communities of immigrant and racialized workers; it must engage young people in the fight for decent jobs; and it must successfully integrate the struggle for jobs with the struggle for environmental sustainability.

In sum, the challenge that was set out so bluntly in *A Moment of Truth* remains as critical, and as daunting, as it was in 2011. But the important victories that our movement has chalked up since the publication of *A Moment of Truth* — victories in which the formation and early work of Unifor have clearly played a leading role — should reinforce our determination and our ultimate confidence in our power to build a better world. Despite the challenges of neo-liberalism, globalization and union busting, workers still possess the power to defend themselves and their communities and win a better share of the wealth they collectively produce. And Canadian workers are clearly better able to carry on that ongoing struggle today thanks in part to the New Union Project and the formation of Unifor.

APPENDIX
The New Union Project Cast

The Proposal Committee
CAW
Peter Kennedy, Secretary-Treasurer
Sylvain Martin, Assistant to the Quebec Director
Deb Tveit, Assistant to the President
Bob Chernecki, Retired Assistant to the President
Tim Carrie, President, CAW Council
Lewis Gottheil, Director, Legal Department
Susan Spratt, Director, Western Canada
Chris Buckley, Chair, GM Master Bargaining Committee

CEP
Gaétan Ménard, Secretary-Treasurer
Michel Ouimet, Executive Vice-President, Quebec
Chuck Shewfelt, Vice-President, Atlantic
Kim Ginter, Vice-President, Ontario
Jim Britton, Vice-President, Western
Peter Murdoch, Vice-President, Media
Angela Adams, Rank-and-File Board Member
Dean Carvery, Indigenous and Racialized Worker Representative

Project Team
Jim Stanford, CAW Economist
David Robertson, CAW Director, Work Organization & Training (retired)
Jo-Ann Hannah, CAW Director, Pensions and Benefits
Fred Wilson, CEP Assistant to the President

Duncan Brown, CEP National Director, Graphical
Patty Barrera, CEP Director, Special Projects

The Working Groups
Communications Working Group
Co-chair Peter Murdoch, CEP Vice-President, Media
Co-chair Susan Spratt, CAW Director, Western Canada
Chris Buckley, CAW Local 222
Shannon Devine, CAW Director, Communications
Angelo DiCaro, CAW National Representative
Chuck Shewfelt, CEP Vice-President, Atlantic
Marie Andre L'Heureux, CEP Communications, Quebec
Barb Dolan, CEP Administrative Vice-President, Ontario
Michelle Walsh, CEP Director, Communications
Roxanne Dubois, CEP Communications

Reference Group
Randy Kitt, CEP Local 79M, Toronto, ON; Candace Lavalley, CEP Local 7-O, Thunder Bay, ON; Daniel St. Pierre, CEP Local 69, Sault Ste. Marie, ON; Jean-Stephane Mayer, CEP Local 6001, Montreal, QC; Mary Croke, CEP Local 410, St. John's, NFLD; Dennis Flood, CEP Local 212, St. John's, NFLD; Dave Kuntz, CEP Local 1-S, Regina, SK; Andrea McBride, CEP Local 2000, Vancouver, BC; Nancy McMurphy, CAW Local 302, London, ON; Nick D'Alicandro, CAW Local 112, Toronto, ON; Jim Sadlemyer, CAW Local 114, New Westminster, BC; Johanne Duplantie, CAW Local 728, Sainte-Thérèse, QC; Jean-Yves Filion, CAW Local 510, Longueuil, QC; Mandy Ryan, CAW-FFAW, St. John's, NFLD; Carolyn Wrice, CAW Local 597, St. John's, NFLD

Constitution Working Group
Co-chair Lewis Gottheil, CAW Director of Legal Services
Co-chair Michel Ouimet, CEP Executive Vice-President
Sylvain Martin, CAW Assistant to the Quebec Director
Bill Murnighan, CAW Director, Research

Rick Garant, CAW National Representative

Alex Keeney, CAW National Representative (retired)

Denise McMorris, CAW Aboriginal and Workers of Colour Executive Board Member

Joseph Gargiso, CEP Administrative Vice-President, Quebec

Angela Adams, CEP National Executive Board Member

Dean Carvery, CEP Racialized Workers Representative on National Executive Board

Rino Ouellet, CEP Administrative Vice-President, Atlantic

Dave Moffat, CEP Administrative Vice-President, Ontario

David Robertson, Project Team

Fred Wilson, Project Team

Reference Group

Carla Bryden, CAW National Representative, Halifax, NS; Jean Upshaw, CAW National Representative, Toronto, ON; Rolly Kiehne, CAW Local 112, Toronto, ON; Christine Connor, CAW Local 414, Toronto, ON; Marcel Rondeau, CAW National Representative, Montreal, QC; Gavin McGarrigle, CAW National Representative, Vancouver, B.C.; Jean Van-Vliet, CAW Local 3000, Vancouver, B.C.; Ian Hutchinson, CEP Local 601-N, St. John, NB; Archie MacLachlin, CEP Local 912, Port Hawkesbury, NS; Mike Baranek, CEP Local 914, Sarnia, ON; Pete Jones, CEP Local 92, Fort Frances, ON; Jean Pierre Lafond, CEP Local 227, Amos, QC; Julie Ferland, Local 146, Montreal, QC; Kevin Bittman, CEP Local 1S, Regina, SK; Trilbee Stirling, CEP Local 191, Winnipeg, MB

Constitution Committee Subcommittees
Strike and Defence Policy

Lewis Gottheil, CAW Director, Legal Services

Rick Garant, CAW National Representative

Alex Keeney, CAW National Representative (retired)

Dave Moffat, CEP Administrative Vice-President, Ontario

Fred Wilson, Project Team

Anti-Harassment Policy
Julie White, CAW Director, Women's Rights
Gisele Pageau, CEP Director, Human Rights

Organizing Working Group
Co-chair Tim Carrie, CAW Council National Chairperson
Co-chair Jim Britton, CEP Vice-President, Western Region
Bob Chernecki, CAW Assistant to the President (retired)
Martin Lambert, CAW Quebec Council Chairperson
John Aman, CAW Director, Organizing
Dave Moffat, CEP Administrative Vice-President, Ontario
Renaud Gagne, CEP Administrative Vice-President, Quebec
Laura Davis, CEP National Representative
Jim Stanford, Project Team
David Robertson, Project Team
Fred Wilson, Project Team
Duncan Brown, Project Team

Reference Group
Anne-Marie MacInnis, CAW Local 598, Sudbury, ON; Dino Chiodo, CAW Local 444, Windsor, ON; Jonathan Blais, CAW Local 510, Longueuil, Quebec; Jeanne Doiron, CAW Local 2107, Antigonish, NS; Tim Carrie, CAW Local 27, London, ON; Gavin Davies, CAW Local 111, Vancouver, B.C.; Lisa Martin, CEP Local 506, St. John, NB; Penny Fawcett, CEP Local 2289, Halifax, NS; Michel Hanfield, CEP Local 145, Montreal, QC; Daniel Lablond, CEP Local 1495, Dolbeau, Quebec; Michel Arruda, CEP Local 6004, Ottawa, ON; Paul Morse, CEP Local 87M, Toronto, ON; Reg Meisner, CEP Local 1115, Quesnel, B.C.; Michelle Moskalyk, CEP Local 328, Edmonton, AB

Implementation Working Group
Co-chair Deb Tveit, CAW Assistant to the President
Co-chair Kim Ginter, CEP Vice-President, Ontario

Peter Kennedy, CAW Secretary-Treasurer
Richard Vann, CAW Assistant to the Secretary-Treasurer
Graeme Brown, CAW Director, Operations and Facilities
Shahmez Khimji, CAW Director, Information Technologies
Martin Lambert, CAW National Representative
Gaétan Ménard, CEP Secretary-Treasurer
Don Boucher, CEP Administrative Vice-President
Line Brisson, CEP Assistant to the Quebec Vice-President
Jasen Murphy, CEP Assistant to the Secretary-Treasurer
Patty Barerra, Project Team
Jo-Ann Hannah, Project Team

Staff Relations Working Group
Co-chair Peter Kennedy, CAW Secretary-Treasurer
Co-chair Gaétan Ménard, CEP Secretary-Treasurer
Ken Lewenza, CAW President
Deb Tveit, CAW Assistant to the President
Bob Orr, CAW Assistant to the President
Dave Coles, CEP President
Jasen Murphy, CEP Assistant to the Secretary-Treasurer
Marie Hélène Sansfaçon, CEP Director, Benefits

Convention Working Group
Co-chair Peter Kennedy, CAW Secretary-Treasurer
Co-chair Gaétan Ménard, CEP Secretary-Treasurer
Graeme Brown, CAW Director, Operations and Facilities
Shahmez Khimji, CAW Director, Information Technology
Karen Davis, CAW Assistant to the Secretary-Treasurer
Shannon Devine, CAW Director, Communications
Angie Niles, CAW Administrative Support
Jasen Murphy, CEP Assistant to the Secretary-Treasurer
Michelle Walsh, CEP Director, Communications
Nicole Brulé, CEP Executive Assistant to the President

Unifor's Founding National Executive Board

President — Jerry Dias (CAW)
Secretary-Treasurer — Peter Kennedy (CAW)
Quebec Director — Michel Ouimet (CEP)
Atlantic Regional Director — Lana Payne (CAW)
Ontario Regional Director — Katha Fortier (CAW)
Western Regional Director — Scott Doherty (CEP)
Quebec Chairperson — Marcel Rondeau (CAW)
Atlantic Regional Chairperson — Penny Fawcett (CEP)
Ontario Regional Chairperson — Dino Chiodo (CAW)
Prairie Regional Chairperson — Christy Best (CEP)
B.C. Regional Chairperson — Andrea McBride (CEP)
Racialized and Workers of Colour — Ruth Pryce (CAW)
Skilled Trades — Dave Cassidy (CAW)
Retirees — Len Harrison (CAW)

Industry Council Representatives*
Aerospace — Roland Kiehne (CAW)
Airlines — Cheryl Robinson (CAW)
Auto — Gary Beck (CAW)
Energy — Angela Adams (CEP)
Fisheries — Earle McCurdy (CAW)
Forestry — Jean Pierre Lafond (CEP)
Health Care — Nancy McMurphy (CAW)
Media — Randy Kitt (CEP)
Railroad — Heather Grant (CAW)
Retail — Christine O'Connor (CAW)
Telecommunications — Marc Rousseau (CEP)

*Some industry councils (railroad, airlines, aerospace, fisheries) were formally constituted in the following months.

Acknowledgements

This book has drawn on the records and notes of participants in the New Union Project. In particular, Jim Stanford kept extensive notes of the project, divided into binders on Phase 1 from 2011 to 2012, and Phase 2 from 2012 to the founding convention. Peter Kennedy's personal notebooks provided insight and detail on key events and evolving perspectives over these two years. Each of them also accepted the burden of reading and commenting on drafts of this book over several months, and I cannot thank them enough. I also relied on the memories of Ken Lewenza, Dave Coles, Michel Ouimet, Kim Ginter and Roxanne Dubois to recreate some of the critical moments that form part of this history. David Robertson made valuable criticisms and suggestions on an early draft. Jerry Dias, Tim Carrie, John Aman, Lewis Gottheil, Deb Tveit, Katha Fortier, Joie Warnock, Patty Barrera, John Cartwright and Gregor Murray also reviewed early versions or parts of later sections of the manuscript.

I am indebted to Linda McCrorie, Sylvie Miron and Brenda MacKay for their help in producing various manuscripts and assisting me with the long list of participants in the New Union Project that deserve recognition.

The people and events in this book are brought to life by the work of John Maclennan, an old friend whose outstanding photography has chronicled picket lines, meetings, marches and demonstrations across the Canadian labour movement for more than two decades.

This work has made it to publication in no small measure because of the patient encouragement of Jim Lorimer and his team. Their insistence that more than an administrative history was called for to bring this story to the labour activists and public it was intended for resulted in something much more than where I started.

Throughout my years in the labour and progressive movement, Pat Wilson has been the constant inspiration and support in my life. That was the case through the intense period of the New Union Project and once again in the writing of *A New Kind Of Union*.

Endnotes

Introduction

1. Unifor was created by the CAW and the CEP. But these founding unions are themselves the product of union development and adaptation from breakaways and mergers. The CAW was formed in 1984 as a breakaway from the US-based United Auto Workers. After the formation of CAW Canada, forty-five mergers with smaller unions brought 146,000 members into the Canadian union. The CEP was formed in 1992 by a merger of the Canadian Paperworkers Union, the Energy and Chemical Workers Union and the Communications Workers of Canada. It was later joined by NABET Canada and the majority of the Canadian members of the Newspaper Guild, International Typographical Union and Graphic Communications International Union.

2. For current information on unions in Canada, see Government of Canada, "Labour Organizations in Canada 2015," www.canada.ca/en/employment-social-development/services/collective-bargaining-data/reports/union-coverage.html.

3. The quality and quantity of statistical data on unions in Canada have accompanied the decline in union influence. Reliable current data on union membership, organizing and bargaining are sporadic and inaccessible for most union members. The data on rates of unionization in Canada in this book are taken from Statistics Canada, "Unionization Rates Falling," *The Daily* (Release date: 2015-05-28). The study found that in 2014, the rate of unionization had fallen to 28.8 per cent from 37.6 per cent in 1981. The decline was greatest for men between the ages of twenty-five and forty-four. The only demographic to increase its rate of unionization is women over the age of forty-five. Public sector unionization between 1999 and 2014 was stable, with the 1999 rate of 70.4 per cent increasing slightly to 71.3 per cent in 2014. In the same period, private sector unionization fell from 18.1 per cent to 15.2 per cent. Regionally, the highest rates of unionization in 2014 were in Quebec and Newfoundland at 36 per cent, whereas the lowest rate of unionization was in Alberta at 20 per cent, www150.statcan.gc.ca/n1/pub/11-630-x/11-630-x2015005-eng.htm.

    In Ontario, the *Changing Workplaces Review* (see Chapter 5 endnotes 21, 25, 26) found that in 2015, the private sector unionization rate was 14.3 per cent.

    A June 2018 Statistics Canada report provided a different measurement of "union coverage." This measure includes all workers covered by the terms of a collective agreement even if they are not members of the union. The coverage rate is somewhat larger than the unionization rate at 30.1 per cent, www150.statcan.gc.ca/t1/tbl1/en/tv.action?pid=1410013201.

    Another important metric for the health and influence of the labour movement is the number of labour disputes. Strikes in Canada have declined as union density has fallen. During the 1980s, there were 756 strikes per year on average. During the 1990s, the average dropped to 394 strikes per year. From 2000 to 2009, the average number of strikes per year was 258. From 2010 to 2017, the average number of strikes per year was 192. These data are from Statistics Canada, "Work Stoppages in Canada, by Jurisdiction and Industry" (Release date: 2018-07-03), www150.statcan.gc.ca/t1/tbl1/en/tv.action?pid=1410035001.

4. By the end of 2016, New Union Project players Ken Lewenza, Dave Coles, Jim Britton,

Kim Ginter, Chuck Shewfelt, Peter Murdoch, Michel Ouimet, Joe Gargiso, Lewis Gottheil, Dave Moffat, Duncan Brown, Rita Lorie, Jo-Ann Hannah, Michelle Walsh, Nicole Brulé, Gisele Pageau, Julie White, Bob Chernecki, Susan Spratt, Alex Keeney and David Robertson had all retired or resumed their retirement. Gaétan Ménard departed Unifor soon after its founding for personal reasons. Others took up positions in central labour bodies: Chris Buckley became president of the Ontario Federation of Labour, Sylvain Martin a director at the Quebec Federation of Labour (FTQ) and Jasen Murphy the chartered accountant at the Canadian Labour Congress. Jim Stanford followed his family to Australia, where he became the director of a new labour research association.

Chapter 1

1. Don Butler, Andrew Nguyen, and Alicja Siekierska, "Paul Dewar Cruises to an Easy Victory in Ottawa Centre," *Ottawa Citizen*, May 3, 2011.
2. The quote from Harper is disputed but has been published multiple times and used in Liberal Party election ads. See Noah Richler, "The Stubborn Persistence of a Canadian Political Meme," *iPolitics*, January 8, 2016, ipolitics.ca/2016/01/08/the-stubborn-persistence-of-a-canadian-political-meme/.
3. Ken Georgetti, Opening Address to the 2011 CLC Convention, May 10, 2011, Vancouver.
4. Steven Pearlstein, "Caterpillar to Unions: Drop Dead," *Washington Post*, August 4, 2012.
5. The *Companies' Creditors Arrangement Act* or *CCAA* is intended to forestall bankruptcy proceedings by allowing companies to negotiate a debt payment arrangement with their creditors. Typically, the courts will appoint a monitor to oversee the negotiation of debt payments, with secured creditors having priority over unsecured creditors. Wages, long-term disability payments and pension obligations fall into the latter category, with the result that the *CCAA* arrangement may result in a court order to cut or waive outstanding compensation to workers. Underfunded pension plans are often the largest such obligation, and both the pensions of retired workers and the pension credits of active workers have been cut by *CCAA* settlements.
6. The list of anti-labour legislation enacted by the Harper government is extensive. The following list cites the year of adoption, not when the legislation may have been introduced:
    - 2007 *Railway Continuation Act*, which forced an end to the strike of 2,800 railroad workers.
    - 2009 *Expenditure Restraint Act* and *Equitable Compensation Act*, which imposed salary caps on federal workers and removed the right of public sector unions to jointly file pay equity claims.
    - 2011 *Restoring Mail Delivery for Canadians Act*, which ordered a return to work for locked-out postal workers and imposed wages less than the employer's last offer. This *Act* was later cited by the International Labour Organization (ILO) for violating freedom of association.
    - 2012 *Protecting Air Service Act*, which intervened in airline bargaining to prevent strike action. This *Act* also was condemned by the ILO.
    - 2012 *Restoring Rail Service Act*, which ended a six-day strike by 4,800 workers.
    - 2013 *Economic Action Plan 2013 Act*, which provided for federal ministers to direct

bargaining and veto bargaining agreements with Crown corporation workers.

- 2014 *Employees' Voting Rights Act*, which eliminated card-based certifications in the federal jurisdiction that had governed union organizing for seventy years.
- 2015 *An Act to amend the Income Tax Act* (Bill C-377), which required unions to publish all expenditures over $5,000, including legal and professional fees, pensions and organizing expenses.

7. Andrew Jackson calculated a remaining deficit of 30,000 jobs since statistic peak employment of July 2009 in his post "Still in the Hole," *Progressive Economics Forum*, January 28, 2011, www.progressive-economics.ca/2011/01/28/still-in-the-hole/.

    Statistics Canada reported average union wages at $25.82 in May 2010, $26.47 in January 2011 and $26.24 in May 2011. The report showed a 1.6 per cent year to year growth in union wages. However the Consumer Price Index for the second quarter of 2011 was 3.4 per cent. https://www150.statcan.gc.ca/t1/tbl1/en/cv.action?pid=1410032 001#timeframe.

    In March Statistics Canada released its report on the wage gap for black workers, reported in: Tavia Grant, "Black Canadians Paid Less on Average than Whites: Study," *Globe and Mail*, March 4, 2011.

    Kevin O'Leary's anti union rant was on *CBC News Morning* on January 10, 2011, and cited by Andrew Jackson on the Progressive Economics Forum. Later in 2011 on the *Lang O'Leary Exchange*, O'Leary said, "Unions themselves are borne of evil, they must be destroyed with evil, so you have to kill their contracts." These and other comments resulted in complaints to the CBC Ombudsperson who reported in November 2011: http://www.ombudsman.cbc.radio-canada.ca/en/complaint-reviews/2011/unions/.

8. The War in the Woods dominated BC politics for several years in the early 1990s over protests to stop the clear cutting of old-growth forests. The protest movement peaked in 1993 at the blockades in Clayoquot Sound near Port Alberni. The NDP government sought to resolve the conflicts through the Commission on Resources and Environment (CORE) land use planning process to designate protected areas of old growth forests.

9. The Social Contract was austerity legislation enacted in 1993 by the Bob Rae NDP government in Ontario to re-open collective bargaining agreements with the province's public sector unions. Provisions in the legislation requiring workers to take unpaid holidays were known as "Rae Days."

10. *A Moment of Truth* can be found here: www.caw.ca/assets/images/CAW_-_CEP_ Discussion_Document-final.pdf.

11. Rachel Mendleson, "CAW, CEP Talk About Creating New Larger Union," *Huffington Post Canada*, December 16, 2011.

12. Richard Littlemore, "Do Unions Have a Future?" *Globe and Mail*, March 27, 2013. This feature was typical of media commentary on the state of the labour movement. Here is a sample:

    > Before the complexion of unionism went civil-servant, workers in the private sector tended to aspire to union membership. But now, non-union members of the public are more likely to resent union protections, especially when it seems that civil servants are getting fat (and retiring happy) on taxes paid by the unorganized. The workforce is polarizing into a public-sector side that has ample benefits, job security and pensions, and a private-sector side that does not.
    > These factors have cascaded into a crisis that at least some union leaders recognize

as life-threatening. "The trade union movement in Canada faces an enormous and historic moment of truth," says a discussion paper that proposed the CEP/CAW tie-up. "If unions do not change, and quickly, we will steadily follow U.S. unions into continuing decline."

Chapter 2

1. The regional officers on the CEP side of the Proposal Committee were also the union's principal sectoral leaders. Quebec's Michel Ouimet was the senior telecommunications sector leader. Ontario's Kim Ginter was from the paper sector and Western Vice-President Jim Britton from the energy sector. National Media Vice-President Peter Murdoch and Atlantic Vice-President Chuck Shewfelt were both from media. The CEP officers held in common a conditional relationship with Coles and Ménard. The CEP rank-and-file board members appointed to the Proposal Committee, Angela Adams and Dean Carvery, were both from Alberta. Adams was from the Suncor mine in Fort McMurray, where she had driven one of its towering trucks before being elected secretary-treasurer of the local. Carvery was also an energy sector worker who was the executive board representative for Aboriginal and racialized workers.

2. The CAW group joining Peter Kennedy included assistant to the president, Deb Tveit; retired assistant to the president, Bob Chernecki; retired B.C. director, Susan Spratt; Lewis Gottheil, director of legal services; Local 222 President Chris Buckley; and Local 27 President Tim Carrie. Chris Buckley was the president of the big General Motors local in Oshawa and represented the historic core of the CAW that remained politically crucial to the union's culture in spite of the downsizing of that sector within the union at large. Carrie was the chairperson and emotional voice of the CAW rank-and-file Canadian Council.

3. A summary version of Gregor Murray's cautionary notes on union mergers can be found here: www.crimt.org/AS_Website/Media/FO_AT2_4/Murray.pdf. In 2017, Gregor Murray joined the Unifor UE North American Solidarity Project as an advisor.

4. The final report of the Proposal Committee, *Towards a New Union*, can be found here: www.unifor.org/en/towards-a-new-union-proposal-committee-final-report.

5. The identical resolution to each union convention read:

    Whereas the Report of the Proposal Committee of the new Union Project has fulfilled the mandate set out in the joint protocol of the CAW and CEP Executive Boards and Whereas the report of the Proposal Committee describes the purposes, goals and objectives, structure, finances and other main operating principles of a new union, Therefore be it Resolved that the (CAW convention) (CEP convention) accepts the recommendation of the Proposal Committee to cooperatively create a new Canadian union based on the proposals set out in the report, and
    Be it further resolved that the Executive Boards of each union establish working groups to prepare the constitution and other founding documents and to organize a founding convention of the new union in 2013.

6. Duncan Cameron, "Building a New Union at the CEP Convention," Rabble.ca, October 16, 2012.

7. Ken Cole would later become a member of Unifor's Ontario Regional Council executive. He retired from his full-time position in Local 333 in 2018, happily reassured that Unifor was a stronger union than its predecessor.

Chapter 3

1. The Communications Working Group's mandate was to design and implement a process to choose a name, a logo and an identity; prepare a communications plan for the founding convention and after, including new union communications services, publications and technologies.

2. The Constitution Working Group's mandate was to map CEP and CAW constitutions; draft constitutional application of final report proposals; identify unfinished business, consult as necessary and draft constitutional language (council structures, delegate ratios, election procedures, membership categories, etc.); map CAW and CEP policies; identify and draft necessary founding policies (strike and defence fund, harassment and equity policies, etc.); identify existing industrial and political policies to be grandfathered into the new union; and develop a broad vision statement of the new union's approach to bargaining/industrial/political issues to fill any gaps in joint policy by the founding convention.

3. The Organizing Working Group's mandate was to draft an organizing plan and organizing fund rules and procedures; propose a design for a national organizing database; consider new membership/services models; conduct research on other union experiences; and organize initial representation from new groups at the founding convention.

4. The Implementation Working Group's mandate was to map CAW and CEP operations, design new union department structures, determine the design and function of the secretary-treasurer's office, servicing map and make recommendations on administrative policies, buildings, technologies and databases.

5. The Staff Relations Working Group's mandate was to map a pension plan analysis, timetable and format for negotiations with staff unions and administrative policies relevant to collective agreement.

6. The Convention Working Group's mandate was to provide oversight for convention logistics, including site, hotels, travel, registration systems, audiovisual needs, guests and speakers, special events and celebrations.

7. This table, circulated to the Organizing Working Group, summarized part of the comparative study carried out by the project team.

New Union Project – Global Survey of New Membership Models, January 2013*

Union	Members	Main Focus	Services	Fees
Unite, United Kingdom	Community	Advocacy Community campaigns	Advocacy, legal, education, information	$41 per year to higher depending on wage levels
Unionen, Sweden	Students and college-age workers	Marketing and web-based campaigns	Consumer benefits	
Together, New Zealand	Non-union workers, community	Campaigns for workers' rights, minimum wages Starting union organizing drives Emphasizing values	Telephone helpline for workers Advice on employment agreements	$42 per year Family memberships available
Unite, New Zealand	Service sector workers Part time and precarious With or without collective agreements	Organizing Political campaigns Collective bargaining		Non-working supporter $20 per year Working without collective agreement $2 per week
National Union of Workers, Australia "Every Worker Counts"	Part-time and casual workers in union jurisdictions	Organizing, negotiating and campaigning for casual and precarious workers		
New Trade Union Initiative, India	Informal workers Worker associations	Advocacy and political campaigns		
United Steelworkers, Associate Members	Non-union workers Family members Community	Community campaigns Advocacy and information	AFL-CIO Union Plus Benefits	
United Food and Commercial Workers (UFCW) USA, Retail Action Project	Non-union retail workers	Advocacy Political and workplace campaigns	Career coaching, job assistance, legal referrals, training	
UFCW USA "Our Walmart"	Current and former Walmart employees	Walmart campaigns		$60 per year
Writers Guild of America Freelancers	Freelance media writers	Advocacy for freelancers with major media employers	Pension, health care, legal and professional benefits, services	
Freelancers USA	Multi-sectoral communicators	Assistance and advocacy for self-employed	Insurance and business services	
AFL-CIO, Working in America	Trade union families Community	Political campaigns on worker issues	AFL-CIO Union Plus Benefits	

*The original table has been edited and condensed.

8.   Richard B. Freeman and Joel Rogers, *What Workers Want,* Cornell University Press, 1999. In 2006, Freeman and Rogers published a second edition of *What Workers Want* with a concluding chapter on their proposal for open source unionism. "We have borrowed the term from software development," they explained, "where open source refers to software created and improved by a diverse community of programmers working with source code available to all rather than by a single vendor or proprietary code. In the same way, open source unions would be available to any employee who wanted to join with others in improving work conditions and opportunity, and would operate through networks of members rather than traditional union bureaucracies."

The argument was that traditional collective bargaining in the United States was in terminal decline and that unions must open their doors to new members not in a position to secure or win contested union elections under American law. Unions would engage in collective bargaining where they could and otherwise represent workers through individual advice and advocacy and through political campaigning. Open source members would be organized into relevant networks as possible across workplaces or even on a national basis, using digital technologies to communicate and make decisions. Actions in defence of workers would be taken through direct action in workplaces and outside, including picketing and slowdowns, pressure on investors and shareholders and legal actions and arbitrations.

The ideas of open source unionism had inspired a short list of new membership initiatives by major US unions, including the Communications Workers of America (CWA), which had launched the "IBM Union," an Internet-based local of CWA members working at the tech giant. The CWA had also organized "WashTech" and "TechUnite" for Pacific Northwest tech workers, which welcomed tech workers as associate members. The United Steelworkers had also announced "associate membership," which the union described as "open to anyone regardless of where they work . . . [and] intended to revolutionize the American union movement and alter how the American people think about unions and belonging to them." Other examples included the UAW, which had joined forces with the National Writers Union with seven thousand freelance members. The International Association of Machinists and Aerospace Workers had established "CyberLodge," a Web-based "guild-like" association of skilled workers in non-union workplaces.

9.   Unite was formed through the 2007 merger of the former Transport and General Workers and the former Amicus, itself a merger of four private sector unions. Unite brought together 1.3 million workers in the United Kingdom and Ireland. However actual density within the union was less than a third of bargaining unit members; only about 330,000 were paying dues as members. Unite went through a major restructuring in 2011 after the election of Len McCluskey as its general secretary. Close to one hundred full-time organizers were added to focus on existing workplaces and in the first year resulted in 40,000 new members.

In 2011, Unite announced a new division of the union that would represent non-working unemployed, students and retired persons as "community members." The community program was directed towards community activists "to ensure they have a voice at a time of economic turmoil and social change." The community members were offered financial benefits and services, a legal advice helpline, a "welfare benefits check up," debt counselling, assistance with job searches and "hardship grants."

10. In 1990, New Zealand's *Employment Contracts Act* outlawed closed shops and replaced collective agreements with individual contracts, requiring unions to reorganize all their members with individual authorizations to continue to represent them. Not unexpectedly, the result was a stunning setback for unions, with density free-falling from 50 per cent of the private sector workforce to less than 20 per cent. In 1999, after a political split in the Labour party, Labour regained power in coalition with the left-wing Alliance party. Some trade union rights were restored, including access to workplaces for union organizers and the ability to conduct multi-employer bargaining, but individual contracts remained lawful, and closed shops were not restored.

11. The project team took note of a New Zealand union that had also taken the name Unite. (There are at least three unions globally with this name, reflecting the trend in unions to rebrand themselves as more than occupational groups.) In 1998, Unite had one hundred members who did not fit existing New Zealand unions, mostly teachers and service workers. Its original strategy was to create a large, community-based union, but after internal debates, it decided instead to launch organizing drives at the big chains in fast food, cinemas and hotels that had been largely de-unionized. The union combined audacious political campaigns around raising the minimum wage with organizing, and by 2008, it claimed 1,300 members at McDonald's fast-food restaurants, as well as members in hotels and casinos. In 2014, Unite had seven thousand members, half of whom were fast-food workers. Its success in these precarious sectors is remarkable given the high turnover of service employees. Unite estimated that it was necessary to organize five thousand workers per year to maintain its membership.

12. UE Local 150, the North Carolina Public Service Workers Union, was founded in 1999. It has chapters in more than a dozen NC cities with members at hospitals and universities, as well as city employees in sanitation, streets, fleet maintenance, parks and other public works departments. There are UE 150 chapters in more than a dozen cities statewide. Local 150 also has a minority union at the Whitakers, North Carolina, plant of Cummins.

13. Doorey's article on Graduated Freedom of Association can be read here: www.yorku.ca/ddoorey/law6022/blog/wp-content/files/Doorey_Author_Proof.pdf.

14. In 2007 the Supreme Court of Canada ruled in favour of the B.C. Hospital Employees' Union in a case known as "Health Services." The union had challenged the legislation by B.C. Premier Gordon Campbell in 2002 to rip up the union's contract and, in violation of that contract, to fire 8,000 workers and cut pay by 15 per cent. The SCC found that "freedom of association" protected by the *Charter of Rights and Freedoms* includes a right to collectively bargain. In 2011, subsequent SCC decisions on the rights of Ontario agricultural workers, B.C. teachers and RCMP officers have built on Health Services reinforcing union rights under the *Charter*.

15. The scale of resources needed to offer general representation to individuals was explained by another presenter to the Organizing Working Group workshop, Alex Farquhar. Farquhar was the director of the Office of the Worker Adviser, which provided health and safety advocacy services for Ontario workers adjudicating compensation claims. The Ontario office responded to over 18,000 cases per year through a network of sixteen regional offices and almost 100 full-time case workers and support staff. That was possible because the $11 million budget was funded from the province's worker compensation system. Although clearly not a sustainable model for new union

organizing and representation, the publicly funded Worker Adviser network would be a willing partner with the new union on community health and safety campaigns and would accept referrals of individual workers for representation on their workers compensation claims.

16. Wayne Dealy, a CAW member completing a PhD thesis on the New Union Project, was another presenter to the Organizing Working Group workshop who asserted that the New Union Project should embrace "a revival of mutual aid" initiatives such as group insurance or direct social services such as union-run daycare centres. He argued that the labour movement was capable of providing mutual aid to fill in gaps in the social safety net. However, Dealy contrasted mutual aid to a "clientele model" that marketed benefits to individuals and their families. The working group already had a consensus that although some benefits could be part of the package they were creating, it could not be based on what some in the room called "1-888-Union."

Dealy also picked up on the proposition of the New Union Project "to go beyond the limitations of craft and industrial unionism." "Of all its goals, none is more ambitious," he said. The goal went to the heart of the debate around new membership categories. When industrial unions replaced craft unions, they did not add industrial workers as a "second tier" to the existing craft union members, he contended; a larger redefinition of membership applied to everyone. The new union ought to do the same if it was to be successful in organizing workers as a class. Or as yet another presenter, Tracey McMaster, put it, workers who have been excluded from the social benefits of unionism must now be "brought into the circle of protection created by labour citizenship."

17. *Broadening Union Citizenship: Unifor's Members in Community Chapters*, August 25, 2014. Unifor's strategy to open its membership to workers without a collective agreement can be found at this link: www.unifor.org/en/broadening-union-citizenship-unifors-members-community-chapters.

18. The links between the anti-labour and anti-abortion campaigns are evident in Campaign Life Coalition publications: www.campaignlifecoalition.com/2013-national-rollout.

19. The political set-up for Bill C-377 is described in detail by Andrew Stevens and Sean Tucker in "Working in the Shadows for Transparency: Russ Hiebert, LabourWatch, Nanos Research, and the Making of Bill C-377," *Labour/Le Travail*, Volume 75, 2015.

Chapter 4

1. The Canadian Labour Congress research was done by Vector Research: www.vectorresearch.com/polls_unions.php.

2. This research was performed by Abacus Data for the agency Public Response and released for Labour Day 2012. Another positive finding in the research was that millennials were the demographic most likely to join a union. "Our research has uncovered a new generation of Canadians willing to sign up to the new union project. We've found that a majority (53 per cent) of younger Canadians under the age of 30 say they would join a union if given the opportunity. That's the highest level of any demographic we asked." Morna Ballantyne and Steven Staples, "Think Unions Are Outdated? A New Generation Disagrees," *Huffington Post Canada*, September 3, 2012.

3. Final report to the Communications Working Group, Stratcom Report 11, 2013. A case study summary of Stratcom's work for the New Union Project is here: www.stratcom.

ca/about-us/case-studies/caw-cep-new-union-project.

4.   The survey garnered a 7.2 per cent response rate and 7.8 per cent in Quebec. These results surpassed average response rates for similar direct mail surveys of 3.5 to 5 per cent.

5.   Grace Macaluso, "CAW-CEP Unveil New Name," *Windsor Star*, May 30, 2013.

6.   "Lewenza Says CAW-CEP Merger Priority Over Leadership," *Windsor Star*, May 6, 2013.

7.   The vision paper setting out the priorities and agenda of Unifor at its founding is here: www.unifor.org/sites/default/files/documents/document/682-new-union-vision-web-eng.pdf.

8.   Allan Gregg's speech to the founding convention can be viewed here: www.youtube.com/watch?v=fT5Y1pa4IUk. Naomi Klein's address is at this link: www.youtube.com/watch?v=6MK3SCCqWag.

9.   Dias's speech to the founding convention can be seen on Unifor's YouTube channel: www.youtube.com/watch?v=J7MyF1CX6P4.

Chapter 5

1.   The Strategic Planning Committee's twelve defining moments for Unifor determined at the September 26–27, 2013, meeting were supplemented in 2014 with a further nine defining moments: public and media awareness of Unifor; a stronger labour movement; defeating Stephen Harper; young worker organizing breakthrough; stopping two–tier wages; defending pensions; carry out the local union task force; advancement of an equity agenda; and go on the offensive on labour rights.

2.   Richard J. Brennan, "Tory Election Document Undermines Ontario Unions, Critics Say," *Toronto Star*, November 11, 2013.

3.   Adrian Morrow, "Jim Wilson Named Ontario PC Interim Leader as Hudak Steps Down," *Globe and Mail*, July 2, 2014.

4.   The new leader of the Ontario Progressive Conservatives, Patrick Brown, made conciliatory statements that union members were welcome in the PC party after his election in May 2015. His meetings with former Premier Bill Davis prompted media attention that he was attempting to rebuild a "red Tory" coalition reminiscent of the successful Davis era. See Steve Paiken, "Can Bill Davis help Patrick Brown end the PC party's losing streak?" TVO Blog, August 29, 2016, www.tvo.org//blog/current-affairs/can-bill-davis-help-patrick-brown-end-the-pc-partys-losing-streak. However the PC party under his leadership opposed the reforms to labour law reforms enacted by the Liberal government in 2017. Brown resigned as PC leader in January 2018 over sexual misconduct allegations.

5.   Kellie Leitch was named minister of labour and minister for the status of women in July 2013. In her role as federal labour minister, Leitch was pragmatic and distanced herself from the anti-union rhetoric in the Conservative Party. She maintained regular communications with Unifor and did not intervene in Unifor federal bargaining in 2014 and 2015. During the 2015 federal election campaign she acquired a more extreme public image after holding a media conference to announce a Royal Canadian Mounted Police "tip line" where Canadians could report "barbaric cultural practices." In 2017 she ran for Conservative Party leader on a platform widely seen as intolerant, calling for screening of immigrants on the basis of "Canadian values."

6.   Unifor National Executive Board Policy concerning Locals Representing Staff of Other Unions — adopted March 2014

UNIFOR members employed by other unions in a servicing and organizing capacity

1. Unifor members employed by other unions participate in the life of Unifor, engage in Unifor education and policy, are subject to the Unifor constitution and work to build and strengthen Unifor.

2. Unifor members employed by other unions engage in collective bargaining and the resolution of workplace issues with the understanding that they work for a social movement of working people. When conflicts or labour disputes arise, they will be dealt with taking into account the interests of the members they serve and the need to maintain labour movement solidarity.

3. Unifor members employed by other unions shall not participate in any action on behalf of their employers that harms or weakens Unifor, including organizing situations. Unifor members employed by other unions will seek language in their collective agreements to protect their right to refuse to participate in situations which place them in conflict, such as raiding and/or publishing and distributing materials which attack or discredit Unifor.

4. The organizing of any new bargaining unit of members employed by other unions must have the advance approval of the President.

5. Unifor members employed by other unions who are also members of that union, eligible to run for office in that union, and subject to that union's constitution are best served by an independent union. Unifor will assist any present bargaining unit in this situation to transition to an independent staff union.

6. Unifor representation of members employed by another union is at all times a mutually voluntary relationship based on a shared understanding of these principles to serve the interests of the labour movement. Unifor shall ensure that members employed by other unions are aware of this policy.

7. Unifor's recommendations on the 2015 federal election:

1. Unifor will focus its political work in 2015 on the issues that directly affect our members, including:

- Labour law and restoration of labour rights in the Canada Labour Code and Public Sector Staff Relations Act, and to have Bill 377 formally withdrawn.
- Comprehensive jobs strategy, including support for manufacturing and public services
- Opposition to current proposals for free trade agreements, including CETA, Korea, TPP and China FIPA
- Renewed Canadian Health Care Accord
- National Child Care Program
- Restoring full OAS at age 65, enhanced CPP and support for DB pension plans
- Restoration of EI coverage for unemployed workers
- Support for Canadian culture
- National transportation strategy, including support for mass transit and high speed rail
- Restoring coast guard services
- Sustainable development and action on climate change

2. Unifor will work with Canada's opposition parties to secure commitments on our core issues, including commitments to reverse measures by the Harper government to ensure that Canadian Laws and social programs reflect Canadian values.

3. Unifor's primary goal is to replace the Conservative government, and towards this goal we will focus our resources in key ridings with significant Unifor presence where Conservative incumbents and challengers must be defeated.

4. Unifor recognizes the strong possibility of a minority government and will work to create circumstances that will ensure the replacement of the Harper government by a progressive minority or coalition government under all circumstances short of a Conservative majority.

5. Unifor welcomes the "wise vote" strategy of the FTQ and will work with the Quebec labour movement towards the defeat of the Conservatives in Quebec.

6. Unifor will work with the Canadian Labour Congress in a national strategic effort to defeat the Conservatives and to elect New Democrats. Unifor will support the re-election of NDP incumbents and support New Democrats in other selected priority ridings consistent with our primary goal of replacing the Harper government. The possibility of electing Canada's first NDP government or NDP-led government is an historic opportunity for Canadian workers.

7. Unifor will develop a detailed organizational plan including with research, education, communications and membership mobilization components and present this plan to the Canadian Council Political Action Committee and National Executive Board.

8. Unifor will hold regional Political Action conferences in BC, Prairies, Ontario, Atlantic and Quebec to further implement our federal election strategy.

8.   Unifor's policy on political relationships and elections:

Unifor's policies on political relationships and elections will be guided by these four guiding statements:

- Principled — Unifor's political policies will reflect the principles in the Unifor constitution, the new Union Project documents and the founding convention documents.

- Independent — Unifor politics is at all times based on an independent analysis and democratic decisions in the interests of the membership and the labour movement. Unifor will develop policies, take direct action, campaign with movements and coalitions, and determine electoral tactics in each concrete political situation based on democratic debate and decisions by Unifor Councils and by accountable leadership bodies.

- Balanced — Independent labour political action, social movements and electoral politics are all necessary components of social change, and Unifor must have the capacity and the will to engage in all of these forms of struggle depending on the circumstances.

- Transformational — Unifor's political analysis is based in an understanding of class and power relationships, including oppression based on gender, race and sexual orientation. Unifor is committed to a transformative politics to bring about fundamental social change for political, social and economic democracy and a sustainable environment.

Our political relationships:

- Unifor strives to develop relationships with multiple political parties, social justice movements, equity seeking movements, NGOs and institutions, and individuals that contribute to the advancement of our political, social and economic goals.

- Unifor recognizes the historic relationship of the Canadian labour movement with the New Democratic Party. Unifor participates in the labour movement's relationship with the NDP, based on the involvement and affiliation of Unifor members who have voluntarily joined the NDP. Unifor's independent relationship with the NDP is based on mutually shared goals but is shaped by our own analysis, policies and strategies which may differ from the party.

- Unifor recognizes the distinct political relationships of the union in Quebec and the decisions of the Quebec labour movement to develop political tactics for each election, including endorsements of PQ and Bloc Quebecois candidates.
- Unifor's political relationships are also internationalist and we will continue to be informed, inspired and motivated by the experiences of labour and working class political movements globally. While many of these relationships are based in global union federations (GUFS) and in the anti-globalization movement, our bilateral relationships with unions in other countries which allow for in depth exchanges of our political experiences are particularly important.

Our electoral policy:

- Unifor may make recommendations to its members regarding any election when the interests of Unifor members and the labour movement are affected.
- Any electoral recommendation shall be debated by the appropriate Unifor Council or the National Executive Board.
- Electoral recommendations for a party or individual should be specific to a particular election.
- Unifor recommendations will not "tell members who to vote for" and will clearly set out the reasons for any recommendation, and also acknowledge the democratic right of each individual to make their own political choice.
- All Unifor members will be supported and encouraged to participate in political debate within the union.
- As we develop our political relationships and electoral policies, Unifor will be guided by the ultimate reality that we can never "contract out" our politics to any other party or structure.

Our political goals will only be achieved through the organized strength of the labour movement and by Unifor's own independent analysis and strategic directions.

9. Unifor's political policy and strategy adopted in 2014 is at this link: www.unifor.org/en/whats-new/briefs-statements/unifor-motion-canadian-council-politics-workers-unifors-political.

    Politics for Workers describes the idea of a political project in these words:

    There is a great need for a new politics that advances the interests of workers, but there are no easy answers for a 'worker politics' that will accomplish this. We describe this process as Unifor's 'political project' because it has both immediate and short term goals. Our Project cannot be described simply by the goal of electing a particular government or by ideological pronouncements about a future society. Unifor's political project is a process of active and ongoing engagement in politics, and continuing discussion with our members to draw conclusions and to define concretely the political and social conditions that will fulfill our long range goals of a new advanced democracy where the interests of workers and the majority of citizens come first.

10. "In most provinces and federally, the NDP has taken steps in recent years to weaken their organic ties to the trade union movement as it has endeavoured to present itself

as a more centrist Democratic Party," Unifor stated. "The party has carefully removed from its statutes and policies almost all references to socialism, public ownership, and redistribution of wealth. Like social democratic parties in Europe, Australia and New Zealand, the NDP has accommodated its policies to global capitalism, free trade, deregulation of labour markets, tax cuts and a smaller role for government. The net result and political problem for social democracy is the consequent inability to present a real alternative from other centrist Democratic Parties."

11.   To drive the point home on excessive partisanship and the need for coalition strategies, Unifor cited former NDP leader Ed Broadbent from his 2014 "Jack Layton" lecture: "Although it was the CCF and NDP that led the Canadian struggle for social and economic rights, it is important to note that other parties played a key role in their implementation. It was John Diefenbaker's Progressive Conservative Party that brought in a national hospitalization program and other progressive measures. And it was Lester Pearson's Liberals who enacted universal health care legislation and introduced the Canada Pension."

Politics for Workers called for an embracing of coalition politics to address twin problems of Canadian political culture. On the one hand, "self-interested partisanship" had facilitated the right wing, which "happily exploits the divisions of the centre-left." But on the other hand, coalition politics represented an alternative to "big tent liberalism." Whether pursued by the Liberals or the NDP, each attempting to displace the other's political base, the result would be a merger of those parties into a centrist "Democratic Party." Pointing to the United Kingdom's "New Labour" and the US Democratic Party, *Politics for Workers* concluded: "There is little space in the big tent for worker politics or labour's priorities . . . Unifor's Political Project therefore has the long range goal of building a political force that will always stand unapologetically with labour on immediate issues and larger social changes, and at the same time engage vigorously in coalitions and compromise with other parties in the governance of the country."

12.   The *Kinnear v. Hanley* decision can be read here: www.dgllp.ca/wp-content/uploads/2017/02/Kinnear-v.-Hanley-final.pdf. At paragraph 9 of his decision, Penny set out these provisions of the ATU constitution that set out its property-like relationship with Canadian members:

d) a local cannot withdraw from International as long as 10 members of the local object. In the case of Local 113, this represents .09% of the membership;

e) if a local withdraws or disaffiliates from International, the local's property is forfeited to International;

f) International may suspend the existing management of a local and place it in temporary trusteeship to, among other things, restore democratic procedures, carry out the legitimate objectives of International and enforce International's Constitution and Bylaws. This includes a local "willfully violating" the Constitution or acting "in antagonism" to International's welfare. If a temporary trusteeship is imposed, a hearing must take place within 30 days to determine whether the trusteeship is justified and should be continued;

g) union officials may be disciplined for "gross disloyalty" or "dual unionism, decertification or secession." When a charge alleges support for any other union or collective bargaining group with the purpose or intent of supplanting International, the charge must, in the first instance, be filed exclusively with the general executive board of International.

13. On March 6, Hanley published a retraction on Twitter:

   I wish to retract and apologize to Mr. Dias for the following comments or statements:
   1. My February 10, 2017 comment on Twitter that he was a disgrace to the labour movement;
   2. My February 21, 2017 comment on Twitter suggesting that he was a poor union leader and a cancer on the union movement;
   3. My February 23, 2017, and February 25, 2017, comments on Twitter suggesting that he was hiding behind another user's skirt;
   4. My February 25, 2017 comment on Twitter that described him as a "corporate sell out."
   All of the above comments were inappropriate, and I should not have made them.
   In addition, I want to clarify that my references to bigotry in my February 13, 2017 comment on Facebook and February 23 and February 25, 2017 comments on Twitter, refer only to the fact that Mr. Dias has made multiple public statements that appear to pit Canadians against Americans, an expression of intolerance which I believe is at odds with the goals of trade unionism.

14. Data on Canadian union memberships can be found here: www.canada.ca/en/employment-social-development/services/collective-bargaining-data/labour-organizations.html.

15. See "Top Five Questions & Answers on Unifor's Disaffiliation," January 30, 2018, at www.unifor.org/en/whats-new/news/top-five-questions-answers-unifors-disaffiliation. This widely distributed statement to Unifor Locals stated:

   This dispute is about the ineffectiveness of the Canadian Labour Congress and its failure to prevent attacks on workers from their U.S.-based unions. The Canadian Labour Congress lacks an effective mechanism for workers to change affiliations and it is a broad problem that has plagued the labour movement and requires urgent change. This difficult decision was made after a year of working with the congress trying to resolve Unifor's concerns about U.S.-based unions trampling on the rights of workers, including their democratic right to choose their own representation or to express dissent about the union. The congress failed to act to address the aggressive and undemocratic tactics shown by U.S.-based unions, against the wishes of members in Canada.
   When Unifor was founded we committed to improve and build the labour movement. That is why Unifor took a stand for union democracy and the rights of workers. Our union is opposed to any union that threatens, harasses, intimidates, or silences workers for simply asserting their democratic rights to choose a union or for the purpose of quelling dissent. It is our hope that the action to disaffiliate from the Canadian Labour Congress will trigger change to ensure that workers in Canada have their democratic rights respected.
   Change never happens without challenge. Unifor's leadership believes strongly that in order to make things better for workers there is a need to advance this issue now, and by doing this Unifor's leadership hopes that there will be a stronger labour movement in Canada. The Canadian Labour Congress must establish a solution that will create a fair process to allow Canadian workers to change their union affiliation, including leaving undemocratic U.S.-based unions, and to prevent, bullying and intimidation of workers should they choose to leave. While Article 4 of the Canadian Labour Congress

Constitution outlines a democratic process for workers to change unions, it is not enforced, which means it is not working for workers. We must fix that.

16. The Unifor-UE co-operation agreement was signed August 27, 2017, in Pittsburgh, PA.

17. Garret Keizer, "Labor's Last Stand," *Harper's Magazine*, September 2018.

18. In a July 2018 update letter from Jerry Dias and UE National President Peter Knowlton, the purposes of the North American Solidarity Project were set out:

The participants are not seeking to establish alternative labor centrals in the US, Canada or globally. Our goal is to work towards new and stronger labor movement solidarity that can bridge the gap to the larger working class excluded and left behind by economic change and outdated trade union models. We share a commitment to independent working class politics that is fully engaged but will not contract out its politics to politicians or parties that minimize or sacrifice worker rights. We are coming together to build solidarity based on shared values of social unionism, rank and file democracy and respect and equality across borders. These objectives start with reflection on our own practices and models and learning from innovative models throughout the labor movement. We are discussing active cooperation in education, organizing, and in core campaigns around issues such as medicare-for-all, fair trade and just transitions. The alliance we envision can provide a collaborative network for learning, innovation and joint action that would be a force for change in the broader labor movement.

19. The Port Elgin statement of the North American Solidarity Project can be read here: https://www.unifor.org/sites/default/files/attachments/nasp-statement_0.pdf.

20. Frank Graves and Michael Valpy, "Ford's Win Exposes the Angry Blind Spot of Canadian Democracy," *Globe and Mail*, June 8, 2018. Graves, president of EKOS Research Associates, and veteran journalist Valpy explained the Ford victory in Ontario:

. . . a majority of males between the ages of 20 and 55 appears to have handed Doug Ford power over the next four years, and his supporters are, by and large, anything but optimistic about the economy or, for that matter, anything else. EKOS research finds them deeply and consistently angry at elites, anti-intellectual, chafing at political correctness, largely tepid toward trade and globalization, staunchly opposed to immigration — and especially to non-white immigration — receptive to bromides about "restoring greatness" and "taking back control" and wanting to bring back lost security and class privilege. The trigger of their discontent is that they belong to that sizeable chunk of the province's population who have been standing still or moving backward in the economy over the past 30 or so years, and who do not see things getting better in the future.

21. The Final Report of Special Advisors John Murray and Michael Mitchell for the Ontario Changing Workplaces Review is at this link: https://www.ontario.ca/document/changing-workplaces-review-final-report_ga=2.158063161.223546592.1547501364-593602922.1533928477.

22. Pam Frache, quoted in Paola Loriggio, "Ontario Government Passes New Labour Laws, Rolls Back Many Liberal Reforms," *Global News*, November 21, 2018.

23. Colin Perkel, "Steve Bannon, Frum Debate Takes Place Amid Protests," *Globe and Mail*, November 2, 2018.

24. The 2018 decision by the US Supreme Court in *Janus v. AFSCME* was a devastating blow to US public sector unions, barring them from charging "agency fees" — or dues

— to the public employees for whom they negotiate pay increases and benefits if those employees decline to join the union as full members. The 5–4 majority decision was written by Justice Samuel Alito. The dissenting opinion cited was written by Justice Elena Kagan. The SCOTUS decision and the dissenting opinion can be found here: https://www.supremecourt.gov/opinions/17pdf/16-1466_2b3j.pdf.

25. Unifor, Response to the Interim Report of the Ontario Changing Workplaces Review, September 2016. Unifor elaborated the organizing and union density challenge in Ontario:

Ontario's 6 million payroll workers are increasing at a rate of 1.5% per year. To maintain the current union density of 28.6% it would be necessary for Ontario unions to organize over 25,000 new members each year. However, Ontario unions are nowhere near organizing fast enough to keep pace. The 2015 OLRB Annual Report cited 412 certifications covering 11,638 workers. The 2014 OLRB Annual Report indicated 405 certifications covering 11,444 workers. Assuming a similar performance in 2016, we can expect the decline in union density to continue.

26. John Murray and Michael Mitchell, Interim Report of the Changing Workplaces Review, July 2016, https://www.labour.gov.on.ca/english/about/cwr_interim/index.php.

In 2015, 87% of workplaces (defined as business establishments with employees) in Ontario had fewer than 20 employees and around 30% of all employees worked in such establishments. To the extent that it is impractical to organize, administer and bargain a collective agreement for so many small units of fewer than 20 employees (union coverage in such establishments in the private sector was only 7.2% in 2015), this means that about 87% of workplaces and almost 30% of the workforce are practically ineligible for unionization (not including construction).

27. Murray and Mitchell gave this description of non-standard work in Ontario, which they found constituted 26.6 per cent of the Ontario workforce in 2015:

From 1997 to 2015, non-standard employment grew at an average annual rate of 2.3% per year, nearly twice as fast as standard employment (1.2%).

Temporary employment grew at an annual rate of 3.5% from 1997 to 2015 – faster than the other component of non-standard employment.

Compared to workers in standard employment, those with non-standard jobs tend to have lower wages, lower job tenure, higher poverty rates, less education and fewer workplace benefits.

Poverty rates of workers in non-standard employment are two to three times higher than the poverty rates of workers in standard employment.

Real median hourly wages were about $24 for workers in standard employment relationships and $15 for workers in non-standard forms of employment in 2015.

In 2011 most workers in standard employment had medical insurance (74.3%), dental coverage (75.7%), and life or disability insurance (68.1%), or a pension plan (53.8%). In comparison, less than one-quarter of workers in non-standard employment relationships had job benefits such as medical insurance (23.0%) or dental coverage (22.8%), while only 17.5% were covered by life and/or disability insurance or had an employer pension plan (16.6%).

In 2015, the median job tenure in non-standard employment was 32 months, less than half the tenure of standard jobs (79 months). The median length of time in temporary jobs was 13 months in 2014.

The industries with the highest incidence or concentration of workers in non-standard employment, in descending order of the percentage of employment in the industry in non-standard employment (relative to the average incidence of 26.6%) are:

- arts, entertainment and recreation (57.7%);
- agriculture (48.9%);
- real estate and rental and leasing (42.9%);
- business, building and other support services (40.0%);
- social assistance (35.7%);
- construction (33.8%);
- professional, scientific and technical services (32.9%);
- other services (32.6%);
- educational services (31.3%);
- accommodation and food services (30.2%);
- transportation and warehousing (28.6%); and
- retail trade (26.9%).

28. "Canadian Franchise Statistics," www.franchise101.net/canadian-franchise-statistics.

29. The fissured workplace was defined in David Weil's book of the same name, *The Fissured Workplace* (Harvard University Press, 2014). Here is his succinct explanation of the problem:

> Fissured employment fundamentally changes the boundaries of firms — whether through subcontracting, third party management, or franchising. By shifting work from the lead company outward — imagine the outsourcing of janitorial or security workers — the company transforms wage setting into a pricing problem. As will be seen this pushes wages down for workers in the businesses now providing services to the lead firm, while lowering the lead business's direct costs. Fissuring results in redistribution away from workers and toward investors. It therefore contributes to the widening income distribution gap.

30. Sara Mojtehedzadeh, "Inspection Blitz Finds Three-Quarters of Bosses Breaking Law," *Toronto Star*, January 20, 2016. The offenders included a number of well-known businesses:

> A Ministry of Labour inspection blitz focusing on precarious employment has found 78 per cent of workplaces in violation of the Employment Standards Act, according to a detailed breakdown requested by the Star. These include household names like Goodlife Fitness, G4S Security, and Bowlerama, who were caught for a variety of infractions including shoddy record keeping, excess hours of work, and failure to shell out overtime pay.
>
> A total of 304 workplaces were inspected in the province-wide blitz, which targeted sectors like cleaning, security services, and recreation facilities. Some 238 were breaking the law. The most common monetary infractions being overtime, public holiday, and vacation pay. The ministry collected $361,000 in unpaid wages for workers following the inspections, according to its website.

Afterword

1. The discussion paper *A Moment of Truth* is available at www.caw.ca/assets/images/CAW_-_CEP_Discussion_Document-final.pdf.

2. This convention document, titled *A New Union for a Challenging World*, was passed unanimously by delegates to the convention and is available at www.unifor.org/sites/default/files/documents/document/682-new-union-vision-web-eng.pdf.

3. The term "right to work," of course, is manipulative and hypocritical. The prohibition of standard union security provisions, now imposed in twenty-seven US states (and, under Donald Trump, likely to be imposed federally), has nothing to do with any worker's right to work. The policy, rather, involves abolishing the ability of workers to decide collectively to form and fund a union and should more accurately be called "prohibiting union security laws."

4. Of course, this historic trade-off embodied in the Rand formula approach included limits on work stoppages during the term of collective agreements and acceptance of general management rights in the workplace.

5. One interesting aspect to the campaign was the Unifor research department's exposure of a major mathematical error in the Conservative election fiscal plan, revealing that Hudak was vastly overestimating the net jobs that would be created under his own proposed economic plan. Public attention to this error dogged the Conservative campaign right up to election day and badly undermined its credibility.

6. Chief among many anti-union policies implemented under the Harper majority government were Bill C-377 (which imposed arbitrary and punitive financial disclosure requirements on unions, including publicly listing any expenses over $5,000, which would have destroyed union-run insurance and benefit programs), Bill C-525 (which made it harder to organize a union in federally regulated industries and much easier to decertify one) and several interventions to forcibly end work stoppages (even lockouts precipitated by employers) and cap wage increases (for workers in the federal public service, Canada Post, Air Canada and CP Rail).

7. WestJet long boasted of its non-union corporate culture, invoking paternalistic "input" schemes and share ownership as alternatives to collective bargaining and binding wage increases; the company successfully resisted union organizing drives for the first two decades of its existence. However, within a year of the restoration of card-based certification procedures in 2017 (itself delayed by the legislative stalling tactics of Conservative senators), new bargaining units were certified for two groups of WestJet pilots (who joined the Air Line Pilots Association) and over 3,000 flight attendants (who joined CUPE). Inspired by important bargaining gains in the pilots' first contract (reached in 2018 after threatened strike action), it is almost certain that WestJet's other workers will also soon unionize. The unionization of this firm, a poster child for union avoidance, is symbolically important for the reputation and future growth of Canadian unions.

8. In France, formal membership in unions is less than 10 per cent of total employment, but this is not an accurate indicator of union power. Unions are supported through universal workplace representative structures, government subsidies and mandatory collective bargaining. Collective bargaining coverage is close to 90 per cent of the workforce.

9. This logic helps to explain the very low incidence of strikes in countries such as Sweden and Germany.

10. See *Submission to Ontario's Minimum Wage Review Panel*, www.unifor.org/en/submission-ontarios-minimum-wage-review-panel.

11. See *Building Balance, Fairness, and Opportunity in Ontario's Labour Market*, September 2015, www.unifor.org/sites/default/files/attachments/unifor_final_submission_ontario_changing_workplaces.pdf.

Index